Kids Like Us

Using Persona Dolls in the Classroom

Trisha Whitney

 Redleaf Press

Published by: Redleaf Press
                  a division of Resources for Child Caring, Inc.
                  450 North Syndicate, Suite 5
                  St. Paul, MN 55104-4125

Distributed by: Gryphon House
                  Mailing Address:
                  P.O. Box 207
                  Beltsville, MD 20704-0207

Library of Congress Cataloging-in-Publication Data

Whitney, Trisha, 1958-
     Kids like us : using persona dolls in the classroom /
Trisha Whitney.
        p.   cm.
     Includes index.
     ISBN 1-884834-65-5
     1. Early childhood education—Activity programs.
2. Teaching—Aids and devices.   3. Toleration—Study and
teaching (Early childhood)—Activity programs.   4. Dolls
5. Storytelling.   I. Title.
LB1139.35.A37W433   1999
372.133—dc21   99-35235
                                                    CIP

For Do Mi

And Alex

With all my heart

Contents

Acknowledgements

The creation of the five-step method and the writing of this book would never have occurred without the help of Do Mi Stauber. Over the years she has spent innumerable hours reviewing stories with me and talking over the details of the *Kids Like Us* Method. She made it possible for me to present *Kids Like Us* workshops by doing them with me. Her confidence in my ability and her willingness to take care of my other responsibilities while I wrote made it possible for me to write this book.

I also want to thank Beth Wallace, my editor at Redleaf, for making the editing process pleasant, Christopher and Deb Michaels, who reviewed the book and gave me excellent advice, and Louise Derman-Sparks, for encouraging me to write.

I am also grateful to all the children and their parents who have shared their lives with me and helped to bring the *Kids Like Us* dolls to life.

And, finally, a big hug and thank you to my daughter, Alex, for putting up with so many hours of "Mama's working" while I wrote this book.

Introduction: A Story to Begin

Hamasi's New Glasses

Hamasi's mom told me the news one morning: Glasses had been ordered for him. My first thought was of Hamasi's fragile sense of self-esteem that was just beginning to blossom in the security of my classroom. This extremely active five year old had experienced a lot of peer rejection in the past due to his impulsive behavior. Now that he was beginning to make friends and to see himself in a positive light, it would be important for him to make the transition to wearing glasses without being teased by the other kids.

My second thought was that this could be a good opportunity for all of my students to learn to respect and appreciate diversity. Glasses would be new in our class since none of the other children wore them. If I could help the kids remain open to the new experience, they would learn about glasses and gain a wider understanding of the importance of treating everyone with respect.

Now I needed the right opportunity to make this discussion and learning take place. Using two of my *Kids Like Us* dolls and an old pair of child-sized glasses, I created that opportunity.

Two days later, when Hamasi was not at school because of a dentist appointment, I brought out two of my 22-inch cloth dolls named Rachel and Mei Lin. These two dolls had been to our circle several times before, so the children were familiar with them.

I sat down in the circle with the dolls, one on each knee, and I settled the children into their places. They began to greet Rachel and Mei Lin immediately.

> *"That's Rachel!"*
> *"Hi, Rachel! I remember you!"*
> *"Is Mei Lin going to tell us a story?"*
> *"Can I give her a hug?"*
> *"Hey! Rachel has glasses! She didn't have glasses before!"*

And so I began my storytelling.

> *"Yes. This is Rachel. And over here is Mei Lin. Do you remember them? They have each been to our circle before. Remember it was Rachel's birthday a little bit ago? She told us about her robot that works by remote control. She got it from her Zaide. That's Rachel's favorite thing—robots. And she has a new pair of glasses. I'll send her around the circle for a quick hug. And here's Mei Lin. She is six, just like some of you."*

> *"I'm six! I'm six just like her! We're both six!"*

" That's right. Mei Lin likes being six. She's learning to read. She really likes hearing Amelia Bedelia books. I'll send her around the circle the other way. Just give her a quick hug and send her on around.

" Rachel asked to come to the circle to tell you about something that happened to her the other day. She asked Mei Lin to come with her to help tell about it. They want to hear what you think."

" We can help 'em. We're good at thinking!"

" Yes, you are all good thinkers. Well, here's what happened. You see, just the other day Rachel went to the eye doctor, the optometrist, and she said Rachel will see much better if she wears glasses. Rachel was excited to get her glasses because she had been getting headaches and things looked a bit fuzzy. But with her new glasses she sees everything clearly and she hasn't had a single headache since she got them! What do you think about that?"

" That's great! I don't like headaches."
" Me neither."

" So Rachel and her mom went to the glasses store and Rachel picked out these red glasses. She had to wait a few days to get the right lenses—that's the glass that helps her see better—put into the frames. Now she wears them all day. See? The arms fit over her ears and the center rests on either side of her nose. That holds the lenses right in front of her eyes, and they help her see better."

" Can she run and play with them on?"

" Good question, Zack. I see you are thinking! Yes, she plays just the same as before she got glasses. In fact, she can catch a ball better now that she can see more clearly. She takes her glasses off when she wants to roughhouse, so she doesn't break them. She has to remember never to leave them on the ground where they might get stepped on. She has a glasses case she puts them into. At school she keeps the case in her cubby.

" After Rachel got her glasses that morning her mom dropped her off at school. Rachel hurried out to play at recess. When she ran up to Mei Lin by the overhead ladder, Mei Lin said, 'Hey! You've got glasses! Look at that! Now you look like you have bug eyes! We'll call you "Bug Eyes!"' How do you think that made Rachel feel?"

" Bad."
" I bet that hurt her feelings."
" I'd feel really, really sad."
" Yeah. I'd feel like crying."
" I think I'd be mad.

" She'd feel sad or mad. You think her feelings would be hurt. Uh-huh. Maybe she'd even be furious?"

" I would be! I'd feel like punching her out!"

"You'd be so furious you'd want to hit her, huh?"

   "Yeah."

"You are doing some good thinking about how it feels to be teased. And, you know, Rachel did feel really, really sad *and* mad when Mei Lin said those things to her. She had been feeling terrific about her new glasses, but now she wasn't sure. What do you think Rachel could do to help herself feel better? Do you think punching Mei Lin would help or make things worse?"

   "No, that would be worse because then Rachel did the wrong thing too."
   "Oh, yeah. Well... she could tell her not to say that stuff."
   "Maybe I'd go tell the teacher about it."
   "Crying makes me feel better sometimes."
   "I think she could go find some other kid to play with."

"What if *you* were another kid at Rachel and Mei Lin's school and you heard what Mei Lin said to Rachel? What could *you* do to stand up for Rachel?"

   "I'd tell Rachel I like her glasses." [She looks at the doll.] *"I DO like your glasses, Rachel!"*

Another student reaches over and holds Rachel's hand.

   "I'd play with her!"
   "I'd tell her not to listen to Mei Lin. I'd tell her glasses are a good thing because they help you see better."

"Why do you think Mei Lin said those things to Rachel?"

   "She wanted to make her feel bad."
   "I think she was surprised when she saw Rachel had glasses. I was surprised when I saw them."
   "Maybe she didn't think how it would feel."
   "Maybe somebody teased Mei Lin about something."

"Could you think of something to say to Mei Lin to help her learn not to do this again?"

   "Yeah. I'd tell her she hurt Rachel's feelings."
   "I'd tell her we all want to be safe in our school and calling names makes us feel not safe."
   "I'd tell her not to say that to my friend Rachel again."

"What would you say, Danielle?" [Danielle has been watching silently.]

   "Let's all be friends."

"Good thinking! If you were there, would you rather be the person that teased Rachel or the one that stood up against that teasing?" [Every hand shoots up into the air.]

   "The one that stood up against it!"
   "I'd stand up for Rachel!"
   "I'd never be the teaser! Not me!"

"Wow! You all have such good ideas. I'll bet Rachel would be glad to have you there to help her stand up for herself. You know, Rachel used several of your ideas that day. She did feel very sad, and mad too. I think she was even furious! She ran over to the corner tree and cried and stomped her foot for a minute. Then she went to her friend Julio and asked him to help her talk to Mei Lin. Julio told her he liked her glasses and held her hand as they went back to Mei Lin.

"Rachel told Mei Lin that glasses help her see better and that Mei Lin should not call her names ever again. She reminded her that their class made an agreement to be sure everyone in their school feels safe.

"And Mei Lin said she was surprised that Rachel had glasses, and that she didn't mean to make Rachel feel bad. She told Rachel that she wanted to be her friend and that she'd never tease her about her glasses again. Rachel was still a little mad, but she wasn't furious any more. Then they all three climbed up on the overhead ladder and pretended to be eagles on a high mountain for the rest of recess. Do you think she chose a helpful way to work it out?"

"Yeah! That's just what I'd do."
"Good thinking, Rachel."

"Thanks for helping them think about this. It often helps to talk things over with people you trust."

Five days later, when Hamasi appeared with his new glasses, several students complimented him on them. A couple asked him if he could see better with his glasses. The rest paid no attention to them at all.

How Can Kids Like Us Dolls Change Your Classroom?

Kids Like Us doll stories can be told to children ages two through eight. They can be about an infinite number of situations. Each story is a link in the chain of experiences you can bring to your students to help them learn important social skills. Through these stories children can deal with common problems, conflicts, and developmental issues.

Children can learn to empathize.

How many times have you heard someone, even another educator, say, "Children can be so cruel. I guess it's a natural part of childhood." This is just not true. What this really means is, "Children can be cruel to one another, and we don't know how to help them learn to treat others with respect." And we *must* teach these skills to our children! Because our children are not learning how to treat one another with respect, many are living with taunting and humiliation, learning to despise themselves. Other children are learning to feel superior because of their race or possessions or their ability to intimidate. Many are lacking empathy, and so they act without any feeling about their impact on other people. Young children *can* learn these skills. All we need are the right tools to help them learn. Using *Kids Like Us* dolls to help tell stories is a simple tool that does just that.

Through doll stories the children learn skills we may have thought were beyond their abilities. In fact, by discussing the events of stories, identifying the characters' feelings, and doing group problem solving, *children teach one another* to feel empathy, to understand others' motivations, and to gain insight into complex emotions.

During this story about Rachel and her glasses, the children were having a real-life lesson in learning to see new things as "interesting," not as something to be labeled "weird" and therefore avoided or ridiculed. Through participation in the doll story, these children had the opportunity to get information, ask questions, and become comfortable with the new experience.

By the time Hamasi appeared at school with his glasses, these children had already absorbed this concept into their knowledge about the world. Glasses were no longer "strange." They had become a simple fact of life. Because of the doll story, they didn't have to explore the subject at Hamasi's expense.

Children can accept difference.

Many times adults take it for granted that children won't like someone who is different in some way. When peers do not accept a child, that child is often blamed for the problem and efforts are taken to "make the child more like the others." What we should do is help the peer group become comfortable with this difference and all individual differences. Telling stories using *Kids Like Us* dolls can do just that.

One of the parents at my school told me horrific tales of receiving glasses at age seven. Harassment, name-calling, and having her glasses ripped off her face were daily occurrences. She cried as she watched Hamasi show his new glasses off with pride to a few admiring classmates. She later told me, "What a difference. How I wish we had lessons like this when I was in school!"

For Hamasi, glasses were not a terrible thing that had happened to him to set him apart from the others. Never once were they used as an object of ridicule. They were just glasses, a wonderful tool to help him see better.

Children can make choices.

Another strand of the glasses story was about making the right choices. For many children it is a revelation to realize that they have choices about how to behave in any situation. During this story they brainstormed their own solutions to Rachel's problem, evaluated the ideas, and discussed which ones would be effective. Then they saw the effect of some of their choices put into practice.

Kids Like Us doll stories are also an excellent opportunity for children to experience how good it feels to step into a helpful role and to give them practice in rejecting hurtful ones. The peer reinforcement each child received for standing up against bias as they looked around at their classmates raising their hands and yelling, "I'd never be the teaser!" was pure gold. An adult could remind children, "Do not tease!" a hundred million times and never equal the learning power of that one moment. These are crucial experiences for kids to have if we are to help them learn compassion, caring, and the importance of standing up against bias. In *Kids Like Us* doll stories these reinforcing moments occur naturally, in a way that is meaningful, and therefore memorable, to the kids.

This book will guide you through the process of becoming a *Kids Like Us* storyteller. We will begin with information on obtaining dolls and inventing their identities. The majority of the book will then cover a simple five-step process for planning and telling stories on many subjects and how to use them to get your students involved and learning from the very beginning. These sections will serve as a constant resource as you delve into telling different types of stories and explore different levels of understanding with your students. Throughout the book there will also be many examples of *Kids Like Us* doll stories I have told. I have found that studying other stories is the best way to learn to develop your own.

Welcome to the magic world of the *Kids Like Us* doll storyteller! I'm glad you've come to join me.

1

A First Look
at Kids Like Us

Dolls and

 Storytelling

The foundation of the *Kids Like Us* storytelling method is a set of dolls. These dolls can be handmade or bought from a catalog. They can be as small as 10 inches or as large as life-sized. They can be made of cloth or plastic and dressed in handmade clothing or thrift store baby clothes that look like older kid clothes. In other words, many types of dolls are useable for *Kids Like Us* storytelling. What is most important is how the dolls are treated. ● *Kids Like Us* dolls are special. They are not the same as the dolls found in the housekeeping area of many classrooms. Classroom dolls are usually babies, meant to be diapered and fed, held as one's own baby in each child's imaginings. *Kids Like Us* dolls are not babies. They are the same age as your students. ● Each doll represents a real person and maintains its own identity: personal traits, family, and culture. Some of these details are invented before presenting the dolls to the children, and some are added as they relate to stories the dolls take part in. But these details stay the same over time, just as the details of a real student's life would.

For example, when I made a doll with dark brown skin and black cornrows, I decided it was a girl, named her Ianthe, and set her age at six years old and her race as African American. I decided that she lives with her mother and father and her younger brother Henry, one of my other dolls. As I told stories about Ianthe, I added to her biography that she is a very close friend of another doll named Julio and that she likes to jump rope and climb trees.

These are the basic facts of Ianthe's life. Children meet Ianthe early in the year and can always say, "I know her!" when she comes to talk with them. All kinds of things happen to Ianthe throughout the year. The children see her at story-telling sessions. They listen to her problems and hear about her joys. They help her think of ways to solve her problems. They are happy for her and sad for her. They relate to her much as they would a classroom friend.

A classroom collection of *Kids Like Us* dolls can be as few as four and as many as twenty. The dolls are introduced one at a time, helping the class get to know each one individually. The collection should represent the population of students in the class and many other kids who are not represented in the class. Take into account a number of details when creating the dolls' lives— gender, age, race and ethnicity, religion, family structure, culture, class, likes and dislikes, languages, special abilities and disabilities. In this way each student will see herself in parts of the dolls and will also become comfortable with diversity.

To make the storytelling situations as real as possible, the dolls are treated much as if they were students in the class. They are kept in a special place in the classroom where they can "observe" what is happening in the room. They are available to come to talk with the group at a moment's notice but are not within a child's reach. When they are brought down from their observation point, they are treated with respect. They like hugs but do not want their hair pulled or their clothes taken off. The teacher sets the tone for this scenario of "real kids, just like us," and the children love to be part of it. "Ianthe has a problem she is hoping you can help her with," is answered with cries of *"What's wrong, Ianthe?"* and *"We'll help you, Ianthe! Don't worry!"*

This set of dolls and a knowledge of the five-step planning process (which begins on page 41) are all you need to tell stories that get your students talking, empathizing, and problem solving.

How I Brought My Dolls to Life

In my first year as the teacher at a small private school in rural Virginia, I was hopelessly lost when it came to dealing with the children's social interactions. I saw exclusion, scapegoating, arguments, and bossy behavior. I heard name-calling and put-downs. This was just an average set of kids thrown together and expected to get along. They needed social skills. None of my college training had taught me what social skills they needed, and even if I could identify them, I didn't have a clue about how to teach them to the children. I had to find my own way.

Over the next years I tried many methods to teach these essential social skills. Just discussing the problems did not help. The kids who most needed to talk about a problem tuned out. Role-playing was fun but put kids on the spot. Puppets in the hands of kids faced with social problems just growled at one another and fought.

Finally I hit on storytelling as a springboard to discussion. I made up several stories about getting along with one another, and I used pieces of felt on a flannel board to illustrate the stories. I told the whole story, including how the characters solved their problems.

The kids loved these stories and requested them again and again. I didn't know yet that the children would learn much more if I let *them* be the ones to brainstorm solutions and decide what the characters in the story should do. I had taken much of the value of discussion away by solving everything myself! Also, I never went further than a few stories because it was so time consuming to create felt pieces for each one. And there was no way I could tell a story spontaneously when a need arose. There was much too much preparation involved.

I was also learning to use conflict-resolution techniques, and I taught them to my students. When individual children or the whole group became involved in a conflict, I would mediate for them, giving each a turn to state their idea of the problem. Everyone would be asked for solutions, and all ideas would be considered. In the end, an agreement would be made based on the solution that was most amenable to everyone.

Conflict-resolution skills helped the children work out their immediate problems, and I continue to use this process with my students. But I wanted something more. I wanted to work on their social skills *before* the problems erupted into arguments on the playground. Once the issues had heated up into conflicts, the students' feelings were in the way of listening, thinking about others, and caring. This is not the best moment for teaching! I needed a technique that presented these same daily situations one step back from reality, where students would feel safe to work on them openly, without defensiveness, fear, or embarrassment. And I wanted to teach the children to care about one another. I wanted them to learn to allow people to be themselves, to help them see their diversity as an asset to the group.

Over the next few years, about a third of the children I taught were African American, the rest were European American. Half were girls, half boys. But beyond these details were a hundred others. Some of the children were not allowed to eat sugar. Some came with cookies and candy bars in their lunch every day. Some ate meat. Some were vegetarian. Some learned to read very quickly. Some had to work long and hard. One had cerebral palsy. One wore

QUESTION #1

Q: *Can children really learn not to tease?*

A: Absolutely! This method is so powerful you will see changes in your children from the first five-step story you tell. Each group has a culture all its own, and it is possible to systematically turn the "kid culture" in your classroom against put-downs, then against hurtful teasing, then against exclusion, then against bias for any reason. Without reinforcement from peers, these behaviors will not work. In fact, children persisting in these behaviors will find themselves facing a group of classmates that demand they change their ways!

Parents of children who have graduated from my program tell me things that let me know this education stays with the children. One young boy came home from a week in third grade and asked, "Why do they think boys are better than girls in my new school? In my old school we never thought that."

(continued on next page)

glasses. One had a heart condition. One was Deaf and was learning sign language. One had lesbian parents. Several split their time between two homes and separated parents. Some lived on a group farm. Two lived in mobile homes. One lived on an old colonial plantation that had been in her family for generations. Many lived on farms.

In other words, the children in my class each year were like children anywhere. They were each unique. They were regular kids in all their diversity. How could I support all of them to feel good about who they were and also teach them to respect one another and treat others fairly? I needed a simple tool to help me do this.

Then I found the *Anti-Bias Curriculum* book and a sample persona doll story by Kay Taus (see resources on page 219). Taus had found that telling a story with a doll as the main character helped to bring the story to life and helped the children make a connection to the discussion about it. After watching a three-minute clip of Taus telling a doll story on the *Anti-Bias Curriculum* video, I was inspired to try this method myself.

The next day I took a small UNICEF doll and a larger doll into the classroom and introduced them to my students. I remember the fear in the pit of my stomach as I tried to recall exactly what I had seen in the video. What was I going to say? I didn't have time to memorize an entire story, so I didn't exactly know what to do. I knew I wanted to address the problem of sharing the outside toys. I held tight to the dolls and launched into a long-winded spiel about the two of them and all they had done that day.

By the time I got to the point of my story, an argument over a jump rope, the children's attention had begun to wander. Without thinking about it, I held up one doll and made a small voice for her, yelling, "I want it!"

As soon as I did it I knew it was the wrong thing to do. It felt false. If this doll was supposed to be real in her own right, I could not speak for her. It also made the kids laugh at my funny voice, which took the focus off the argument between the dolls. I continued the story, this time using my regular voice to tell the two dolls that they should share the jump rope and practice saying, "Could I have that next, please?" The kids sat and watched.

I had made just about every mistake possible. I took control of the whole story and left no room for the children to participate. I went on and on and on, longer than small children can usually attend. I didn't know how to make the dolls seem real without dramatically acting out their characters. Somehow I muddled through to the end, sure I had blown it and the kids would gain nothing from this attempt.

I was surprised, then, when we went to the tables to draw the story and I heard, "Could I have the orange marker next?" It didn't matter that I thought I had bungled the effort. The kids were right there with the dolls and understood what they had been through. They listened and they learned. This is the power of storytelling with dolls.

It took me several years to put together my collection of dolls. It took me longer to devise a simple method to help me plan and tell my stories. I had to learn to step back and allow my students to identify the dolls' feelings and to solve the dolls' problems. Over time I learned what works and what doesn't. I learned from the kids, story by story.

I named my dolls the *Kids Like Us* dolls because they represent the kids in my class, as well as kids everywhere. I know my story is right on track when one of my children, on hearing about a problem the dolls are having, calls out excitedly, "Just like us!"

By 1995 I had refined my five-step method and begun using it to train teachers and caregivers in Oregon, where I then taught. Many educators had heard of Taus' work by this time. Some had purchased dolls and even created personalities for them, but they did not know how to proceed from there. The dolls were sitting on classroom shelves, unused.

With two hours of practice in the five steps of a *Kids Like Us* doll story, the teachers and caregivers had the tools, vision, and courage to use storytelling right away. The success of these workshops was remarkable, and I soon had more requests for them than I had time to fulfill. So I decided to write this book, including all of the information you will need to get started storytelling right away. The five-step method will enable you to easily plan and present your own stories.

Ten Goals of Kids Like Us Doll Stories

Having a group of *Kids Like Us* dolls in your classroom gives you a powerful and flexible tool. *Kids Like Us* dolls can be used in interactive storytelling sessions to help create a caring classroom community of eager learners.

Telling stories with your dolls will allow you to easily involve your students in practicing pro-social skills, problem solving, cooperation, and dealing with emotions. Being involved in discussions about the stories enables each student to develop empathy and anti-bias attitudes. Doll stories are the perfect opportunity to gently correct incorrect beliefs or stereotypes your students may have picked up. The dolls can even be used to introduce new topics of study, catching the students' attention and making them eager to learn about the subject, just like the dolls.

Let's examine some of the goals that can be reached using your *Kids Like Us* dolls (each one will be discussed in more detail beginning on page 49). The skills being taught in these stories build on themselves over time. I have

A European American child came home from school and told her mother that she needed her hair done in many small braids. When her mother asked her about the reason for this urgent need, she replied, "There's only one African American girl in my class. The other kids tease her about her braids. I want braids too, so she won't be the only one." This child wore her braids with pride and showed the other children that it is possible to stand up against bias. I have also seen my classes play together without harassment, encourage each other to learn, console each other when things don't go well, and celebrate with each other when they are successful. *Kids Like Us* doll stories have made this possible.

started with the simplest goals that can be addressed by the beginning stories appropriate for the youngest children (ages two to four) and children who are new to *Kids Like Us* stories. More advanced goals, which appear later in the sequence below, can be reached by telling stories that provide opportunities for children to discuss and problem-solve more complicated problems. These stories are most appropriate for children ages four to eight who have had experience with *Kids Like Us* stories. (More information on best goals for different ages of children can be found in chapter 10.)

1. To Bring Up a Subject; To Begin a Theme Study; To Give Information

Any subject you would like to study with your children can be introduced through a doll story. Stories that introduce a topic are especially good stories to tell to two and three year olds, but older children enjoy them as well. It is a very effective way to get your children's attention and begin to build their enthusiasm for any subject. It's also a lot of fun! You could begin a theme study by describing a doll's interest or experiences, as in the following examples.

> "Rajit loves insects. He likes to take his magnifying glass out into his backyard to look very closely at the bugs that he finds there. He loves to count their legs. How many legs do you think he finds?"

> "Mei Lin went somewhere with her grandfather this weekend. She wants to tell you all about it. Do you think you can guess where she went? I'll give you a clue. She saw lots of water and she walked in the sand."

Discussing the doll's interest or the doll's experiences gets the children involved immediately in the subject you would like them to study. The doll serves as a positive peer role model, representing another child who is fascinated by a subject. Your students will love to tell the doll (and the class) all that they know about it. And this discussion can be a springboard to further study. The following story was told to a group of three year olds:

> "Melly has been learning about farm animals at her school. She loves to make their sounds. Do you like to do that?"

> > "*I know 'moo, moo!' That's a cow!*"

> "Yes! Melly learned that one too! Let's all be cows. Moo! Moo!"

> > *[Various moos.]*

> "Why do farmers keep cows?"

> > "*Milk comes out of 'em!*"

> "Uh, huh. That's where we get milk, alright! Melly wants to learn about all the farm animals and what they can do. Would you all like to learn about that too?"

> > "*I know lots about them. I'll tell you, Melly!*"

"That's great, Nancy. Tell us about a farm animal you know. Melly would love to hear, and so would the rest of us."

"I know chickens make eggs and they go 'cluck cluck.'"

"Terrific! Thanks for telling us about chickens. They are important farm animals. What farm animals do other kids know about?"

"Me! Me! I know about cats 'cause I have one."

"It seems we know a lot about farm animals already. Melly has had a fun time talking with you all about it. Let's go make some pictures of all these animals to put up on our wall. Then we'll sing the 'I Have a Rooster' song and see if we can remember the animals' sounds."

After a doll story, the kids have a special interest in the subject discussed and will refer to the doll's interest many times. These dolls become so real to the kids that they will take their paintings and other creations over to the dolls to show them what they have learned.

2. To Undo Incorrect Information

It is very easy for children to misunderstand the grown-up world. There is so much to learn and understand. Many times they get things just a little bit wrong.

"If you cross your eyes, they'll get stuck that way."

"When a kid is really bad, parents get divorced so they don't have to live with you anymore. That's what my dad did."

"When you turn out the light at night all the monsters come out from under your bed!"

Telling a doll story can help to undo these incorrect assumptions and also let the children discuss their worries. *Kids Like Us* dolls give teachers a simple method for creating opportunities to bring up just such topics. The discussion that follows the basic story presentation allows students to relate to the dolls' experiences and feelings and to express their own. It also allows the teacher to present clear and correct information in a way that catches the children's attention and allows them to take in the information, even about subjects that carry strong emotions with them.

"One day Saed practiced crossing his eyes. It felt really funny. And then he thought maybe his eyes got stuck that way like his brother said they would!"

A *Kids Like Us* story can feature a doll who learns that his eyes won't stay crossed by discussing his concern with his mother. A story about a doll whose parents are divorcing can include clear information about *why* parents divorce, along with the strong message that the divorce has nothing to do with the parents' feelings for the children. And giving correct information about monsters is as simple as telling a story about a doll that begins the story afraid and then learns that there are no monsters.

While telling *Kids Like Us* doll stories, teachers get to know more about their students. The children's reactions to the problems the dolls present reveal issues that are important in their lives. Comments made during one doll story will make a teacher aware of a need for another story. This is especially evident when children have picked up incorrect information. For example, while telling a story that modeled continued involvement of a noncustodial father taking his child to the beach, one of my students made this comment:

> *"Mickey better not put his toes in the water 'cause a shark will bite 'em right off!"*

General head nodding from others in the group made me aware that this was a generally held fear. During the story I made sure to have Mickey paddle happily in the waves without experiencing a shark attack. I also added a study unit on ocean animals to our schedule. As part of the unit, I told a doll story about being scared of sharks. This allowed all my students to express their fears and to get correct information about the safety of swimming in the nearby ocean.

3. To Introduce a New Emotional Vocabulary Word; To Teach Skills for Handling Emotions

Young children are bursting with emotions. Minute by minute they experience great joy, sadness, fear, amazement, disappointment, and anger. Recognizing their own emotions and knowing good ways to deal with them are important personal and social coping skills that all children need to develop. In addition, the understanding that all people experience strong emotions can help children accept their own feelings.

Kids Like Us doll stories create opportunities to enlarge your students' emotional vocabulary. Presenting situations, bringing out the feelings experienced by the doll or dolls in the story, and discussing how they deal with these feelings gives the children a real-life understanding of the words. It also gives children a safe place to examine and share experiences when they have dealt with the same feelings.

In helping my class enlarge their feelings vocabulary, I told the following story. My main purpose was to give my students the meaning of the word *disappointed.*

> "On her birthday, Marcy wanted a tricycle. But she didn't get one."

This simple situation led to questions for the kids to think about, such as the following:

"How do you think she felt?"

"Have you ever felt disappointed?"

"What did you do when you were disappointed?"

Students who have not discussed emotions with the *Kids Like Us* dolls usually label most emotions either "bad" or "good" or sometimes "happy" or "sad." That is the entire range of emotions they understand and can express. Through doll stories they become familiar with *frustrated, furious, jealous, surprised, worried* and *thrilled.* Experiencing these emotions through the dolls' lives gives the words real meaning and makes it possible for the children to apply the words to their own lives.

The problem-solving process gives your group of children a common vocabulary and set of skills for dealing with emotions.

> "So Ianthe learned that hitting Julio because she was mad at him just made both of them upset and didn't solve the problem she was mad about. What do you think she should do next time she's mad? What can she do with her anger that won't hurt anyone but will help her deal with her mad feeling? Who has an idea?"

When they have helped the dolls solve problems, children are able to use those experiences to help solve their own problems, with the teacher's help.

> "Remember when Rachel's block tower fell down? She was upset just like you are now because your Lego car broke. What did she do when she felt all mad and sad at the same time?"

> "I know you are both feeling very angry now. What did we decide Ianthe should do when she was mad at Julio? What's a good way to handle those strong, angry feelings?"

4. To Teach a Pro-Social Skill; To Teach a Classroom Skill

As children mature and function at higher and higher levels of cognitive development, they are able to gain more and more pro-social skills. But how are they to learn them?

Modeling by adults and peers is a very effective way for children to learn these skills. So often, though, in these days of violent television shows and hours spent "killing" video game enemies, teachers despair of getting children to value cooperation and kindness in their play and social groupings. "Fighting and pretending to kill the bad guy are the only games they know," so many teachers say. "They don't know how to work in cooperative groups. They just end up arguing." How can kids learn to comfort others, cooperate, and think about others' feelings when they don't see their peers doing it?

Some Goals for Kids Like Us Doll Stories

- To bring up a subject; to begin a theme study; to give information
- To undo incorrect information
- To introduce a new emotional vocabulary word; to teach skills for handling emotions
- To teach a pro-social skill; to teach a classroom skill
- To practice problem-solving skills
- To support a child or all the children by mirroring their situation
- To help children become comfortable with diversity
- To undo learned stereotypes and biased beliefs
- To help children develop anti-bias attitudes
- To help children learn to stand up against bias

Modeling by the *Kids Like Us* dolls, on the other hand, is easy to make happen. All *Kids Like Us* stories help children learn pro-social skills as the children help the dolls find solutions to their problems and identify with their feelings. Specific pro-social skills can be taught through a series of doll stories, such as the following:

> **Helping:** "Umoja realized her mom was really tired because she was just getting over the flu. So she told her mom she would take care of her little sister, Imani, while her mom took a nap. Why do you think she did that? Have you ever helped out someone that way?"

> **Caring:** "Henry saw Julio fall down and skin his knee. He ran right over to see if Julio was all right. When he saw that Julio's knee was bleeding, he helped him go to the office."

Sometimes the dolls do not have the focus skill and learn it during the story:

> **Sharing:** "Elizabeth and Ricky both wanted the jump rope. They ran over to it, yelling 'It's mine!' and each grabbed an end of the rope. They started pulling and pulling on it. How do you think they felt?"

> **Empathy:** "Rajit saw some kids pointing at Henry and calling him 'Dummy.' He saw that Henry was starting to cry. How do you think Henry felt? How do you think Rajit felt when he saw that?"

> "One day when Rachel and Lucia were in the bathroom, Lucia slipped and fell. She landed right on her arm. She grabbed her arm and started to scream because it hurt very much. How do you think Lucia felt? How did Rachel feel?"

Empathy is one of the most important pro-social skills learned through *Kids Like Us* doll stories. Stories designed to encourage children to understand the feelings of the character or, most especially, of two or more characters, give children direct experiences with empathy. According to researchers, children who engage in violent behavior are unable to empathize with others. Without empathy, we have no guidelines for behavior.

Children are not born understanding how their behavior affects others. Empathy does not naturally occur without being modeled and valued repeatedly. All children need to practice putting themselves in someone else's shoes. This is a crucial skill for children to gain if they are to grow up as caring adults who take the needs of others into account. Practicing this essential skill is simple with the *Kids Like Us* dolls. Many stories can be told that lead to a discussion of the feelings of others.

Classroom skills can also be modeled and encouraged in this same way:

> **Waiting a Turn:** "Ricky was really thirsty. He ran over to the drinking fountain. Just as he got there, so did Lucia and Marcy!"

> **Using Glue Neatly:** "Rachel made a turtle out of felt. But when she went to glue the eyes on, she forgot she had the glue bottle upside down. She started talking to Mickey and poured glue all over her turtle when she wasn't looking."

Coming to School on Time: "Umoja just wouldn't get out of bed yesterday. Steve had to come back to her room three times to tell her to get up. She was an hour late getting to school that day. When she got there the other kids were all excited because a clown had come to visit their room! He had just left and Umoja didn't get to see him."

Taking a Rest: "Henry was really tired at rest time yesterday. He went right to his cot and lay down with his blanket from home. He made a special dream in his mind that he was floating in the sky on a white fluffy cloud."

Admitting Mistakes: "When Umoja went home on Thursday, the last thing the teacher said was, 'Be sure to study your spelling words for the test tomorrow!' But when Umoja got home she put her books down in her room and watched TV all afternoon. She didn't even look at those words that night."

The dolls are very willing to talk about mistakes they have made—much more willing than the real children would be! Having the dolls tell stories about their mistakes models open discussion of a problem and accepting help from friends. It gets the kids involved in problem solving on issues that are relevant to their own lives.

All of these stories give children a chance to rejoice in their own skills. They love to give the dolls advice and to relate times when they have used the skill needed.

> "You should keep your eyes on the glue next time, Rachel."

> "I know how to share better than that, Ricky. You should say, 'Can I be next?' That's what I said to Kenji when I wanted the red marker."

> "I help with my little brother all the time! I'm a good big brother."

Children will identify themselves with the positive role in *Kids Like Us* stories and work to find ways to bring themselves closer to that role. They will happily report to the teacher when they have found an opportunity to use the skills that have been discussed.

> "I helped my dad set the table last night, 'cause I'm a good helper at my house like Umoja is at her house."

> "Look! I'm good at waiting in line, just like Ricky!"

The *Kids Like Us* discussion is also a chance for children to plan for how to act when these skills are necessary in their own lives.

"Everyone was all stressed out at my house because my baby was sick last night. I remembered how Umoja helped when her mom was sick. So I stayed quiet while my parents were trying to calm the baby. When it was bedtime, I got my own self ready without them even telling me!"

"Nekicia and I both wanted to paint at the same time, so we decided to share the paper, just like we told Rachel and Saed to do with the jump rope. We made a painting together. I'm glad we didn't fight about it."

5. To Practice Problem-Solving Skills

Most *Kids Like Us* doll stories will contain discussion centered on helping the doll or dolls solve a problem or decide how to act in some situation. There are four problem-solving skills children should learn. They must be able to

- accurately describe the problem and listen to everyone's version
- think of multiple realistic solutions
- choose solutions that have the best chance of success
- find a solution that meets the needs of everyone involved

To help your students learn the skills to do this effectively, and thus to be able to problem solve in their own lives, they must practice the skills themselves. To help students practice these skills, a teacher can tell some *Kids Like Us* doll stories that focus on these problem-solving skills. These stories are designed to have many possible solutions.

"River was playing with his new slingshot at home yesterday when something happened. By mistake a rock shot right through one of the windows in the garage. No one saw it happen, but the window is very broken and River is trying to figure out what to do."

The children will identify River's feelings—worried, sad, upset, scared, sorry, guilty. Then, the majority of the storytelling session will focus on helping River think of solutions for his problem.

The following problem solving was done with six year olds. The main goal of the session was to help students think of multiple solutions and then to evaluate those solutions. The teacher led the students through this process because they were new to these skills.

"Yes. River was feeling all those feelings. He was worried and scared his parents would be very angry with him. He was very, very sorry he had broken that window. But he knew that he couldn't go back in time, even though he wished he could undo his mistake. What do you think he really could do now to take care of this problem?"

"He could try to fix the window."
"Maybe he could go and tell his parents."
"Maybe he could go away from there and pretend he didn't do it! Then he won't get in trouble."

"Those are all possibilities. Can you think of any other solutions he might try?"

"He could tell a friend and maybe the friend could help him fix it."

"Carrie, what do you think?"

"I think he should say sorry."

"Good thinking! Well, that's a lot of solutions you have thought of. Let's see—River could pretend he didn't do it, tell his parents, or say he is sorry. He could even try to fix the window and maybe get a friend to help. Which solutions do you think are the best? "

"I still say he should just pretend he doesn't know about it."

"Okay, let's look at that solution. Do you think that might work?"

"Yes. I do it all the time."
"No. I think they'd find out."

"Would this solution get the window fixed? Or make River feel better? Would it make up for the mistake River made? Or let his parents know he won't do that again?"

"No. I think it would make things worse."
"I think he should tell. They won't be that mad."
"At least he wouldn't have to be worried they'd find out anymore."
"And he could say sorry too."

"Let's check out the idea of saying he is sorry. Do you think River really IS sorry? That means he wishes he hadn't done it and he plans not to do it again."

"Yes, he is sorry. Maybe he could fix the window first, though, before he tells."

"That's right. One solution was that he might fix the window. Could that work?"

"I don't think so. Windows are sharp. My sister told me not to touch broken glass."

"You have all done some really good problem solving for River today. He even used some of the ideas you came up with. He decided to tell his parents right away, so they wouldn't think he tried to hide it from them. He told them he was really sorry and promised to be more careful with his slingshot. Then he went with his mom to the glass store to get a new pane for the broken window."

6. To Support a Child or All the Children by Mirroring a Situation

The *Kids Like Us* dolls can also be used as a mirror for the children in your group. When one or all of your students are experiencing a difficult situation or could use some guidance in a particular situation, creating a *Kids Like Us* story that is similar can be very helpful.

"Henry is having a problem he wants to tell you about. Sometimes when things don't go his way, he gets soooo mad, and before he even thinks about it, he bites someone."

Seeing someone else, even a doll, going through the same struggles and emotions that a child is experiencing can be enormously supportive. This gives children a chance to share their emotions with their teacher and their friends.

"Rachel had to pack up all of her toys and things into boxes. She and her mom moved out of their apartment yesterday. Rachel really misses her old house."

"Hey, Rachel! Me and my dad just moved too! I didn't like it either. Did you cry too?"

In this type of story, when the children problem solve for the doll, they are actually helping the real child find possible solutions. For some children it can be important just to hear that there *are* possible solutions.

"What do you think Mei Lin can do next time she is tempted to take candy off the shelf? She needs some good ideas. Who can help her?"

"How can Melly make up for that mistake? She knows now that she shouldn't call names, and she wishes she hadn't done that to River. Is there anything she can do to let River know she's sorry and she won't do it again? Who has an idea?"

When the whole group is experiencing or anticipating a difficult situation, problem solving during a *Kids Like Us* story can help each student deal with the problem better.

"Melly heard on the TV news last night that soldiers are being sent to Iraq. She heard they were going to drop bombs on Iraq. That made her think maybe the war would come here and the Iraqi people would drop bombs on *her* house! Can you imagine how she was feeling?"

"Yeah. Really, really scared! I hid under my bed when I heard about the war!"

"I think maybe lots of kids have been feeling this way. How many of you have been scared about bombs?"

What a relief to have a chance to tell someone about these secret worries and to find out that you are not alone! This type of story also creates an opportunity for the teacher to present correct information to alleviate fears for the whole group.

I always make sure the situation I present does not exactly represent the child I am mirroring. Instead, I use just the general situation that the child is experiencing as the basis of my story. Often just changing the gender of the main character is enough. Then these stories can be used effectively even in very difficult situations or when children are very upset.

"Julio really misses his mom. He hasn't seen her in a long time because she is way far away in Guatemala. Sometimes he worries that he won't see her again."

When I told this story, the child who I knew was crying herself to sleep at night because her mother had moved away sat up straight with excitement on her face and volunteered the following:

"Just like me! I miss my mom, too, Julio! My mom is far away, just like yours!"

At the end of the story this child asked to hold the doll. She took him into the pillow pit and spent twenty minutes whispering into his ear. After that day, from time to time, she would ask to talk with Julio and would spend some quiet time with him, sharing her concerns and fears. He had clearly become a symbol of support that helped her through this difficult situation.

7. To Help Children Become Comfortable with Diversity

Kids Like Us dolls are an important part of a multicultural, inclusive classroom environment. Having *Kids Like Us* dolls as respected and loved members of your class sets the tone for respect for diversity. The dolls represent many cultures, families, races, and religions. They have their own distinct features, skin color, and clothing styles. As the children get to know the dolls, they learn and accept that each doll has its own type of family with its own traditions, foods, activities, and religious beliefs. To love and care about the doll, the children have to accept all aspects of the doll.

And this is very important for even the youngest children. Research shows that by age two, children begin to notice and categorize differences between people. By age three, children begin to place judgment values on these differences. Too often our society's push toward conformity translates into negative values being associated with these differences.

As children go through the process of learning about their world, they will be curious. They will need information. If they are not directly given this information, they will ask for it. Unfortunately, it is not unusual for a curious child to ask:

> *"How come your teeth stick out crooked?"*
> *"Are you black all over 'cause you forgot to wash?"*
> *"Where'd that kid with the funny eyes come from?"*

Children need to get information, and using *Kids Like Us* doll stories can give that information to them *before* they subject other children or adults to such questioning. Without information and positive experiences with diversity, children learn to classify anything different from their own experience as "weird." This is why teachers and caregivers need to be proactive about giving our children the information they need.

Kids Like Us doll stories create many opportunities to help children become comfortable with diversity. During doll stories they will be exposed to many new diversities and will have the opportunity to ask all the questions they have about them. They will discover common experiences, feelings, and actions between themselves and dolls that are otherwise different from them in many other ways.

Using *Kids Like Us* dolls gives a teacher a ready-made, simple method to introduce diversity issues and discuss them naturally and in a nonstressful environment. Any classroom with an established population of *Kids Like Us* dolls has a whole set of diversity lessons just waiting to be discussed.

> "Henry's ears don't hear very well. He can hear big trucks when they go rumbling down the street, but he can't hear you when you talk. Since he hasn't heard people talk, he doesn't know how to make the right sounds for talking. He is learning sign language now so he can talk with his hands."

> "Melly lived near the Siletz homeland when she was little because her family belongs to the Siletz tribe of Native Americans. When Melly was three, her mom and dad moved with her to our town, and she has lived here ever since. Sometimes they miss living near other Native Americans. They like to go to powwows because at powwows lots of Native Americans come together to celebrate their cultures. Melly really likes the dances and the food at powwows. She wants to learn some dances next summer when she goes to visit the rest of her family near the reservation."

"When Umoja's teeth came in, there just wasn't enough room on her jawbone for all of them to fit. They had to overlap a little and the front ones made room by sticking out a bit. She can chew all right and everything. That's just how her teeth are. She is careful to take good care of them by brushing after she eats. She wants her teeth to last her whole life long."

These stories create an opportunity to do three important things: model comfort with diversity, talk calmly about many issues, and give children basic information.

8. To Undo Learned Stereotypes and Biased Beliefs

Stereotypes lump together everyone who shares a trait. Stereotypes simplify things by allowing us to feel that we know all about someone before having met them. But this type of "prejudging" is exactly what "prejudice" is made of. It is judging a person without knowing them individually. Some stereotypes have negative connotations and some are positive, but all stereotypes are harmful because they keep us from seeing the individual.

Children are attracted to stereotypes as a way to organize their world. And we present stereotypes to them constantly through television shows, books, toys, and movies and all the paraphernalia marketed with them. Stereotypes are created in our children's minds about gender, race and ethnicity, religion, culture, class, body size, and anything else that makes one person different from another.

Research shows that teachers and other adults in children's lives encourage and reinforce stereotyped beliefs by our unconscious actions and expectations of children. For instance, even parents who insist that they treat boys and girls the same were shown to describe a child's personality and interests differently depending on whether they thought the child was a girl or a boy. This experiment was described first in a journal article, "Maternal Behavior and Perceived Sex of Infant" (*American Journal of Orthopsychiatry*, 1976, 46, 1). It is discussed fully in *Growing Up Free: Raising Your Child in the '80s* by Letty Cottin Pogrebin, which is out of print. A newer book, *Beyond Dolls and Guns* (see the resources section), also discusses these issues.

Teachers notice children expressing stereotyped beliefs but often do not know what to say to the children, or even how to bring up the subject.

"That doll's the bad guy. Look at its slanty eyes!"

"Boys have short hair. Girls have to have long hair. You're a boy 'cause your hair is short."

"He's really good at basketball. All black kids are."

Using *Kids Like Us* dolls is a gentle and yet direct and effective way to undo children's incorrect or prejudiced beliefs. Discussing the dolls' experiences, feelings, and mistakes allows the children to admit their mistakes and learn some new ideas.

Presenting a doll story about stereotypes allows a forthright conversation to take place without putting any of your students in the position of being shamed for their beliefs or behaviors. Children need information and the *Kids Like Us* dolls can give it to them in a way they can hear and understand.

Learning the five-step method for telling *Kids Like Us* stories will enable any teacher to present simple stories about any subject—even those that are difficult for us to talk about. Rather than fretting and worrying over what to say about race, religion, or the death of a parent, it becomes a simple matter of taking out one of the dolls and putting together a story about the subject.

One way to use this method to undo stereotypes is to bring *Kids Like Us* dolls to the group to tell about something they used to believe but have since learned was not true.

> " Julio used to think Mickey couldn't be his friend because Mickey can't walk by himself. But now he knows a person doesn't have to walk to be a good friend. He and Mickey have so much fun drawing together. Julio is really glad he learned that he doesn't need to be afraid of people who get around in wheelchairs."

It is much easier for dolls to bring up these feelings and mistakes than it is for your students. And yet your students will relate to the dolls' stories as though one of the kids in the class is telling it. And many times the students who had believed those stereotypes will be the most vocal in their rejection of them during the discussion, almost as if they were pushing that old notion firmly away from themselves.

When I heard a gender-based stereotyped comment at the computer *("You girls go away! Boys are the only ones who like computers!")*, I told a similar story that happened to a *Kids Like Us* doll.

> " When Rachel was in the sandbox, Rajit told her she couldn't have the dump truck because trucks are for boys."

A general discussion followed about what girls can do and what boys can do. This gave the girls a chance to stand up for their right and ability to do anything, even though they had just come to that understanding the moment before. Several of the girls took the opportunity to assert their love of trucks. Several of the boys stated most emphatically that they always share the trucks with everyone. This led to a discussion of other things people claim are "not for girls," including the class computer!

When the dolls model being willing to talk about such things, you will find that your students will also be willing to talk about their mistakes and how they have learned to correct them. It is very common to have a child eagerly admit that they have just learned a lesson from the dolls.

> *" I used to think girls didn't like computers!"*
> *" Yeah, I used to tell the girls that computers are for boys, but I won't say that anymore."*

9. To Help Children Develop Anti-Bias Attitudes

By age four, many children discover the power of biased behavior through put-downs, name-calling, and exclusion.

> *"Beaver! Beaver! Don't bite us with those crooked teeth!"*

> *"Gimme that swing, fag!*

> *"Quick! Run away! That scary slanty-eyed kid is coming!"*

A preschool teacher once told me that she had heard several children excluding another with the words, *"You can't play here. Only white kids are allowed in this fort!"* She said she had not intervened because she "didn't want to interfere with their play" and because the excluded child went on to do something else anyway. All of the children in that fort learned that racial exclusion is a way to take power over someone. The excluded child sobbed at bedtime. The event told her that there was something wrong with her race and that it was acceptable for her to be excluded because of it.

Many parents and teachers take what they subconsciously consider to be the "safe road"— saying nothing about such tension-filled issues as race, religion, or disability. Many times parents feel, "I don't want to make a big deal about these things, so I just don't say anything about them."

But saying nothing simply leaves the children without input from the adults in their lives. And while the children are sorting it out for themselves, they are having an effect on all the other children they interact with—both those being hurt by the bias and those benefiting from it.

Children exhibiting these behaviors are not thinking about the feelings of the child they are excluding. Often their biased behavior is not motivated by some deep-seated hatred but simply by its effectiveness and because others seem to approve. Other children may be mesmerized by this type of behavior and wait to see what happens. Children interpret adults' silence as acceptance of this behavior. And, when it serves to give a child power over the group, it looks to others like a good way to behave.

Stories that introduce bias situations take the discussions one step further than stories that teach comfort with diversity. Here the focus is on helping children learn to recognize bias and to reject it.

> *"When Henry went out to recess, one of the big kids came up to him and said, 'Ewww! What are those things hanging from your ears? Ewww! Let's get outta here!' Then he and his friends laughed and ran away."*

By having the *Kids Like Us* dolls experience bias in a story, the teacher has an opportunity to discuss these situations before they occur among the students. In fact, these experiences preempt this kind of behavior because students learn how much bias hurts and empathize with the doll that has lived through it.

"When Ianthe was out riding her bike yesterday, she rode by two kids on the sidewalk. When she was past them, they yelled out to her, 'Hey, brownie. Get off our street!' How do you think that made her feel?"

"When River first came to his school, some of the boys teased him. They called him a girl and pretended they were going to cut off his long hair. How do you think that made him feel? How would you feel if that happened to you? Do you think River should cut off his hair? What do you think he should do?"

For students and teachers alike, everything is easier to talk about when it is one step removed from reality. If any of these situations had just occurred on the playground, the student who had been harassed would be crushed, and the students who harassed him would be defensive. Instead, all the children are open to the subject and interested participants in the discussion. They are all free to consider how everyone in the situation would feel and what they would do if they were in a similar situation. They search inside themselves for answers to many questions:

"Why do you think those kids said that?"

"What do you think River could have done after they did that to him?"

"Would you have said those things to River if you were there? Why not? "

An incredible change in children's behavior toward one another can be brought about by their growing awareness of how their behavior can affect other people. During *Kids Like Us* discussions, kids unerringly place themselves on the side of the characters doing the right thing and reinforce their feeling about themselves as someone who cares about others.

"I wouldn't say that to River. I don't think that's right. It could make him feel real bad to say he's a girl when he's not. That's a stereotype about long hair. I don't believe it."

10. To Help Children Learn to Stand Up Against Bias

It is an easy step from helping children understand how bias hurts to helping them plan how to stand up against it. All of the children will experience bias in their lives—aimed at them and at others. To give them tools to deal with bias *before* they have experienced very much of it is an invaluable gift they will use the rest of their lives.

"Mei Lin heard the kids whispering, 'China girl,' when she walked down the hall."

With one sentence, a teacher launches her students into a discussion that will teach them to stand up against bias rather than being a part of it. They will consider the motivations of people acting biased toward others.

"I think those kids said that because they were trying to act cool, but it's not cool to make people feel bad."

They will discuss and learn what to do when they are part of a group that is being biased against someone:

> "What if your friends were the ones whispering? What would YOU do?"

> > "If my friends said that, I'd tell them that's not nice! I'd tell them to stop it or I'd leave."

They will empathize with the dolls experiencing the bias and learn how to support them:

> "What if you were there with Mei Lin? How could you help her?"

> > "I would tell her to come away from those kids. I'd tell her to come walk with me!"

They will listen to one another's answers. They will encourage one another to be supportive, to be a friend, to do the right thing. They will turn the classroom culture toward caring and support and away from teasing, name-calling, exclusion, put-downs, and other biased behavior and attitudes.

> > "One time some kids next door called my sister 'snot nose.' I told her they just wanted to make her mad, and we ignored them."

When a *Kids Like Us* doll story helps children think, insights can occur. A five year old in my class made this comment:

> > "I think she teased him about his name because she was afraid they would tease her about her glasses. She tried to make everybody tease somebody else instead of her."

These ten goals and many others can easily be reached using *Kids Like Us* dolls and the five-step storytelling method described in chapter 3. Teachers will find their own uses for the dolls. You will use a doll story to meet any immediate need you see in your classroom, regardless of the progression of skills listed here. It is easiest and best to start with the skills at the beginning of this list of goals; however, sometimes you will need to tell a story that deals with a more advanced skill, so it's helpful to be familiar with all the possibilities.

CHAPTER 2

Creating Your Collection of Kids Like Us Dolls

our dolls will be the center of all your storytelling sessions. They will become more and more real to you as you use them, so take great care to get dolls that will be able to come to life for you. ● You'll need four to seven dolls to begin, and you can add to your collection over time. It is true that storytelling sessions can be told using any doll, but if you are going to take full advantage of the *Kids Like Us* technique, you will need to establish a set of dolls, each with its own identity. ● I bought my dolls as blank doll bodies, and then added hair, bought clothes, and got a friend to paint realistic faces on them. I began with four and, as I completed new ones, added them to the dolls the children had already met. After several years of adding a new doll now and then, I have seventeen dolls.

Buying Dolls

QUESTION #2

Q: *I can't afford expensive dolls. Can I still do this?*

A: Yes. Any dolls will do, as long as you can bring them to life for the kids and yourself and you use the dolls only for *Kids Like Us* doll stories. Some teachers even use large photographs to represent the kids in the story. Get started storytelling in whatever way you can. And reach out to the parents in your program. You may find someone who can sew simple dolls for just the cost of a couple of yards of material.

I find it best to either buy or make cloth dolls. These dolls can be hugged and have their hands held, and they feel more like living beings than molded plastic dolls. It is also easier to give cloth dolls racially accurate features, because the features are already molded into plastic dolls, and most manufacturers use the same features for all their dolls regardless of skin color.

Some of the best dolls available are the People of Every Stripe dolls (see the resources list on page 219). They have realistic faces and come in a wide variety of skin colors, hair, and facial features. These dolls come in a couple of sizes, and they are available fully clothed, even down to tiny sneakers, shiny shoes, or cowpoke boots! In addition, these dolls can be fitted with glasses, braces, hearing aids, or a prosthetic leg. Wheelchairs and walkers are available as well. Some plastic dolls are available in a variety of skin tones, but most of these dolls, no matter the skin tone, have the same European American features. Children need to see that noses, eyes, mouths, and ears come in different sizes and shapes. Don't buy these dolls thinking that they'll be good enough. These dolls perpetuate the Eurocentric view many children have already formed. (For information on companies that sell dolls, see the resources list on page 219.)

Making Dolls

If you'd like to have a variety of cloth dolls but can't afford to buy them, it is possible to make them. If you or someone you know can sew (possibly a talented parent?), it is not that difficult. There are four elements to making a doll: skin, hair, faces, and clothes.

Making the doll's basic shape in a variety of skin colors will require a pattern for a rag doll, which can be found in any doll-making book, and skin-tone fabric. When looking for a good body pattern, keep it simple. Unless the person doing the sewing is highly skilled, a flat face and body will do very well. The dolls should be stuffed loosely enough so they are able to sit down and bend their arms, but they should have stiff necks so they can hold up their heads. (An exception to this is when creating a doll to represent a child with little muscle control.)

Kids Like Us dolls can be any size, from 10 inches to life-sized, but I recommend that you make them between 20 and 25 inches. These are large enough to really be a presence in the room but small enough to be passed around the circle and stored on a shelf in the classroom. Clothes for this size of doll are easy to obtain. It is much harder to find them for smaller dolls.

All children are not the same size and neither should your dolls be. To represent the real diversity of people, it is important to make some dolls a bit smaller, some a bit taller, some thinner, some fatter. You may want to make a doll that is missing an arm or leg.

It's not easy to find fabric in a full range of skin tones. You may have to search several fabric stores to find what you need. You will want at least six colors, from a light tan to an ebony brown. Unless you are making an albino doll, none of the dolls should have absolutely white skin. Likewise, none of your dolls should be made with entirely black skin, although having very dark brown dolls is a good idea. Black and white are only labels that people have invented—they don't really reflect what people look like.

Once you have the doll bodies sewn and stuffed, you are ready to bring your dolls to life. This is the fun part!

Hair can be added in several ways. Make sure you make the type of hair appropriate to each doll's racial and ethnic background, and make it strong enough to stand up to handling. These dolls will not be dragged by their hair around the dramatic play area, but they will need to be sturdy enough to be passed around, hugged, and stroked.

The simplest and most durable way to add hair to a doll is to buy a doll wig. These are available in doll-makers' catalogs and magazines, but they are expensive and might not fit the doll you have made.

To make hair for your doll, I recommend using hot glue. This is the fastest way to attach many strands of hair. It dries clear and very quickly.

Yarn makes good straight hair. It can be braided and then sewn or glued on at the part and around the ears and nape of the neck. It can be attached across the top of the head and then left to hang down to the doll's shoulders. Very fine yarn can be braided into many small cornrows and then glued into place. Beads glued at the bottom of each row make this an outstanding "do."

Curly hair in a couple of colors can be purchased at craft stores. It comes in long, loose strands. Spreading a line of hot glue across a piece of the doll's scalp and then quickly sticking strands of this hair into it works well. Going piece by piece across the doll's head and putting the strands as close together as you can will give the doll a thick head of hair. This type of hair can also be rubbed between your fingers to create kinky hair. I have made long black curly hair, a frizzy mop of hair, and a short flattop of tight, kinky hair using this product.

Finally, very short hair can be painted on. I used thick acrylic paint and spread it on lavishly, making ridges to represent strands of hair. Faces can also be created using acrylic paint. Using a few lines and a bit of shading, you can create many different faces with ethnically accurate features, and each one is unique.

QUESTION #3

Q: *Why shouldn't I let the kids play with the dolls? It seems a waste to have them sitting there.*

A: There are two reasons: First, your dolls are likely to need more careful handling than the baby dolls in the housekeeping area that get dragged around by their hair! If you have invested time or money in your dolls, you will want to make them last many years.

Second, in order to create the feeling that the dolls are real kids with their own lives, you need to encourage the children to treat them as small people. With this in mind, it is appropriate to take one to sit in your lap to talk to, or even to invite one to come listen to a story being read, but not to use them for imagination games.

TIP!

Getting Acquainted

Spend a bit of time getting to know each doll individually. Read over the biography you create for her. Take her home for a few days. Put her somewhere you can see her often. The more alive the doll seems to you the easier it will be to first introduce her to the children and to help them see her as real too.

A full-size, copyable set of these doll faces can be found in the resource section (see page 216). Use these faces as guidelines, or use tracing paper to transfer the drawings right to the face of the doll. Use a very small brush and thick acrylics to paint the faces. Start with the eyebrows and eyes and then work your way down the face, letting the paint dry between applications of different colors. Keep the face simple and the doll's personality will jump right out at you. Vary the faces a bit for each doll. Remember that they don't have to be perfect, and each one should be unique.

Clothes are easy to find. Any thrift store with a collection of baby clothes will have what you need. Tiny jeans, sweat suits, T-shirts, and even bathing suits and winter coats are made for infants. Put onto your *Kids Like Us* dolls, they immediately become kids' clothes! Dress your dolls last so you don't get glue and paint on their clothes. Then they are ready to receive their identities.

Creating a Balanced Collection

The process of creating your dolls' identities begins with a close look at your current classroom population. You will do this to identify both the children's characteristics that you want your doll collection to reflect and the characteristics that are missing from your classroom. Both sets of information will be included in the lives of your dolls.

Remember that we are not talking only about race or skin color. Your doll collection will model many different physical and nonphysical characteristics. When selecting dolls for your collection, be sure to include physical diversities such as hair and eye color, size, and other special details.

After you have represented a diverse set of physical characteristics, you will also give your dolls diverse personal identities. These identities will consist of facts about your dolls' lives that, over time, you will relate to your students' lives as part of the stories you tell. You will consider such factors as family structure and history, age, language spoken, cultural background, economic class, religion, home, parents' occupations, favorite activities and foods, and individual behaviors.

Student Population Record

Filling out the two pages of the Student Population Record (see page 206) will help you see the full range of diversity in your group. Never again will you feel that your students are more or less the same! You also want to communicate this perspective to your students. We have so much in common, but each of us is an individual in so many ways. Understanding this yourself is a first important step. To begin, fill in the top boxes of the Student Population Record with information about the children in your class. In addition to helping you choose

	Names	Race/Ethnicity	Physical Appearance/ Other Characteristics	Favorite Activities and Foods	Individual Behaviors
My Class					
New					

	Family Structure	Economic Class/Home/ Parent Occupation	Recent Family History	Family Culture/ Language	Religion
My Class					
New					

dolls and assign them identities, getting to know the children in your class will help you see which issues would be good to use as story lines. Looking back at this chart often as you plan your stories will enable you to create situations that the children can relate to and that help them discuss and problem solve issues they are dealing with in their own lives.

Using details from the children's real lives will make the dolls' identities ring true to your students. They just love to be able to say, "She's just like ME!" When a European American boy from a single-parent family that lives in a small apartment says this about a Native American girl doll from a large extended family that lives in a large house because they both like playing soccer best, you know your children are learning already.

When you begin to go through the questions about your students, you may be surprised to see that you don't know much about them in one category or another. You may have to request some information from families for categories like family culture and recent history. Some categories, like favorite activities and foods, can be fun to learn about by interviewing the kids themselves. In some categories you will have to use whatever information you have picked up from the children and your observations of them.

Here are the notes I took one year about the family structures of my students. (See page 32 for guidance on how to use this information when creating the dolls' identities.)

Family Structure	Economic Class/Home/ Parent Occupation	Recent Far
My Class - single moms: some contact with dad occasionally; visits dad most weekends; no dad - single dad: sees mother occasionally - mom and dad together at home - lives with grandma and 2 older siblings - lives with 2 lesbian moms - adopted: by single mom; by mom and dad; from India - siblings: two older brothers; much older sibling; no siblings; expecting a new baby; expecting to adopt a new sibling - other adults: very close to grandma and grandpa; to baby-sitter; to "aunt" - has very ill parent - household: two households; in group situation with two other families - three interracial families		

Questions to Help You Think about Your Students

Names

- Do any children share the same name? Which name?
- Are any children named the same name as a parent? As another family member?
- Do any children have a first name that's traditional in their family?
- Do any children know a special meaning for their names?
- Are any children named after a famous person? A season? A plant? An animal?
- Do any children have nicknames? What are they?
- Do any children have names that come from their cultural background?
- Do any children have a name made especially for them?
- Do any children have different last names than one or both of their parents?
- Do any children have hyphenated last names?

Race and Ethnicity

- What races/ethnicities are represented in your class?
- Are most of the children of the same race? Which?
- Are any children in interracial families?

Physical Appearance

- What hair textures are present in your group (straight, wavy, curly, kinky, very kinky)?
- What hair colors are present in your group?
- What hair lengths are present in your group?
- What are some of the ways children wear their hair?
- What skin colors do your students have (tawny, russet, golden, peach, ebony, cinnamon, olive, cocoa, light tan)?
- What are some of the facial features you see in the children?

Size

- Are some children much shorter than others? Much taller?
- Are there any children who are very thin? Any children with a large build?
- Are there any children with special growth conditions?
- Are there any children with body parts of an unusual size (ears, feet, head)?

Other Physical Characteristics

Do any children have the following?

- birthmarks
- scars
- an overbite
- visible disabilities

Do any children wear the following?

- glasses
- hearing aids
- braces (teeth or leg)
- a prosthesis
- special clothing
- torn or ragged clothing

Do any children use the following?

- a walker
- a cane
- a wheelchair
- a communication board
- Braille books
- a computer (to communicate)
- special pencil grips
- an inhaler

Favorite Activities and Foods

Do some of your children

- like to play sports? Which sports?
- like to draw? What does each of them draw? What other art activities do they like?
- have favorite recess games? Which games?

- have a favorite pretend game they play? What stories do they imagine?
- have favorite lunch foods? What are they? Favorite dinner or breakfast foods?
- have a favorite treat? What is it?
- enjoy certain books over and over? Which books?
- have special places on the playground where they especially like to be? Where?
- have favorite activities they do at home? What activities?
- have favorite toys or cuddle animals? What are they?
- have favorite places they like to go with their parents? Where?

Individual Behaviors

Do some of your children

- suck their thumb or fingers?
- twirl their hair?
- get bloody noses?
- stutter?
- get the hiccups a lot?
- run everywhere?
- constantly whistle or sing?
- talk quickly or like to talk all the time?
- fall asleep at school?
- come to school late a lot?
- play at the sink when washing hands?
- whoop and yell as soon as they get outside?
- complain about everything?
- feel afraid of everything new?
- hate to get messy?
- love to get messy?
- pick at their food?
- fall down a lot?
- raise their hand to talk all the time?

- never talk unless called on?
- head to the block area every day? Or the dramatic play area?
- cling to the teacher?
- eagerly make new friends?

Family Structure

- Who does each child live with?
- Who are the important adults in each child's life? What roles do these adults have in the family?
- Do any children live with other siblings? Do any have siblings they do not live with?
- Are there any siblings who are very close or very different in age to the children in your class?
- Do any children have people they love and count as family that they don't see often? Or don't see at all?
- Do any children have people of different races in the family?
- Are any children adopted? Are their adoptions open or closed?
- Do any children have adopted siblings?
- Do any children live in foster families? If so, how long have they been with their current families? How long have they been in foster care?

Economic Class

- Are any children from families with an upper-class lifestyle? Middle-class? Working-class? Poor?
- Are any children on welfare?
- Are any children homeless?
- Do any children come to school without breakfast?
- Do any children have difficulty buying school materials?
- Do any children have all the latest toys or clothes?

- Do any children travel a lot?
- Are any children able to obtain whatever they want?

Homes

- Do all children have a home? Are some homeless? Are some living somewhere temporarily?
- What type of homes do your children live in (mansion, trailer, ranch house, apartment)?
- Have any children moved to new houses a lot? Have any moved recently?
- What neighborhoods do the children live in?
- Do some children have their own bedroom?
- Do some children share a room? Do some share a bed? Who do they share with?
- Do some children sleep in a bed with their parents?
- Do some children live in two homes—each with a different parent?

Parents' Occupations

- What occupations do the parents of the children have?
- Do both parents work?
- Does only one parent work? Which parent?
- Do one or both parents take care of the children in each family?
- Do some families have parents who work at night or in the afternoon and evening?
- Do any children ocassionally go with a parent to work?
- Do any children stay home alone while their parents are at work?
- Do any children stay in child care while their parents are at work?
- Are any parents going to school?

Recent Family History

- Are any of the children's parents new to the area? If so, where did they move from?
- Have any of the families lived in the same place for a long time?

- Did any of the parents grow up in this area?
- Did any of the parents grow up far away? In a different country?
- Do any families have ties to another place (friends and family, language, culture)?
- Have any parents recently divorced or separated?
- Have any families been newly formed (stepfamilies, recent adoption)?
- Have any family added new members recently?
- Are any families expecting or planning for a new sibling?
- Has there been a death in any family recently? Are any expected?
- Have there been any other big occurrences in any family?
- Have any children been abused by a family member?
- Have any children been removed from their family? For what reasons?

Cultural Backgrounds

- What cultures do your children come from? (Remember, every child has a culture.)
- Do the families have much awareness of their cultural backgrounds?
- What special events are part of your children's cultures?
- What foods from their families' cultures are special to the children?
- What traditions do the families participate in?
- What kinds of music are part of the children's family lives?

Spoken Languages

- What languages are spoken in your children's homes?
- Do the children's parents speak English?

- Can any children speak or understand another language besides English? Which one? Are they fully bilingual?
- Are any children just beginning to learn English?
- Do any children refuse to speak their home language at school?
- Do any children know other children or adults who speak a language that they do not know?

Religion

- Is religion important to some children's families?
- To which different religions do the families in your class belong?
- Are there special things some children must do or wear because of their religion?
- Are there religious holidays that are important to your children? Other important religious traditions?

Adding Missing Diversity

After you've looked at the characteristics in your classroom, the next step in creating a balanced collection is to add to the Student Population Record the items that are *not* present in your classroom. Look at the details in each category and ask yourself, "What is missing? Who have I left out of this picture?" Think about the people in your community who are not represented in your classroom. Go through each category on the Student Population Record again and add these missing characteristics in the boxes labeled "New."

Choosing Your Dolls' Characteristics

Now that you have information at your fingertips about the details of your children's lives and about those not represented in your class, you will begin to create your dolls' identities. Of course, you have just accumulated a huge amount of information and will not be able to assign every detail to a doll! You will have to decide which details to use.

An easy way to do this is to go through the Student Population Record and circle the details you think are most important to include in your dolls' identities. Some of the characteristics you choose will come directly from your students' lives. There are several things to keep in mind as you do this:

- Be sure to include characteristics you think will reflect the most important elements of your students' lives. For example, if one of your students is trying to adjust to living in a new stepfamily configuration, be sure to circle that family structure for inclusion in one doll's life. If you have students who are bilingual, make a couple of your dolls bilingual.
- If one of your students has low self-esteem or has been teased because of an identity detail, include that detail in your list. This will allow you to show a doll being self-accepting. For example, if you have any children

who are teased for their accent, freckles, frizzy hair, or hippie clothes, these should be part of your dolls' lives.

- Include any characteristic on your list that is true for only a few children. You want all the children to see themselves in various parts of the dolls, but children in the minority or those with special issues in some ways have an even more urgent need to have their lives acknowledged in your classroom. Children who do not have as many opportunities for validation from the general society have an extra need to see themselves in the lives of the *Kids Like Us* dolls.

- Include characteristics that you think many children do not have any information about. This will help the children understand their classmates' lives better. A doll's identity is a simple way to help your children learn about a classmate's religion, medical condition, or family structure without making the child tell this information.

- Finally, some of the characteristics you give to your dolls should come from the list of characteristics that are *not* present in your classroom. If your class has very little diversity in one category, first present a couple of dolls that are like your classroom population. Then use other dolls to create the diversity you would like your children to become familiar with.

Keeping these points in mind, you can give the *Kids Like Us* dolls characteristics that will both relate to the children's experiences and provide diversity. For example, a class might have almost entirely "mom and dad" families, with only a couple of children living in different family configurations. These children may not even be aware that there are other ways to be a family. Through their own experiences, books, movies, teachers' comments, and people's assumptions, children in a class like this will learn to assume that the only "real" family consists of a mom, dad, and kids. This also means that children living in different family configurations may believe the same thing and feel that there is something "wrong" with their family. In a situation like this, when the classroom population fits the mainstream stereotype of "who everybody is," it will be especially important to widen the children's view of the world by adding new diversities to the lives of your *Kids Like Us* dolls.

In my own example about family structure on page 28, I found that my class contained quite a variety of family structures and that I did not need to add diversity to this category. On the other hand, I found very little racial or ethnic diversity—all of my students were either European American or biracial (African American/European American). I added the following to my notes in this category: Mexican American, Guatemalan, Chinese American, Native American, Greek, East Indian American, Japanese American, Egyptian, Albanian, and Iranian. When creating my doll collection, I created two European American and two biracial dolls. Then I made two of my dolls Hispanic (Mexican American and Guatemalan American) to represent a large part of our local population. Later I made dolls that were Chinese American, Native American, East Indian American, and Iranian. In this way you can create a collection of *Kids Like Us* dolls that can easily represent a full spectrum of people's lives and give your students a more realistic view of the world in all its wonderful diversity.

Kids Like Us Identity Planning Chart

Now that you have chosen some characteristics you would like to represent, you will combine them to make full biographies for your *Kids Like Us* dolls.

The *Kids Like Us* Identity Planning Chart (see page 208) will help you to do this. Each chart can hold information about four dolls. Copy the chart as many times as necessary to make a space for each doll that you plan to have in your collection. Use a pencil to fill in the chart. You can then rearrange the characteristics you've assigned to the dolls after you've had some time to reflect on how well they mirror the children in your class and introduce diversity. Then lay the charts in front of you so you can see them all at once.

Name	G B	Age	Physical			Family			Behaviors/ Activities/Food
			Race/ Ethnicity	Physical Appearance	Other Characteristics	Family Structure	Class/Home Parent Occupation	History, Religion Culture, Language	

Follow these guidelines as you choose and combine details from each category to describe each doll's life:

- Balance the characteristics of your doll collection between those shared by your students and those that are *not* present in your class. Put a priority on including details that reflect your community's diversity. Make sure that each category (family structure, class, and so on) is represented in many different ways in your set of dolls.

- Avoid inadvertently reinforcing any stereotypes with your dolls' biographies. For instance, be sure not to make all of your African American dolls live in single-parent families or all of your Hispanic dolls unable to speak English. Dolls with physical disabilities should come from wealthy as well as poor families. Create a mom who's a surgeon and a dad who takes care of the kids.

- If you are creating a doll that is not like your students in several ways, be sure to give it some characteristics to share with them. For example, a doll with a race that is just being introduced to the kids can match some of them in family structure or individual behaviors.

- If you are creating a doll that shares a detail that is true of only one child in your group, be sure to make the doll very different from the child in other ways. For instance, if you have a European American boy who stutters, make an Asian American girl who has a stutter. Usually, the children will not feel they have been imitated if the gender of the doll is different from their own (which tells us how strong a factor this is in young children's lives), but it is best to vary several characteristics.

Leave the name category on the Identity Planning Chart blank for a while since you need to know more about each doll before you can assign it a name.

The first category to fill in is gender. Your dolls should represent roughly an even mix of girls and boys, unless your population is greatly skewed one way or the other. It is especially important to include some boy dolls when you first introduce the dolls since many children assume all dolls are girls.

Age comes next. Again, this should roughly represent the ages of the children in your classroom. If your students are all near the same age, vary the dolls' ages by a year or two for a bit of variety. If you have a child that is either much younger or older than all the rest, be sure you create a doll that reflects this as well. If you will have more than five dolls, it is a good idea to have a couple of the dolls be siblings.

Many of the physical characteristics (such as race/ethnicity and physical appearance) will be represented in the construction of the dolls themselves rather than at this point. One thing to consider at this point, however, are physical conditions that are not visible, such as asthma or a heart condition.

The next three categories all relate to the dolls' families. It is important here to do a little research to be sure to create a family history, culture, language, and religion that are culturally accurate. If you do not have experience with these details (for instance, to know that a child from Mexico would most likely be Catholic), it can help to think of a child you have taught in the past who was similar to but not exactly the same as the doll you are creating. You may want to talk to someone who knows about this culture. The children's families can be helpful and are usually pleased that you are making a doll that includes them. (For more ideas, see chapter 10.)

Once you have the basic facts filled in for each doll, step back and look at the collection as a whole. Rearrange details to make the dolls balanced, both as individual characters and in relation to the other dolls. Consider each doll to be sure you have created an identity that fits together and feels like a real child.

The last set of details to include in each doll's identity will come from the two categories of individual behaviors and favorite behaviors and food on the Student Population Record, as well as from your imagination. To fill in a bit about each doll's likes, dislikes, and idiosyncrasies, start by thinking about three or four personal details about each doll. You might make one doll interested in insects. Another might hate to go to bed. These characteristics can be about anything from favorite sports to an experience with a broken leg—anything you might tell your students about the doll to help them get to know one another. You can use the information you noted about your own students here, but also feel free to let your imagination roam.

You will also be able to break some stereotypes your students may have formed by carefully combining certain identity details. Here is how I created some details in each doll's biography to create role models of children who are free of gender stereotypes:

- Rachel loves robots and wants to be a scientist when she grows up.
  (Stereotypes: Girls don't like science; girls don't like machines.)
- River never cuts his hair. No one in his family does. He wears it in a ponytail down his back and likes to brush it.
  (Stereotype: Boys have short hair.)
- Ianthe and Julio are best friends.
  (Stereotype: Boys and girls don't play together at all or they are sweethearts.)
- Ricky's favorite color is pink.
  (Stereotypes: Girls like pink; boys like blue.)
- Marcy builds amazing things with blocks.
  (Stereotypes: Only boys like blocks; girls can't build.)

- Umoja's dad, Steve, makes her lunch every day and helps her get ready for school.
  (Stereotypes: Moms take care of kids; only moms cook.)
- Brad likes to play nurse. He wants to be one when he grows up.
  (Stereotype: Girls are nurses; boys are doctors.)
- Elizabeth loves the computer. She's learning to make a Web page.
  (Stereotype: Only boys like computers; only boys are good on computers.)

Many more of these details will become part of each doll's identity as you tell stories about them, but it is a good idea to come up with a few to use right from the start. These few details will then help you develop even more details.

Once the dolls have been given their details, you will have a full and interesting identity for each of your dolls all laid out on the Doll Identity Planning Chart. The only thing you are missing is the name of each doll. Leave this until you actually have the dolls in your hands and have gotten to know them a bit. Then you will be able to get a feel for the doll and its personality and choose a name that really fits and is culturally accurate. Be sure also to reflect in some of your dolls' names the kinds of names you find among your students. Refer to the information you have gathered on the Student Population Record.

Several examples of identities I created for my dolls using an Identity Planning Chart can be found on the following page. These are some of the dolls you will be getting to know in the examples throughout this book.

Although developing your dolls' identities is a long process, it is well worth the time and energy it takes. In the end you'll have an inclusive collection of dolls that will validate the children in your class and introduce them to new diversities simply by coming to meet your group of children.

You won't have to create identities for your dolls each year. Although your classroom population will change a bit from year to year, your dolls can stay mostly as you first created them, with small changes in family structures or personal details to fit some new need. For example, when one of your new students is expecting a new sibling, you can just add this to one of your dolls' identitites. You won't need to start planning all over again!

When you begin telling stories, you will use a separate Biography Page for each doll. These pages have room for you to fill in this basic identity information for quick reference and also a place to keep track of stories and new details added over time. (You will find more information about this in chapter 10).

QUESTION #4

Q: *Where should I keep my dolls?*

A: My dolls sit on a shelf right inside the front door, over the kids' cubbyholes. The children can look up and greet them when they come in, but they can't reach them. Parents and visitors can see them too. And from their shelf, the dolls can "see" much of what goes on in the room. This allows me to begin a story with, "Umoja saw some kids having trouble sharing the little cars yesterday. That reminded her of something that happened to her. Can she tell you about it?"

Many other arrangements will work. Some child care programs have one set of dolls to share among all the rooms. In this case it would be best to choose two or three to be in the classroom with you for a while, tell a story or two with each, and then trade them for some others that will "come visiting."

Kids Like Us Identity Planning Chart

Name	G/B	Age	Race/Ethnicity	Physical — Physical Appearance	Physical — Other Characteristics	Family — Family Structure	Family — Class/Home Parent Occupation	Family — History, Religion Culture, Language	Behaviors/Activities/Food
Ianthe Singleton	G	6	African American	- deep brown skin - tightly curled black hair - dark brown eyes - big smile	- left-handed - short for age	- mother - father - brother Henry - 5	- middle class - lives in suburbs - has own room - father bank manager - mother nurse	- Henry is Deaf - mother ill - Baptist church, sings in choir - Christmas, family reunion each summer - all learning sign language	- special friend Julio - hopscotch, jumprope with Julio
Rachel Kahn	G	5	European American/Jewish	- peach skin - very short straight brown hair - pug nose - big light brown eyes		- adopted by single mom - very close to Bubbe and Zaide, visits every week	- small house - mom is librarian	- lights Sabbath candles with mom Friday night - Temple Saturday, whole family - grandparents moved from Russia, speak Yiddish to her	- science: robots, astronaut - books
Mickey Jenner	B	7	European American	- light tawny skin - wavy brown hair - large brown eyes - long nose - crooked smile	- cerebral palsy - loose muscle tone - wheelchair - beginning to sit, hold head up	- lives with mom, stepdad, 3 brothers, 3 sisters - father in nearby town	- working class - lives in country - old house, needs repair - mother manicurist - stepfather construction sometimes	- don't know about country of origin - difficult birth - family camping - 3 oldest siblings in orchestra	- drawing - laughs at jokes - Cheerios
Rajit Morton	B	5	East Indian American	- short straight black hair - dark cinnamon skin - thin	- asthma - uses inhaler	- two moms: Momma Betty Momma Asha - adopted at 1 year - baby sister	- apartment - Momma Asha is teacher - Momma Betty runs women's bookstore - will share room with sister	- Momma Asha is 2nd generation East Indian American - some Hindu culture - vegetarian - no war toys - Momma Betty is European American	- drawing - insects - doesn't like yogurt - sucks thumb

CHAPTER

3

Storytelling with Kids

Like Us Dolls

in Five Steps

You now have a collection of dolls and have created their identities. After you spend a bit of time becoming familiar with each doll, you are ready to tell your first story. We call this "storytelling," but the process differs from the way a traditional storyteller "performs" for an audience. You will not need to rehearse and memorize paragraphs, but instead you will let the story flow along through five simple steps, interacting with the kids and having fun as you go. ● Telling a *Kids Like Us* doll story is a very informal and interactive process. You will be the interpreter for the dolls, telling your students what the doll has come to say to them. This scenario will then be the basis for a group discussion and problem-solving session as your students identify the doll's feelings and discuss what the doll should do or how they could help the doll in that particular situation.

Q: *Do I have to use the five-step system to tell my stories if it feels awkward?*

A: No! The five-step system and all the other planning sheets and suggestions are designed to make storytelling easier for you. I expect that, over time, teachers will find their own style of storytelling.

You will do most of the storytelling at the beginning of the session, but the goal is to get the children involved in thinking, identifying feelings, discussing, putting themselves into the doll's place, and problem solving. The children will do much more talking during the rest of the session than you will. During most of the story your job will be to facilitate the discussion, making sure to listen to everyone, supporting anyone with strong feelings about the subject, and reflecting back to the students what has been said.

The five steps of a *Kids Like Us* doll story are introductions, situation setup, identifying feelings, discussion and problem solving, and resolution. Once you are familiar with the five steps, you will find it easy to plan and then tell a story based on them. You will learn to use a simple planning sheet based on the information you will need for each of these steps. Memorizing the goal of each step will allow you to easily and naturally tell *Kids Like Us* doll stories that really get kids thinking and discussing. The steps also help to keep you on track. Without needing to memorize a script, you will know at all times where you are in the story and what is coming next. The five-step method also helps to prevent you from saying too much. In several of the steps you will primarily ask questions of your students and facilitate discussion. The structure will help you remember to ask for your students' input instead of telling them everything yourself. This will be the most valuable part of *Kids Like Us* doll stories.

The following example of a *Kids Like Us* doll story will unfold with the discussion of each step in the process. This story was told to a group of six-year-old children who were already familiar with some *Kids Like Us* dolls and had been introduced to the doll in the story.

Step One: Introductions

This step begins the story and lets the kids get to know the characters involved. It includes some basic details of the doll's life and personality, as well as a reminder of other stories the doll may have been involved in. The introductions bring the dolls to life and focuses the group's attention on the dolls. In this story, I reminded the children of Mickey's family members because this is important in the story. I also took a moment to review what cerebral palsy is, which had been discussed a week earlier when the children first met Mickey.

"Is everybody settled? Great, because here's Mickey. Remember Mickey? We met him the other day. Let's pass him around the circle for quick hugs before we start."

"I remember him. Hi, Mickey!"

"Yes, and Mickey remembers some of you too. You remember I told you before that Mickey is seven and lives with his mom, his stepdad, his three older sisters, and his three older brothers."

"Yeah. And he can't move around so good."

"That's right. Mickey has cerebral palsy, which makes it hard for him to get his muscles to do what he wants them to. We talked about that when you met Mickey. And remember how much he loves Cheerios? He eats them every morning."

Step Two: Situation Setup

In the second step, the teacher outlines very simply the situation to be discussed. In a few sentences, the teacher explains what the doll wants to tell the children. This may mean giving the students some information about a new subject or describing a problem the doll is having. In this case, I first told the children why Mickey had come to see them. Then, in a few sentences, I explained the situation I wanted them to discuss.

"Today he has some special news he wants to tell you. You know I told you before about Mickey's family. Well, he came today to tell you that his family has changed. Last week his new baby brother, Donny, was born!"

"Hey! Just like ME! I have a new baby too, Mickey! My new baby is a sister!"

"That's right, Emily. You have a new baby at your house, don't you? Well, you'll understand what it is like at Mickey's house right now.

"Mickey says that he could hardly wait for the baby to come and he thinks Donny's neat. He likes being an older brother, and he's going to teach Donny how to read when he's old enough. But right now he cries a lot. He woke Mickey up three times last night. And his mom and dad are so busy with the new baby they haven't played with Mickey at all."

Step Three: Identifying Feelings

In this step, the kids get involved, and it will be their story from now on. All the teacher needs to do is to *ask* the children how the doll is feeling. Leaving space for the children to respond to this question is the most important part of this step. Here, I used active listening: repeating the children's ideas to make sure the whole group heard them and validating their thinking. I was also sure to quickly reinforce Emily for sharing her feelings with us.

Q: *What if my students come up with ideas that I hadn't expected?*

A: That would be great! It means they're thinking. One of the things you are trying to do is to get the children to think of multiple solutions to any problem. Congratulate them on being so inventive, and then take a moment to consider if maybe their idea is better than the ones you thought of yourself!

Sometimes kids come up with incorrect or inappropriate ideas. My favorite is the child whose answer for every social conflict is, "She could say, 'If you let me…I'll give you a present.'" There are two ways to handle a situation like this. If many children are eagerly waiting to respond with other ideas, listen to three or four more in a row. Then, when you review what has been said, leave out the inappropriate suggestion. If, however, this idea is being carefully considered by all the children or if you feel it is important enough to address, ask the group to evaluate the idea. Guide this process by quickly figuring out why you feel this response is inappropriate and asking questions that help your

(continued on next page)

"As you can guess, Mickey has a lot of different feelings about this new brother. Can you tell how Mickey is feeling?"

> "Sad."
>
> "He's mad 'cause that baby's crying all the time."
>
> "I'd be mad if my mom spent all her time with some new baby."
>
> "Maybe he feels lonely."
>
> "I bet Mickey's tired 'cause Donny won't let him sleep."

"Wow. That's a lot of different feelings Mickey might have—sad, mad, lonely, tired. Do you think he likes having the baby at all?"

> "Yeah. He's excited about that."
>
> "He's proud 'cause he's a big brother now."
>
> "He's happy too."

"So you think Mickey is feeling tired because the baby cries so much, and mad because his parents are so busy taking care of him. But he's also happy and excited to have a new baby, and he feels proud to be a big brother.

> "That's how it is at my house. My baby is very cute and I like her. But you've got to hold her every minute! I get tired of everybody looking at her all the time. Nobody cares about me now that SHE'S around."

"Thanks for telling us about it, Emily. Mickey's feeling that way about his baby too. He likes Donny, but he wishes he could get some attention once in a while. Is that how you are feeling?"

> "Yeah."

Step Four: Discussion and Problem Solving

In the fourth step, students are encouraged to discuss the situation and, when appropriate, think of possible solutions for the problem that was presented in the situation setup. This may include thinking about why the dolls acted as they did or practicing putting yourself in the dolls' places. It encourages creative thinking toward the goal of finding multiple solutions for any situation, and it gives practice in choosing the best solution for all the characters in the story.

When students are skilled in such problem solving, a further step can be added to have them put themselves in the scene. In this way they practice empathy, learn to make good choices in peer situations, and practice skills needed to stand up for what is right.

Children are always glad to have their peers listen to their ideas. In this case, I repeated ideas as they came up and picked a few to remember for use in the last step (resolution). I directed the conversation toward ideas that would help

Emily speak up at home (and at the same time encourage the other children to do the same). I reinforced all of the children's thinking about how to help someone else and for listening to what the others had said.

"What do you think Mickey could do about this problem? How can he enjoy his new brother and still have his parents' attention sometimes? Does anybody have some ideas that could help Mickey?"

> *"He could yell and scream like the baby. They'd all pay attention to him then!"*
>
> *[Much laughter.]*

"He could yell and scream like the baby. Would that help him feel better?"

> *"No, because they'd get mad at him."*
> *"He could play with his parents when the baby is asleep."*
> *"He could take turns with the baby."*
> *"He could go play outside with some friends."*
> *"My mom and dad are always busy, and I don't even have a baby!"*

"How do you get time with your parents even though they are so busy, Jamal?"

> *"I go shopping with my mom and we talk in the car. Sometimes we sing."*

"Maybe that would work for Mickey. Or he could talk to his mom and dad when the baby is asleep. Joy thought he might feel better if he gets some attention from friends. I can tell everyone is really thinking. Has anyone else had this happen in their family?"

> *"I remember when my little brother was born last year."*

"What did you do, Charlie, when your parents were really busy taking care of him?"

> *"I helped out. I can give him a bath now! And sometimes Gramma came."*

"Maybe Mickey could help take care of Donny. Or maybe someone could come help take care of the baby while Mickey spends some time with his parents. How do you think Mickey could let his parents know he wants to talk about this?"

> *"He's gonna hafta tell 'em."*

"Yes. They can't read his mind! He'll have to tell them. How do you think he could let them know that he needs some time to talk to them?"

> *"He could say, 'I wanna talk to you.'"*
> *"He could tell at dinner."*
> *"He could tell in the car, like Jamal said!"*

"Excellent ideas! I can see you've been listening to what everyone has said too!"

students consider this aspect of the situation.

If I asked my students what they thought of giving presents just to get their own way and they all seemed enthusiastic, I might ask, "Do you think it would be fair for one person to go first every time if they promised presents?" Then, if even one child says no, you can ask why she thinks this is so. Other children can respond to her comments, and you are once again discussing the issue you were hoping to explore.

Finally, if a child expresses a biased idea, you must intervene immediately. If it seems the bias was due to curiosity or incorrect information, directly tell the child what she needs to know. Whatever the child's reason for making this comment, you must let this child and all who heard it know that bias can be hurtful and won't be allowed in your classroom. If a child has clearly been the victim of this bias, let him know that he should not have to listen to such things and that you are sorry he has been subjected to it. You will also be aware that your group needs more education on this subject.

Your First Story

- Keep it simple! One doll, one situation, one main feeling to identify. Do not mirror a child.
- Ask, don't tell. Let the children tell you what the doll is feeling.
- Don't go into other issues that the children bring up.
- Keep the story to ten minutes at the most (five minutes for two to three year olds).
- Ask quiet children what they think.
- Take time to look at each child to gauge reactions to the story.
- Summarize and reflect back to the children what has been said.
- When you are done, congratulate yourself! You are now a *Kids Like Us* doll storyteller!

Step Five: Resolution

This step brings the story back into the teacher's hands. The teacher's job here is to help the children leave the story and to bring a sense of resolution to the situation. In this step the teacher tells what the dolls actually did in their situation, often incorporating ideas that the children contributed during the problem-solving stage.

"Mickey is glad to hear all of your ideas. He was feeling pretty left out for a while. But he did just what you said and told his parents how he was feeling. One day at dinner Mickey said to his mom and dad, 'I need to talk to you about something important.' So that night before bed, when the baby was asleep, he told them all the feelings he'd been having. His dad gave him a big hug and said he was glad Mickey told them about this.

"Then they worked out a plan. Every day they take turns, like Lizzie suggested. Either his mom or his dad plays with him for half an hour before bed while the other watches the baby. His sisters and brothers agreed to watch the baby sometimes. They also decided Mickey could sit with Donny on the couch and sing to him every morning to help out. Now things are going pretty well at Mickey's house. The baby still takes a lot of his parents' time, but he feels better about that. And he enjoyed telling you. It can really help to talk over your problem with friends. Thanks for helping him!"

Now that you understand the basic five steps of almost any *Kids Like Us* story, turn to the next chapters for a discussion of each step in detail.

CHAPTER 4

Step One: Introducing the Dolls

The first step in telling a *Kids Like Us* doll story is the introduction. But before you begin to tell the story, remember to *relax!* You are not about to go on stage at Carnegie Hall—you are just going to have a conversation with your students and use a doll as the main character and a visual aid. Your kids will be eager to hear what you have to say, and they will forgive any repetition or backtracking you find necessary. If you need to, give yourself time to think, or tell the kids you made a mistake:

"Wait. I need to think a minute about what I wanted to say."

"Let me think a bit. I have to remember what Ianthe told me about this."

"Oops. I just remembered that River has two sisters. I said he had two brothers. I just forgot for a minute."

Relaxing and letting your story flow as it comes to you is the most important thing you can do to prepare for a storytelling session. I always gather the children in our traditional circle on the rug. I find that storytelling sessions work best with groups of ten or fewer. This allows all the children to have a chance to take part in the discussion, and it allows you to keep track of how each of them is responding to the story. If you must work with a larger group, take extra care to look around at all the students throughout the story to keep track of how they are feeling and to encourage their participation.

After gathering, I give everyone a chance to focus on the dolls in the story. I do this by passing each doll around the circle for a quick hello.

> "Umoja really wanted to come to the circle today. I'll send her around for a hello with each of you. She's so glad to be here to see you all!"

With the youngest children (ages two to four) it is often a good idea to hold onto the doll yourself during this greeting so this does not take too long. It is hard for young ones to let go of the doll once they are holding it. Older children can be gently reminded to, "give her a quick hug and send her on around the circle."

Once the dolls have been around to most of the children, you are ready to begin your story introduction. There are two types of introductions to *Kids Like Us* doll stories—the first introduction and the reminder introduction.

First Introductions

At the beginning of the year or when you are first starting to use *Kids Like Us* dolls with your students, you will need to introduce your dolls one at a time. During this stage, and any time you have a new doll for your children to meet, the introduction and the questions it brings up will be the whole story; you won't go on to the other four steps.

During the introduction you will tell the children a few basic things about the doll. You will include things like name, age, gender, family structure, language, friends, race, and personal preferences. You will not tell all of these details at once, but choose a few of them to tell at this initial session. If you have created a Biography Page for each of your dolls, you can choose these basic details from the information at the top of the doll's page. (You can find more information about making Biography Pages in chapter 10.)

In addition, you can organize your thoughts with a First Introduction Planning Sheet. Note the basic facts you have decided to include in the story. Then, though you will not read aloud from it, you can use it as a memory aid during your storytelling session.

Doll(s) to be introduced:

Children who may need support:

1. Greeting the children

2. Basic facts

Name:
Age:
Gender:
Family structure:

3. Important characteristics to be introduced (one or two most important—plan the details)
languages, race, religion, special abilities, disabilities, parent's jobs, family history, home, some detail of the family's culture, issues central to the child's personality

4. Favorite activities and foods (choose one or two to tell a bit about)

5. Other dolls that are close friends (if any—plan what they do together)

Include some of the small fun details of the dolls' personalities. It is most important to use details relevant to your student's lives. Favorite foods, clothes, games, movies, colors, and toys are all things your children can relate to. Remember to look beyond popular culture assumptions of what children like so your stories show that kids can and do like things other than McDonald's and Barbie.

Here are examples of some first introductions:

" This is Julio. He's a boy and he is six years old. He lives with his dad and his brother, who is sixteen. His mom and his baby sister are still living in Guatemala, where they all used to live. He misses his mom and hopes to see her soon. He likes school and is very good friends with Ianthe. Julio knows mostly Spanish and

Ianthe knows English, so they play together without a lot of talking. They have a great time playing chase and being wild bears together every recess. Julio can really growl just like a bear!"

"Mei Lin just loves to jump rope. She's just learning to jump to a rhyme, just like some of you. Her favorite food is noodles or chocolate cake! She plays almost every day with her plastic horses. She likes to make up stories about them."

"Umoja has a huge yard at her mom's house. She plays outside a lot. She loves to climb trees. At school she likes to climb into the loft. She loves to feed the guinea pig, and her favorite area of the classroom is the computer center. She likes to do Reader Rabbit and Putt-Putt." *[I chose these details because I had a girl who was a tree climber, we have a loft in our classroom, and the two computer programs mentioned were the current hot topics of discussion.]*

"Melly and her family are Siletz Native Americans. That means that her family has always lived around here, even a long, long time ago. Some people think that because they're Native Americans they live in teepees. That's not true, though. It's just a stereotype made up about Native Americans. Melly's family lives in a green house with yellow doors. Melly has her own room. Melly's dad is a doctor. He works at the hospital in town. Her mom works with computers."

"Josh likes to play with his little brother. He also really likes to dance. He says it feels good to move his body just the right way. He is taking ballet lessons and his teacher says that he can be a very good dancer if he really practices. He's getting very strong from all the dancing exercises he does."

This first introduction is also a chance to present a calm, comfortable feeling about diversity simply by presenting the different characteristics of your dolls in a calm, comfortable manner.

"Umoja lives with her mom in her house one week and with her dad in his house the next week. She takes her cuddly kitty that she always sleeps with to each house."

"River is a boy. I heard some of you saying 'she.' Did you think River was a girl? I wonder what made you think that?"

"Those are Henry's hearing aids. His ears don't hear sounds very well, so he has little hearing aids that fit in his ears to help him hear a little better. Would you like to see a hearing aid up close?"

The children are most likely to notice physical differences. You will also want to raise some issues, such as family structure, economic class, or culture, that are not physically evident. Creating details of your *Kids Like Us* dolls' lives that include these issues give you the opportunity to discuss them. Include a detail in this first introduction if you feel that it is central to the doll's identity. You should also include it if this is an issue that you feel your students need to discuss right away, either because you have become aware that they have incorrect information about it or because some children in the class need the support of seeing themselves represented by a doll. For example, I had heard a child being questioned about the skin color of her parents, so I told this part of Umoja's identity during her first introduction:

"Umoja is biracial. That's because her mom is European American and her dad is African American. So Umoja is part of both."

I overheard one child say to another in incredulous tones, "You DON'T have a *TV?*" So when I introduced Elizabeth I made not having a television a part of her family culture.

"In Elizabeth's family they don't watch TV. They are very busy doing lots of other things like reading to each other and doing jigsaw puzzles."

Because an adopted child's homecoming was to be celebrated soon, one year I included this information when I introduced Rachel for the first time. In other years I have left this part of her identity for a later story.

"Rachel was adopted by her mom when she was a tiny baby. Rachel doesn't remember this at all because she was so little. But her mom sure remembers the day the social worker from the adoption agency met her at the airport

QUESTION #7

Q: *What if my kids don't believe the dolls are alive?*

A: We must have a storyteller's attitude about the dolls. We don't want to insist that the children believe the dolls are alive. We just want the children to *feel* as if they were. You bring the dolls to life by talking about them and treating them as if they were alive. You let your students know this is storytelling by admitting that they are dolls. And you will candidly tell them you have a "story" to tell them about the dolls. Don't insist that these are real events.

One day I said River had to cut his hair a bit because he got gum stuck in it. While holding River, one of the kids asked, "If we cut his hair, will it grow back?" I answered that it wouldn't "because River is really a doll." I gave that response in an almost whisper, as if I didn't want to spoil the illusion or didn't want the doll to hear me say it, and all the kids giggled and nodded, pleased to keep the secret with me.

Occasionally children will note, "She's five years old, like me. But look at how

(continued on next page)

much taller I am!" Then I can admit, "That's because she's a doll."

If you have a student or two who seem to be uneasy with the pretend aspect of the stories, briefly talk to your whole group about it.

"You know, I've known Ianthe a long time, and she is very real to me. I think as you get to know her she will seem very real to you too. I know she's actually a doll, but I like to feel like she's a friend you can all get to know. Do you think you can see her that way too?"

I would probably ignore anyone who said no at this point. If a child continues to interrupt the stories with this issue, take her aside at another time and listen to all her problems with the dolls. Then explain that you intend to have a good time discussing doll stories with the group and that you cannot allow her to ruin that. Tell her that she does not have to believe in the dolls, but she does have to stop interrupting the stories. I have never had a child continue to disbelieve past a first general discussion about the issue. Even children who tend to be oppositional are entranced by the dolls.

with Rachel in her arms! They celebrate that day every year. They call it Arrival Day and they go out for ice cream. It's kind of like Rachel gets two birthdays—one when she was born and one when she came home to her family!"

You must be prepared to answer your students' questions when they first meet these dolls. They will be unable to focus on other story elements until their curiosity is satisfied. (We will discuss this in depth in chapter 7.)

Some issues will be appropriate to bring up during the doll's first introduction. Some should wait for a story on another day. The main goal of the initial introduction is to establish your students' relationship with the doll.

Reminder Introductions

A reminder introduction is much shorter and less involved than the doll's first introduction. It is a lead-in to later steps in the storytelling process rather than being the story itself.

A reminder introduction begins with the same greetings and focus on the doll as the first introduction. You may be presenting more than one doll now, if you want to represent more than one point of view in your story.

During the greetings at the very beginning of a reminder introduction, you may want to refer to the situation that will be the main focus of the story to come.

"Melly and Julio have something they want to talk to you about today. They're a little nervous to talk about it, so they'd like to have a bit of a hug with each of you before we start. Let's pass Melly to the left, like this. And we'll send Julio to the right. Just give them each a quick hug and pass them on."

As the children greet the dolls individually, you will tell a few details about the dolls. You can repeat any details that you used in the first introduction. This is also a good time to tell other small details, such as likes and dislikes, friends, family, and happenings in the dolls' lives.

"Ianthe is happy to see all of you. She has a story to tell today. Do you remember Ianthe? She has a little brother named Henry and she is six years old. She has been playing on a soccer team."

"Hey! I'm on a soccer team too!"

"Wow! Just like Ianthe! Her team wears red and she loves to play because she loves to run fast."

This can be a fun part of the storytelling because you can really tell anything that fits the identity of the doll you are introducing. Get inside your doll's life and let your imagination go!

"Saed and his two brothers built a tree house this weekend. It has a real ladder to climb up into it and everything. They want to sleep up there this weekend."

"River has a pet alligator at home. He keeps it in the bathtub, except when he takes a bath!"

"Rajit played hide-and-seek at school yesterday and nobody could find him! He curled up small as a mouse and hid in the ball box. He was so quiet they never knew he was there! He thought that was really fun."

"Mickey's favorite color is purple. He likes to make pictures with lots of purple flowers and sunsets with purple and pink and orange in them."

Including details that you know your students will relate to helps them to feel in tune with the dolls. This is very important, because in the next two steps it will be one of your main goals to get the children to do just that—to relate their own feelings, needs, and experiences to what the dolls are going through. I often choose to put in details that correspond to things I have seen the children being excited about at school.

"Rachel loves building with the big blocks. She made a whole zoo with them the other day and put the zoo animals in it."

> "I love the block center at MY school!"
> "Yea! Me too!"
> "I made a farm yesterday. I put animals in mine too."

"Elizabeth really wants to climb the rope at her school. She has been practicing and practicing, but she just can't do it yet."

> "That's just like me! I want to climb the rope too!"
> "And I just learned! I can do it now."
> "I can climb it! I can climb it, Elizabeth!"

During a reminder introduction, it is not a good idea to put in a detail that your children will need to discuss, unless you are planning to tell a story about it. For instance, if you are planning to tell a story about Julio having a hard time sitting still in circle, but you put into your reminder introduction the fact that his mother is living in Guatemala, the children may need to spend the story time discussing his mother instead. This is especially true if the distracting detail has not already been discussed in that doll's first introduction. Here's an example of a reminder introduction I once told that backfired in just this manner.

"This is Rachel. She came to our circle to meet you last week."

> "I remember her. Hi, Rachel!"

"She is very pleased to come and talk to you today. Do you remember that Rachel lives with her mom in a little house? She has a kitten named Marmalade that she loves very much. Rachel is really afraid of the water because she fell out of a boat once. She's trying…"

Goals of the Reminder Introduction

• To welcome the dolls to the circle and to focus the children's attention on the dolls
• To begin the story and set the tone for an informal storytelling discussion
• To remind the kids of the name and characteristics of the dolls to be used
• To model your fondness for a wide variety of people and to model acceptance of all the dolls' characteristics as a natural part of them
• To start the story in a fun, relaxing way

Q: *Is it really right to show girl and boy dolls being best friends when my boys and girls don't play together at all?*

A: Yes. Your group may be making cross-gender friendships off-limits. If *some* of your boys and girls play together occasionally, the division may be happening because many of the children have not considered the possibility of finding a friend of the other gender. In this case, your *Kids Like Us* dolls can be the perfect role models to show the children that they do not have to segregate.

If *none* of your boys and girls ever play together, a different dynamic is most likely at work. The segregation is probably the result of the children teasing anyone who plays with a child of the other gender. When this occurs, just being seen talking with a girl can bring heavy penalties to boys from the other boys. In this case, the work you do against bias with your *Kids Like Us* dolls will help the children let go of these prejudices and biased behaviors and to see children with all different kinds of characteristics as possible friends.

" *How'd she fall out of the boat?"*

" *Did she drown?"*

" *I'm scared of the water too."*

" *Yeah, me too. I'm never going swimming."*

" *What does that mean, 'drown'?"*

" *Falling out of a boat is scary! Who saved her? Did she get saved?"*

And on and on and on. If this happens, let go of the story you had planned to tell and deal with what is important to the children at that moment. You can always tell the planned story the next day.

Some details you tell about the dolls will cause a spate of comments. Listening to these responses just takes a minute, tunes the kids into the doll, and gets them involved. It is an easy bet that this will happen when you tell the dolls' ages, when their birthdays are, or what their favorite colors are. Sometimes it's fun to put one of these details in just to see how each child responds. This is usually best when your group is small enough to allow them all to talk at once.

You may want to remind the children of the facts that they will need to understand the story you are about to tell.

" Do you remember that Ianthe is really good friends with Julio? Yes, they usually play together at every recess. They play chase a lot."

This detail was part of the introduction to a story I told about a day when Ianthe was upset because Julio went to play with some other kids.

Over time you and your children will know many things about each of your dolls, including memories of the different stories they have been involved in. You will not tell everything you know when you introduce a doll. You will choose a few details each time, using some that are familiar and adding a new detail or two to make the doll more interesting. It will be important to use Biography Pages to keep track of what you tell the kids about the dolls so you don't contradict yourself weeks later.

A Sequence of Introductions

Here is a sequence of introductions for one doll, Umoja. Each begins with a greeting and sending the doll around the circle.

First Introduction: "Umoja is very glad to meet you all. Thanks for giving her such nice hugs and being gentle with her. Umoja is a girl and she is five years old. She likes horses and puppies and lizards. Umoja has a little sister named Imani. She and Imani live one week with their mom, Nancy, and the next week with their dad, Steve."

"Why do they do that?"

"Because Nancy and Steve don't live together anymore, but they both still want to live with Umoja and Imani. So they share houses."

"I stay with my dad sometimes on the weekend."
"My mom lives far away. I hardly ever see her."

"Yes. Families work things out in many different ways. Sometimes Umoja misses Steve when she is staying with Nancy. And sometimes she misses Nancy when she's staying with Steve!"

"Uh huh, I miss my mom lots."

"I'll bet that's hard. Umoja likes it at Steve's house because there is a puppy named Marigold. At Nancy's house she has her pet lizard, Glick. She really loves animals. She wants to be a vet when she grows up."

"I'm gonna be an astronaut!"
[Many excited comments on future plans.]

"Are there any questions you would like to ask Umoja? Anything you would like to know about her?"

"Where'd she get that funny name?"

"Umoja's name isn't funny to her and she doesn't like people to make fun of her name. I'm sure you can understand how she feels about that. Can't you?"

"Yeah."

"Umoja is actually very proud of her name. She is named for the first principle of Kwanzaa. That's an important African American holiday at Umoja's house. And Umoja means unity—being together. Do any of you have names that mean something special like Umoja's name does?"

"Alex means something, but I forget what."
"I'm named for a flower! That's why my name says Rose."

"Yes. Umoja's name is like that. And she is very glad to be able to come here and meet all of you. Can she come back another time to tell you a story?"

"Yeah! I like her!"

After this storytelling session, I made a note to read *Chrysanthemum,* a book about a mouse who is teased about her name. I also made sure to have some extra cuddle time with the child who was missing her mother and to discuss this issue with her father. Later I had one of my dolls experience a divorce and separation from his mother. This doll became the child's special friend and confidante.

It is interesting to note that although Umoja's race was mentioned during the discussion of Kwanzaa, neither the African American nor European American children felt a need to comment on this part of her identity. Representing many different races of children in your doll collection and in the stories that you tell will affirm each child's place in the world and increase their comfort with racial diversity. Racial and other bias will be the focus of some stories you tell, but do not make race the focus of every story.

Second Introduction: "Oh, Umoja is excited to come to the circle. Do you remember her? Remember she is five?"

"Uh huh, she's the same age as me!"

"Yes, and she has a little sister named Imani and two pets. She really loves to eat Popsicles on a hot day. Orange is her favorite flavor."

"I like the red ones."
"We make Popsicles at our house—with juice."

"Yum! I bet Umoja would like those! Umoja loves to paint at school. Yesterday she made a beautiful picture of the sun and a bird. She is very proud of it. Another thing she likes to do is to build sand castles. The other day, when she was in the sandbox…"

Third Introduction: "Umoja wants to say hi to all of you. Remember she loves to paint? And she came to tell us about how upset she was when one of the kids wrecked her sand castle one day?"

"I 'member that. She stompted her feet."

"Yes. She was really mad that day. She has been having a good time outside lately. She is trying to learn to ride a bike, but she keeps falling over."

"Me too! I keep falling over too! See where I scraped my elbow?"
"I can ride already! Well, with my training wheels."
[All at once, the children offer details of their experiences with bikes, and I listen attentively to everyone at once.]

"I see lots of you know about bikes. Umoja keeps her bike at Steve's house and practices when she is staying there. Her puppy, Marigold, likes to run along with her when she rides. Well, Umoja wants to tell you…"

Once you have completed the introduction step, your students will be focused on the doll, interested in what happens to her, and ready to listen to the situation setup—the basic plot of the story you are about to discuss.

CHAPTER 5

Step Two: Setting Up the Situation

Once your students are familiar with some *Kids Like Us* dolls, you are ready to move on to step two, the situation setup. During this step you will present a specific situation you would like the kids to discuss. You can begin this process after introducing two or three of your dolls—you don't have to wait until you have introduced your entire collection. (For more, see chapter 10.) ● The situation setup is the nucleus of the *Kids Like Us* doll experience. It sets the stage for the discussion you want your students to engage in. It brings to life a moment in the dolls' lives. During later stages in the story, your children will identify the feelings of the dolls, put themselves in the dolls' situations, empathize with them, and problem solve with them. All of this discussion springs from the plot you have presented to them during this step—the situation setup. ● Creating and presenting a situation setup is easy. Each one will have two parts: the lead-in and the story line. Together, these parts will require you to say only a few sentences. It is as easy as telling a friend what one of your students did yesterday.

"Rajit wants to come to talk with you today about something that happened yesterday. Sometimes it helps to tell a friend about what is bothering you. Okay? Good. He's glad to have friends who will listen to what is bothering him.

"Well, Rajit sat down at snack time yesterday and, before he knew it, he knocked his elbow into his juice and spilled it all over Henry, who was sitting next to him."

. . .

"Saed asked me to bring him to the circle because he is upset about something that's happening at home and he wants your advice. Will you all see if you can help him? Great!

"The problem is his older brothers. Saed really likes them and he likes to do things with them, but they are always telling him to go away. They say he is too little to do lots of the things they do."

. . .

"Julio could hardly wait to come today to tell you his good news! His dad just got a really good job! Julio and his brother and father had a big celebration last night!"

Use the Five-Step Planning Sheet to plan stories (see chapter 10). It will help you organize your decisions about what details to include in your story and plan the story you will tell.

Setting Up Situations

Goals

Before you can set up the situation, you must decide your goal for the session. Why are you going to tell this story? What do you want your students to learn or experience?

Your first goals with a group of students who are new to *Kids Like Us* dolls will closely parallel the five–steps planning method. Stories focusing on introducing the dolls come first. Then you will tell stories with the goal of teaching children to identify and discuss the feelings involved. When your students can do this with ease, practicing problem-solving skills will be your goal.

Once these basic goals have been practiced, or at any time that you have a specific classroom need, you will branch out into stories with many different goals. In the following chapters, we will discuss stories based on the goals discussed in chapter 1.

Similarity to Actual Students

When you plan the lead-in to the story and the basic story line, you will use settings and details from the lives of your students. It will be important to do this in order to make your stories as believable as possible and to help your children relate to the events and emotions in them. I usually imagine my dolls attending a school exactly like the one my students are in. I take the dolls' interests from things I hear my students discussing—dinosaurs, robots, the Magic School Bus, swimming, playing tag, and so on.

Before planning other details, however, you must decide how close to real life you want the events of this story to be. Because your dolls' lives are based on the lives of the children in your class, every story will mirror the children's lives in some way. Some stories will come directly from an incident or situation in your classroom or the homes of your students. You will need to decide how closely to mirror these events, keeping in mind the comfort level of the children being mirrored. If one child's situation would benefit from a story told exactly like it, would this put any of your students on the spot? Will the other children recognize this child's situation and single out the student? It is best to vary your story enough to keep this from happening, but keep it close enough to real life to allow the child involved to relate to it. This allows the children involved to speak about their relationship to the story if they feel comfortable doing so.

Many stories can be told just as effectively with a situation setup that is similar but not identical to an actual event. When I had a student who was attempting to bribe other students into being friends with him by offering to invite them to his upcoming birthday party (or to not invite them if they did something he didn't like), I told a story about a girl doll who thought the other kids would like her better if she gave them candy.

The discussion centered on what makes a good friend and how kids choose their friends. Several children talked about worrying that they might not have friends. One boy realized the kids might say they liked the girl in order to get candy, but they wouldn't really mean it. We ended the discussion with suggestions for how the doll could make real friends.

The birthday boy said not a single word during the whole story, and the other students did not connect his behavior to the doll's story. He was listening intently, though, and the threats and bribes did not recur.

Before telling any story, it is important to think about who will be most affected by it. Will they be ready to hear it? You will want to remain aware of this student's reactions to the story at all times while you are telling it so that you are ready to give support as needed.

QUESTION #9

Q: *Where do I come up with issues for my stories?*

A: Once you have started using your dolls and see how the children react to them, you'll begin to see story lines everywhere. Good stories to use at the beginning of the year are about fear of separation, reaching out to make friends, how to share, any theme that the group will study, pride at accomplishing some classroom skill (writing your name, for example), impatience while waiting for a snack, and falling down and skinning a knee. Anything your students are trying to learn themselves can make a good issue for the dolls to be learning too.

Dolls to Use

If you want to mirror a specific characteristic of a child, choose a doll that has already been given the same characteristic (or assign it to one of the dolls that seems best suited for it), but be sure that the doll is different from the child in other significant ways. For example, for a story to support a boy who is having difficulty learning to read, I would choose a girl doll who is experiencing the same difficulty. I would use a doll that is the same age as the child I am mirroring, since age is often important to children. I would vary the characteristics by choosing a doll with a family configuration that is different from the child I am mirroring, and I would give the doll a variety of favorite things that differ from the child's. I rarely find it useful to mirror a child exactly, and I want the dolls to retain their own identities separate from the children in my class.

Many times the goal of the story to be told will determine the characteristics of the doll you will want to use. A story about missing dad will be told about a doll that lives with mom and does not see dad. A story about hating to have hair combed will be told with a doll that has long hair. A doll that is teased about celebrating Chanukah would come from a Jewish family.

Often, considering the personalities of each doll will point you toward the one that would be best suited to the story. Over time you will get to know and be fond of each of your dolls, and this knowledge will help you to pick the best doll for each situation. Scanning the identity information and the "Stories Told" section on your Biography Pages (see chapter 10) can help you get a feeling for which doll fits the story.

If you are planning a story that needs more than one doll, think about the relationship between them that has been built up in stories already told. Two dolls that have been special friends in one story could be a good choice for a story about two friends standing up against a bully. A doll that has been the main character in a story about dealing with a pesky younger sibling would be a good choice to include in a story about a doll who feels left out by the birth of a baby in the family.

Just as you did when creating the dolls' identities, you will need to be careful not to perpetuate stereotypes in the stories you tell. For example, choose a boy for a story about a fear of spiders, not a girl. Let the child that uses a wheelchair be the one who wins the art contest. Use a doll from a working-class or poor family to tell about the excitement of winning the spelling bee. Don't use an African American doll for a story about stealing a candy bar. Never reinforce society's stereotypes, and always seize every opportunity to counter the propaganda that insists these prejudices are real.

To avoid "good guy/bad guy" thinking, consider the negative or positive consequences of the doll's situations. When making stories about a doll having done the wrong thing or making a mistake, be sure to use that doll soon in a story that shows the doll acting in a more positive way. A doll that calls someone a name in one story should be used the next week to tell about sharing cookies with friends. Two dolls who fight over a toy one day can later welcome a new child into their class.

Another detail to think about when choosing a doll is frequency of use. Over time, it is very important to use all your dolls somewhat evenly. Even though you may have your favorites—dolls you feel you know the best—it is important not to play favorites in assigning story lines! Modeling comfort with all the dolls' diverse characteristics is a basic benefit of having dolls in the classroom, but that only occurs if you do the modeling by telling stories with all of them.

You also need to think about how many dolls to bring to the circle. When you tell your first stories, you will use only one doll. This way you have only one point of view to present, one doll's experience to discuss, and one set of feelings to identify. This does not mean that you will have only one character in each story, however. A story can have as many other characters as needed for the plot, but you will focus on the dolls you actually bring to the storytelling session. Their feelings and points of view are examined and some resolution is described for each of them. Because they are there with you as you tell the story, these are the characters your children will empathize with.

Once you are up to the challenge of presenting more than one doll in a story, consider what the children will learn from each doll's experience. You may want to use two dolls to help the children fully consider two sides of a problem. You may even want to help them learn to consider the needs of an entire group by bringing five or six dolls into your story.

Setting of the Story

Stories can take place anywhere. Some will have a setting determined by the goal. Stories with a goal of teaching a classroom behavior will, of course, take place at school. Stories dealing with family issues will take place in the dolls' homes. But many stories can be placed in a variety of settings. Consider having a doll meet a new friend at the library, get in an argument while walking home from school, or have a good time at grandma's house. Interesting settings help make the stories seem real and catch the children's attention.

Feelings to Be Discussed

The first subject your children will discuss in each story will be how the dolls feel about what has happened. You will ask the children to consider this immediately after you relate the situation setup. Identifying feelings may be the entire focus and goal of your story (see chapter 7), but even if a given story has another goal, every story will examine the feelings of the main characters to understand their motivations.

Possible Settings for Doll Stories

- in the classroom
- on the playground
- at home
- in the school bathroom
- in the lunchroom
- on the school bus
- while waiting for the bus
- at after-school care
- on the couch
- in the backyard
- at a relative's home
- at a friend's house
- on the street
- at a store
- at the library
- at a restaurant
- at the zoo
- on vacation
- in the park
- at the lake
- in an airplane
- on the beach
- in the woods

Q: *Wouldn't a story about a doll's mother being sick or a doll's parents divorcing scare the children?*

A: There are some issues that I do not bring up with my class unless a child in the class is actually dealing with it in her own life. Death of a parent or other important person, divorce, violence, serious illnesses, and natural disasters are all issues that are in this category. Each teacher needs to be aware of the issues that children are dealing with. When these issues DO arise, the support a doll story can provide is invaluable.

In most populations, for instance, several children in any group will be dealing with divorce or separation at any one time. Many others will already be adjusted to it. A doll story told about a doll's family deciding to split up is very reassuring to a child experiencing the same situation. The discussion and problem-solving step would encourage other children who have split families to tell how they have handled it, letting the child know she is not alone. The resolution step

(continued on next page)

Lead-In to the Story

I usually start a story with some reference to the dolls' wish to discuss this situation. This makes the storytelling feel more realistic and models talking to people you trust. This reference can be planned or just come off the top of your head as you begin your story.

> "Mickey asked to come to the circle today because he wanted to talk about what happened at recess yesterday when he was playing with Ianthe."

> "Mei Lin needs help with a problem she has. Will you listen to her story and see if you can help her figure out what to do?"

> "River wanted to talk to you about something that he said to Elizabeth. You know, sometimes it helps to talk to someone you trust."

Now that you have set your goal and background details for the story, you are ready to create the actual story line.

Creating the Story Line

Now we will combine all the choices you have made into a short story line. The story line is the basic plot—the "what happens." You will describe this situation in three or four sentences, keeping your description as brief as possible.

As adults, we all have a tendency to go on and on, inventing a tangle of small details, settling in to storytelling mode until we glaze over in confusion, unsure as to where we were trying to go! Instead, present the situation setup briefly, leaving space for children to ask questions, for examining the feelings of the story characters, and for group problem solving. Keeping your part of the story short will enable you to spend time on all these points of discussion without losing the students' attention.

> "Lucia really wanted to play in the sandbox. When she went over to it, Rachel said, 'Go away. You can't play with us!'"

> "Saed came to his first day at school. He had never been to that school before, and he didn't know anyone there."

> "Ianthe's mom is very sick. She's in the hospital right now."

> "Mickey went to the library and got his very own card yesterday."

> "Rachel was standing by the slide when she saw another kid push Henry off the swing."

The specific story lines you use will depend on the goal of the storytelling session. Here are some methods for creating story lines designed to meet ten common goals.

1. To Bring Up a Subject; To Begin a Theme Study; To Give Information

Any subject you would like to study with your children can be included in a doll story. This is a very effective way to get your children's attention and to introduce them to new themes. This type of situation setup usually tells two or three things the doll has learned about a subject and then ends with an open-ended question to begin the discussion.

> "Henry went to the fire station this weekend with his dad and his sister, Ianthe. He saw the fire engines and met the firefighters. He even got to try on a firefighter's big boots and hat. Have any of you been to a fire station?"

> • • •

> "At River's house they are planting their garden now. The earth is warming up because it is spring, so it's a good time for new seeds to start growing. River planted peas and lettuce in his own little patch of garden. Do any of you have gardens?"

> • • •

> "Rachel just loves to learn about outer space. When she grows up she wants to be an astronaut, you know."

> > "I remember that, Rachel! She told us before!"

> "Yes! I remember that too. Rachel made this picture of the solar system for all of you to see. She wants to travel to Venus first. Can you find Venus on her picture?"

The dolls model interest in the subject you want your students to find interesting. After describing the doll's interest in a few sentences, you can draw your children into discussion of the subject by asking a leading question. This gives the children an opening to chime in with their own experiences. Stories in which a doll wants to know more about a subject are also effective for giving children information.

> "Umoja is having a hard time understanding what *plus* means. She knows it has a little symbol that looks like this *[the teacher draws the symbol on a large piece of paper]*. But she doesn't understand what it means. Can some of you tell her about it?"

> "Melly has tried and tried to remember the sound for this letter *[the teacher shows the letter* f *on a large card]*, but she just can't remember it. Can some of you help? Who knows what sound it makes?"

This type of story will get everyone involved in trying to help the doll. The children who have had trouble with the subject being discussed will most actively try to help, because they are thrilled to see someone else who understands what they have been feeling. And, as they listen to the discussion, they learn about the subject themselves.

would show that the doll can adjust to the new situation and feel all right about it. And for children who do not have to deal with the situation in their own lives, this kind of story can help them understand and support friends.

When something really scary has happened to one child, like the death of a parent, it might be best to tell a "private" doll story for just that child. A short "Ianthe's mother died too. She's really needing a hug. Will you hold her for a while?" might give the child someone to help her through the tough times. But if one child is experiencing something difficult, the others are likely to know about it. In this case a *Kids Like Us* doll story can provide the forum to safely discuss situations that they would otherwise worry over alone. When telling these stories, be ready to support anyone who has strong reactions. Tell the story matter-of-factly, without drama, and emphasize diversity—this does not happen to all the dolls, it is just something one of them is dealing with.

Another type of story line that is a good method for giving information is one in which a doll experiences a new thing and is fascinated by it.

> "Elizabeth went to the art museum with her dad this weekend. She saw statues and quilts and lots of paintings. Her favorite painting was this one. She got a postcard of it so she could keep it with her always. Let's pass that postcard around for everyone to see and have you tell one thing you notice in the painting."

Throughout the discussion you can give more information about the subject. You will also have an excellent opportunity to assess what the children already know about the subject and to pick up on any misinformation they may believe to be true.

2. To Undo Incorrect Information

Teachers may notice children expressing incorrect beliefs in the classroom.

> "When you go to the dentist he's gonna stick you with a looooooooong needle! Then he's gonna cut your teeth out with a knife. I know 'cause my brother told me so."

> "When I'm all grown up I'm going to be a police officer. They get to shoot bad guys every day. That's what I want to do."

It is important to undo these incorrect assumptions, and with *Kids Like Us* dolls, this is easy. A simple story line in which a doll believes the incorrect information gets right to the core of the problem.

> "Mei Lin cried and kicked and said she wouldn't go to the dentist, even though one of her teeth was hurting very badly. She was afraid the dentist would stick her with a long needle and then cut her tooth out with a knife!"

Later, during the identifying feelings stage of this story, the children will name Mei Lin's being upset and her feelings of fear and worry. This will be an opportunity for them to tell of similar feelings about the dentist. During the discussion and problem-solving stage, the children will tell Mei Lin about their own experiences at the dentist. The teacher will reassure the children that the dentist is careful and never cuts people with knives. The resolution stage will tell about Mei Lin's actual visit to the dentist and how her tooth was taken care of so it didn't hurt anymore.

> "When Marcy first met River she told Umoja, 'Come meet the new girl!' So then River told Marcy that he is a boy. But Marcy said, 'No, you're not. You're a girl. Look at your long hair!'"

The discussion examines both River and Marcy's feelings. River feels annoyed at not being believed about his own identity. Marcy, faced with having to change what she has believed to be true, feels confused. It is a big stretch for young children to understand both of these feelings, as they prefer to label everything either good or bad. Focusing on each doll in turn helps them to make this stretch and strengthens their ability to empathize with the feelings of the people in their real lives.

Another effective method for undoing incorrect information is to tell a story in which a doll believes incorrect information and then learns the truth.

> "Brad always told everybody he would be a police officer when he grew up. He always said he would get to shoot bad guys every day, because that's what he thought the police always did. Then, two days ago, Brad was downtown shopping with his mom and he got lost! He was looking in the window of a store, and then he couldn't find his mom! *[Pause to identify Brad's feelings at this point.]* Yes, he was frightened and scared and upset—all three. He started to cry. And then a police officer came up to him. Brad thought the police officer was going to shoot him for getting lost!"

As this story progresses, Brad learns that the police are there to help when help is needed, not just to catch criminals. This story is also a good way to bring up the "good guy/bad guy" value system so many children learn from watching television. Many children are petrified to admit to making mistakes because, in their minds, it means they become the "bad guy." According to the "good guy/bad guy" values system, *anything* can be done to the "bad guys" simply because they are the "bad guys."

> "Julio hit River on the leg at recess today. When the teacher asked him about it, he said he had to hit River because River wrecked the little house he was building."

Finding out about the feelings of *both* characters in this story is important. Bringing out the point that now *both* dolls have done the wrong thing in this situation takes away the permission that children often believe they have to do anything they want to "bad guys."

Sometimes, when you are in the middle of a story about something else, children's incorrect assumptions will take you by surprise and you will need to add the correct information to your basic story.

> "Mickey lives with his mom and his stepdad and lots of sisters and brothers. This weekend they all went on a picnic, and Mickey got to use the swing set."

> > "*What's a stepdad?*"

> "Mickey's birth dad doesn't live with him anymore. His mom and dad got divorced when Mickey was three."

> > "*Yeah. Parents get divorced when kids act really bad and make them yell. I'll bet Mickey was really bad and that's why his dad left him.*"

Although this story was originally planned to be about Mickey trying something scary—going on a swing— that part of the story was dropped and divorce was discussed instead. The need for correct information was obviously of first importance.

> "Really, when adults decide to get divorced it's because they don't like living together anymore. It has nothing to do with the kids. In Mickey's family, his dad and mom started arguing all the time. They couldn't agree on just about anything. So they decided Mickey's dad would go live in his own apartment."

Throughout any story, always pay attention to what children say, as well as their nonverbal reactions. This can help make you aware of the children's incorrect assumptions. The following story was planned as part of a study unit on community helpers. The goal of the story was to give the children some general information about what doctors do. Note how the children's comments and nonverbal reactions signal their incorrect assumptions.

> "When Mei Lin woke up yesterday morning her ear hurt. So her dad took her to see Dr. Emily. Mei Lin got her ear checked with a little tiny light that the doctor put into her ear. What else do you think the doctor did to be sure Mei Lin was healthy?"

> *"She used one of those listening things, I bet!"*

> "A stethoscope! Yes, Dr. Emily put a stethoscope in her ears and put the other end of the stethoscope on Mei Lin's chest and listened to Mei Lin breathe. She heard Mei Lin's lungs breathe in and out."

> *"Did she put a stick down her mouth to see into her stomach?"*

> "She did use a tongue depressor stick. She asked Mei Lin to say 'Ahhhhhh' so she could look at the back of her throat. Have you ever had a sore throat?"

> *"Oh, yes. That's owie. Did Mei Lin have an owie throat?"*

> "No. Her throat was fine. The doctor just had to check everything to be sure."

> *"I bet she got a great big shot! Every time you go to the doctor you get a shot with a great big needle!! Owwwwww!!"*
> *[Several children nod their heads in agreement.]*

> "No, she didn't get any shots. In fact, most of the time you go to the doctor there are no shots. She got some pills to take for the next few days, and she got a sticker from the doctor too. Then she went home."

Although the story had already been long enough for the four year olds in the class, I picked up on the fear about doctors and shots expressed by one of the students, which was reaffirmed by several children nodding their heads in agreement. I made a note to tell a story a few days later about a doll who was afraid of going to the doctor for his immunizations. In the story, the doll got help by telling his parents how frightened he was. I also mentioned that the doll coped with the situation by closing his eyes and holding his father's hand, and that the shots were over quickly.

3. To Introduce a New Emotional Vocabulary Word; To Teach Skills for Handling Emotions

The third step of every doll story is to identify feelings, but stories can also be created with the specific goal of introducing a new vocabulary word pertaining to emotions. Often, these sessions will include discussion of how to handle the emotion involved.

Introducing a new vocabulary word that names an emotion will be a very important goal during the first few stories you tell with any group. Your students will need the skills of identifying emotions and using words to describe emotions before they can put themselves in the place of the characters in the stories and empathize with them.

Most groups of children should hear at least ten stories in which the main goal is to introduce words that name emotions. For very young children (two and three year olds), discussing the feelings of the characters in a story will be the major focus of the *Kids Like Us* doll stories. With older children, stories that identify feelings will begin with an identification of the emotions involved and move on, during the problem-solving step, to dealing with these feelings.

It is simple to create story lines that introduce a certain word for an emotion. Start with the word or words you would like the children to learn. Then think of an event that would make a child feel that emotion, and then include that event in a story about a doll.

Silly: "Elizabeth told a funny joke to Rajit and Rajit got to laughing so hard he snorted like a pig. And that got Elizabeth laughing. Pretty soon they were both rolling on the floor making pig noises and laughing like anything."

Proud: "Julio practiced and practiced writing his whole name. Then, when he went to the library yesterday with his dad, he signed a paper and got his very own library card!"

Frustrated: "Ianthe wanted to draw a really neat tiger, just the way she could see it in her imagination. She tried, but the head came out too big. She tried again, but the legs were lumpy. She tried again, and it didn't look anything at all like she wanted it to."

Worried: "River is going to play his violin at a recital next week. He has been thinking that he might trip on the way up to the stage. Or maybe he'll get up there and forget everything he is supposed to play! He can hardly sleep at night because he's thinking about all the things that might go wrong."

Sympathetic: "Julio saw Henry trying to tell one of the other kids something. He didn't know the words for what he wanted to say, so he kept pointing and trying to make them understand. Julio knew just how he felt, because before he learned English he used to have the same thing happen to him."

Outraged: "At the park the other day, Rachel saw Ricky with a bigger kid. The bigger kid grabbed Ricky's lunch away from him and ran off yelling, 'Baby lost his lunch!' Rachel couldn't believe he had done that! She wanted to chase after him and get that lunch back!"

In addition to telling stories that give the children vocabulary words that name emotions, focusing on how to deal with these emotions is extremely valuable. These stories give children an opportunity to learn coping skills and gain an understanding that they are not alone in having these feelings. Learning to deal with their emotions is one of the major developmental tasks young children are engaged in during their early years, and *Kids Like Us* doll stories are the perfect method to help them work on it.

These story ideas can come from needs you see in your classroom. When a parent reported to me that a child was waking in the night and screaming in fear of the dark, I created a story that lead us to a discussion of fears.

"One day last week at recess, Umoja fell off the swing. She fell backwards and hit her head a bit. Now she doesn't want to ever get on a swing again!"

After this simple situation setup, the children identified Umoja's feelings: scared, afraid, worried. I introduced the word *frightened*. I asked who else had felt these feelings, and accounts of other scary experiences flew around the room. We discussed what the children did about their fears. We discussed trying a scary thing again. We discussed how to get help when you are afraid. During the resolution stage of the story I told how Umoja told three friends about hitting her head and got reassurance from one that she wouldn't fall off if she held on with both hands. The story ended as Umoja and her friend went off to try the swings together.

Dealing appropriately with anger is a very difficult but essential skill for young children to acquire. Watching the *Kids Like Us* dolls in situations that make them very angry and helping them problem solve for these situations can prepare children for times when they are overtaken by this powerful emotion and will not be nearly so able to think about appropriate behavior choices.

"Mickey spent two hours setting up a block tower. Then Rajit and Umoja ran by him and knocked it down."

"Rachel was cleaning the paintbrushes when Saed came up to the sink. 'Move over! I need to wash my hands!' Saed said, and he shoved Rachel away from the sink."

After this situation setup, the teacher would ask the students to identify the feelings of all the characters involved, which helps to make young children aware that everyone has feelings in every situation. Then the discussion would center on what the two should do now that they are both feeling such strong emotions. Remember that many emotions should be explored, including positive ones.

Friendship, happiness, inclusion, encouragement: "Elizabeth was making a wild horse club. She called across the playground, 'Hey, River! You wanna be in our club?'"

Love, caring, surprise, excitement, happiness: "When Ricky got home from child care there were balloons all over his room. On his bed was a big sign that said, 'Happy Birthday, Ricky!' His brother Brad had decorated his room for a surprise."

4. To Teach a Pro-Social Skill; To Teach a Classroom Skill

One of the simplest ways of using dolls is to directly teach a pro-social or classroom skill. I present many of these stories early in the school year to create a set of social skills that my whole group shares. I use the stories as springboards for role-playing in which my students practice the skills themselves. Then, in real-life situations, I can refer to the story and the skills the dolls learned, when it is appropriate.

To create a story line to meet this goal, think of a situation in the children's lives in which the skill you want to teach is needed.

Helping: "Saed's mother came into the house with two bags of groceries in her hand and her house keys in her mouth. She looked hot and tired. She said there were five more bags of groceries out in the car."

Caring: "River noticed the new boy was standing by himself on the side of the playground, looking around at all the kids playing."

During the problem-solving step of these stories, your students will easily tell you what pro-social behavior the doll should exhibit and positively state that these are the choices they would make in the same situation. Another way of introducing pro-social skills is through a "Mistake Story" in which dolls demonstrate their lack of a pro-social skill.

Lack of caring, empathy: "When Julio tried to kick the soccer ball, he fell down and skinned his knee. Ianthe thought the way Julio fell looked funny and she laughed and laughed."

Not helping: "Elizabeth's mom asked her to fold the laundry and put it away when she got home, but Elizabeth didn't want to. So when she got home from school she ignored the laundry and played with her little cars all afternoon."

This type of story is also a good way to help the children discuss and learn classroom skills. I always tell the following story, or one similar to it, near the beginning of the year. My purpose is to discuss the pro-social value of sharing as well as to help the children learn specific methods for taking turns.

"Yesterday Elizabeth and Ricky both wanted to jump rope. They started pulling on the rope and yelling at each other."

Listening to others is an important skill that can be explored in discussion started by story lines like these:

> "The teacher told everyone to get some crayons and sit at the tables, but Umoja was thinking about going camping on the weekend and didn't hear anything the teacher said. When everybody got up and started moving around, Umoja didn't know what to do!"

> "Yesterday, River's whole class talked about where they wanted to go on a field trip. Kids thought of the aquarium, the zoo, the swimming pool, and the Museum of Natural History. River was busy playing with a piece of fuzz he found on the carpet during the discussion. Then the teacher said, 'Write on a piece of paper which trip you would most like to take and give it to me.' But River didn't know what his choices were!"

Other important classroom skills that can be introduced through doll stories like these are turn taking, cooperation, waiting, encouraging one another, responsibility for work and materials, doing careful work, and being on time. In fact, the *Kids Like Us* dolls can be shown to be learning any skill you would like to have your students learn.

> "Rajit made a snake with some playdough. Then Mei Lin came to play at the table and said, 'Oh, Rajit, I like your snake!'"

> "Elizabeth wanted to paint at the easel, but when she went over there, Mickey was already using it. So together they painted a picture. Then they showed their picture to the whole class."

The following situation discusses a very common experience. It gives children an opportunity to discuss feeling angry, frustrated, impatient, bossy, and cheated. They can then work on the skills of sharing, turn taking, and being fair to everyone, even when they have the power to be unfair.

> "Brad was at home yesterday, playing with his little brother, Ricky, out on the sidewalk. Ricky was riding the Big Wheel, but Brad wanted it. So Brad pulled Ricky off the Big Wheel and told Ricky he got to ride it because he is bigger than Ricky."

Some story lines will come from your awareness of the group's need for a specific skill. When I heard some name-calling going on among my students, I pulled down two dolls and told this impromptu story, which focuses on how hurtful name-calling can be. Allowing oneself to make mistakes and to take responsibility for them is part of this story as well.

> "Saed made a really cool sand castle. Then Rachel stepped right on it. Before he could even think, Saed said, 'I hate you, stupid!' Rachel ran and hid in the bathroom."

Through discussing this situation, my students learned some awareness of how their actions can affect others. They also realized that none of them wanted to be called names, and so they made a group agreement not to do so anymore.

One of the most important skills to model with *Kids Like Us* doll stories is empathy. This is central to children being able to care about the characters in the stories and, therefore, to caring about the people in their lives. Dolls can be shown in situations that will make your students empathize with them.

> "When Melly was trying to hit the ball with the bat, she missed three times. Then she missed two more times. One of the kids on her team yelled, 'You're no good!'"

Identifying the doll's feelings will make even self-centered young children understand and stretch their understanding of the world to include the feelings of others. Story lines in which dolls have difficult things happen to them will help your students identify with the dolls' feelings, especially if the stories are situations the children have seen or experienced themselves.

> "Brad had to go to the bathroom, but he stayed in the sandbox to finish the hill he was building. By the time he ran to the bathroom, it was too late. His pants were wet all over the front."

> "Elizabeth was walking down her street the other day when some teenagers came around the corner in a car. When they went past her they yelled, 'Jelly belly!' at her in really mean voices."

When I told this story to a group of five year olds I knew they were empathizing with Elizabeth even before we began the discussion by the looks of disapproval and sadness on their faces. The child nearest to the doll reached out and held her hand for support.

5. To Practice Problem-Solving Skills

Just as some stories will be constructed to emphasize discussion of the feelings involved, some will also be told to focus mainly on problem solving.

The ability to problem solve in a variety of situations depends on four skills. First, children need to be able to describe the problem and listen to everyone's concerns. Second, and most important, children need the ability to think flexibly and imagine multiple solutions. Without this skill, children are stuck in a futile one-track method of thinking that skips over the problem and goes immediately to the solution. Third, they need the ability to choose solutions that have a good chance for success. Finally, they must be able to work with a group toward a solution.

Telling *Kids Like Us* doll stories with a focus on the problem-solving step is especially important for groups that have not yet gained these skills. Working on problem-solving skills through doll stories will enable your students to use the skills in later story situations for which you have other main goals. And the more comfortable your students become with problem-solving skills, the more likely they will be to use them when faced with personal problems and social conflicts in their own lives. They will also see themselves as being able to solve problems and will willingly work toward solutions to classroom problems that you would like to have them address.

If your goal is problem solving, you will need to create a story line that is based on any situation common to your students' lives and lends itself to multiple solutions. Brainstorming many solutions to a problem and then choosing the ones that will work the best can then be practiced during the problem-solving step of the story. Many types of stories can lead your students to an active discussion of how they can solve this problem.

Here are some situations that have many possible solutions (how these story lines can be used to teach problem-solving skills is discussed in chapter 7):

Problem Solving for Family Situations

" Rajit loves to draw. He especially likes to use markers and colored pencils. But now, every time he gets his drawing things out, his baby sister grabs them and starts chewing on them. His Momma Betty keeps telling him he better put them away so the baby doesn't get into them. But then he can't draw!"

" Lucia wants to go to Brad's house to play. Her mom says she can't go because her room is all messy. Lucia wants to clean it up, but she feels like she'll never get it done."

" At Mickey's house it is always busy. His mom and stepdad are always busy trying to get the housework done and do their jobs too. Mickey really wants to go to a baseball game. You know how much he loves baseball! But he's sure his folks won't have time to take him."

Problem Solving for Peer Situations

" All the kids ran out onto the playground for recess on Tuesday. These three kids jumped onto the swings. Melly started singing, as loud as she could *[the teacher sings the following in a very loud voice]*, 'This is the song that never ends. It just goes on and on, my friends....' Umoja and Brad both told Melly to stop singing that song. But Melly just went right on. 'This is the song that never ends....'"

" River really wanted to play with Umoja at recess. But Umoja was already playing hopscotch with Elizabeth and Julio."

Problem Solving for Classroom Situations

" Elizabeth had to sit out the other day because she was talking while everyone was supposed to be working silently. When she sits next to Julio, she just always wants to talk to him and she forgets she's not supposed to."

" Lucia has a real problem. She can't tell which bathroom is for boys and which is for girls. She's been trying not to have to go to the bathroom because she thinks she might mix them up and everybody will laugh at her."

" Rachel took her work to her desk. The teacher said to work quietly by yourself, but Rachel couldn't figure out how to do the work. She looked and looked at it, but she didn't know what she was supposed to do."

" River didn't know the spelling words last Friday. So he looked over at Elizabeth's paper and copied them from hers. Now the teacher says he's doing so well with spelling that he can practice the really hard words on the Super Spellers list!"

6. To Support a Child or All the Children by Mirroring a Situation

Kids Like Us doll stories created to be similar to a real child or event can have a profound effect on your students. Whether created to help a single child or to discuss the concerns of the entire group, these story lines most directly support and guide your children because they deal with the issues closest to their lives.

Telling a story similar to but not exactly the same as what is happening with one of the students in your group can help you reach four goals: supporting the child by showing him someone else experiencing the same problems, finding solutions to individual problems, changing the child's perception of the problem or of himself, and changing the child's perception of the group's feelings about his situation or about themselves. These stories should not be told until the group has experience with many other *Kids Like Us* discussions and has developed the ability to empathize with the doll in the story and, therefore, with the real child the story reflects.

In planning for this type of story, it is important to prepare to support the children whose experience is being mirrored, to be ready to call on them in the discussion as soon as they indicate they have something to say, and to create an opportunity to spend a little time with them after the story if they seem to want it.

The simplest story to tell is one that supports a child by introducing a doll that shares her experience. Relating the simple story line and having the group identify the feelings the doll is experiencing is all that is needed in this situation. By surreptitiously watching the child you have created this story for, you will be able to tell how she is reacting. Young children experiencing these stories often call out gleefully, "just like *me!*" Others listen to the story silently but with great intensity. Some will not recognize their own story but will gladly participate and understand the feelings involved in the situation.

I told the following story after one of my students lost a grandmother who had been very involved in her life. I varied the gender of the child and of the grandparent. When the children asked, I changed the place the grandparent was at the time of death (at home rather than in the hospital), but I left most other details the same. During the discussion, the children were very sympathetic with Rachel and told her to get hugs and cry a lot. The child who had been inconsolable at the loss of her grandmother told her, "You will always have her 'cause she's in your memory."

> "You remember that Rachel lives near Bubbe and Zaide, her grandparents, so she can visit them every week? Well, Rachel came to circle today because she wanted to tell you about something that happened last week. Her Zaide she loved so very much died. She misses him very much."

For a child who is having a difficult transition from being at home to being in child care, a story about a doll that feels the same way can be supportive.

> "Marcy likes child care lots, but she misses her mom. Sometimes she cries and cries all day because her mom is not there."

How reassuring it can be to know we are not alone in feeling what we feel! Sometimes worries just do not seem so large when we know others are experiencing the same thing.

> "Elizabeth is having a very tough time at school right now. She is just practicing and practicing to learn to read. It's very hard for her. She wants to read very much. But sometimes she thinks she's never going to understand how to do it."

These stories support children by showing someone else having the same struggles. They also give the children an opportunity, during the exploring feelings and problem-solving steps, to express their own pent-up feelings about the situation and to work out solutions to their own problems.

Sometimes a problem will be focused mainly on a child's self-perception or what she assumes the group thinks of her. Telling doll stories that mirror situations in the children's lives can bring up a discussion of the issue so the child gets to see what her peers and teacher really think. If your students have learned, through other *Kids Like Us* doll stories, to put themselves in another's place and understand their feelings, the child will hear, indirectly but clearly, support from her peers and her teacher. Sometimes this kind of indirect support is more easily believed than what teachers and others tell the student directly.

I told the following story, for example, when I had a student who was wearing anything to look "cool." This story was designed to open the discussion to the issue of cool and what the group thought was and wasn't cool. This story line was followed with the question, "Do you think River was being cool?"

> "River really wanted a group of kids that hangs out near his house to like him. He thinks they are really cool. So he went into his mom's purse and took ten cigarettes. He took them to the other kids and shared them."

Stories that mirror one child's situation also help the entire class deal with something they are all experiencing or have all heard about. These stories also give the teacher a chance to provide correct information about the situation and an opportunity to have the children problem solve together. When I was expecting to be absent for a week, I prepared my students for the new teacher with the following story:

> "Mickey's teacher is sick this week. She has the flu and she won't be back for at least five or six days. Mickey doesn't know the new teacher, and he isn't sure he'll like her. He thinks maybe she won't know it's his turn to pass out the snacks this week."

When told near Halloween, the following story causes much discussion of the children's fears of monsters, witches, and ghosts. It also provides an opportunity to reinforce that all the Halloween decorations they see are made of paper and plastic and can't hurt them.

> "Brad doesn't want Halloween to come. He thinks some monsters will grab him and eat him! He saw a mask in a store of a monster. He did NOT like it and he screamed. He doesn't like ghosts or bats, either."

When our field trip was rained out and I was faced with a full day of moping children, I got them involved in solving someone else's problem with a story about a similar situation.

"Rajit and Saed and Rachel and Julio came to tell you that they didn't get to go on their field trip yesterday because their bus broke down. So then they just sat in class complaining about not being able to go."

7. To Help Children Become Comfortable with Diversity

Story lines can also be designed to directly address diversity issues. During these storytelling sessions the children will see you model *your* comfort with and interest in diversity and the information you are discussing. They will learn basic information and will be free to ask questions about diversity issues and bias. Through these stories, they will come to understand how bias hurts everyone and experience empathy for the dolls who are hurt by it.

The most basic of story lines—simply giving information about the doll and its family—is the perfect way to begin using *Kids Like Us* dolls to directly introduce diversity information to your students. The more they know, the more comfortable they will feel. It is also the easiest way to address these issues yourself, if you have never done so before. These stories do not have any conflicts or problems that need to be solved. You will simply be presenting information about some aspect of the doll's life and then helping your students to relate their own experiences to that of the doll's.

Any aspect of your dolls' lives can be turned into a story line designed to help your children discuss and become comfortable with diversity. When inventing these stories, remember to consider *all* aspects of the lives of the children in your class. Diversity is not just about race or religion. It is not just about one "diverse population." It is about all of us. The more your students discuss all the variables that come under the heading "human," with your modeling of interest and comfort, the more they will be interested in and comfortable with all the people they meet in their lives. It will also help them appreciate their own individuality.

To come up with subjects for diversity story lines, think about the students in your class, much as you did to create your dolls' basic identities. None of the children is exactly like another. Look past their similarities into what makes each of them unique. The possibilities are endless. You can tell stories about food, games, families and family histories, clothes, hair, customs, television habits, likes and dislikes of all kinds, special abilities and disabilities, traditions, special events, hopes, and fears.

"Umoja has a mom and dad and a little sister, Imani. They were both named with Swahili names. Swahili is an African language. Africa is important to Umoja's family because some of their ancestors came from there long ago and Umoja's family feels proud to be African American. Do you know where your name came from?"

"At Elizabeth's house they don't have a TV. They used to have one, but they decided they want to spend their time doing something else. So they gave their TV away. Now they have more time to read books together and go for bike rides and things like that. That's the way Elizabeth's family lives. What does your family do together?"

"Rachel is Jewish. She and her mom light candles and say the special Sabbath prayers together every Friday night. Sometimes they get together with Rachel's Bubbe and Zaide on the Sabbath too. And on Saturday they go to pray at Temple Beth Israel with lots of other Jewish people."

"At Ricky and Brad's house they have a special birthday tradition. When it is their birthday they get to choose what they want for dinner. Ricky always picks hot dogs. Brad wants tacos every time. They are brothers, but they like different foods."

"Ianthe and Julio both LOVE to play jump rope. They would play all day if they could. Elizabeth likes jump rope a bit, but she would rather play soccer. What do you like to play?"

These straight information story lines allow children to ask questions and openly discuss the subject in further steps of the storytelling session. It also gives them the opportunity to express their own individuality as they relate *their* favorite game or tell *their* family birthday tradition.

If you have a child or children in your class who you think might feel bad about some aspect of themselves, a story in which a doll shows that she is comfortable with or proud of this aspect of herself can help the children see themselves in a new light.

"Rajit and his moms had lentil casserole for dinner last night. It was really yummy, so Rajit ate two pieces. Rajit and his moms don't eat any meat. Rajit is proud that he doesn't kill animals to get his food. He and his moms eat lots of other things, like bread and potatoes and carrots and cheese and ice cream and cake. What do you eat at your house?"

An easy way to create story lines that give information and allow for diversity discussion is to put a doll into a new situation in which the doll learns the information herself.

"Umoja went to church with Julio last Sunday. Julio is Catholic and goes to St. Anne's church every Sunday with his brother and his father. Umoja really liked the pretty church. It had windows with lots of pieces of colored glass in them. She liked the songs they sang too. Do any of you go to church?"

"When Ianthe went to River's house to stay the night, she was surprised by something. River's dad said River's hair was all oily so it needed to get washed. But Ianthe's mom is always telling her she needs to put more oil in her hair!"

Story lines can also be designed to introduce books that will give children information about a subject. The doll involved can tell the group that she has learned a lot from a book and then present the book to the group.

> "Julio has been wondering why his skin is light coffee brown and his friend Ianthe's is darker mocha colored. He found this book that talks about skin colors in his school library, and he brought it to share with you today. It's called *All the Colors We Are*. Shall I read it to you?"

Another effective way to begin a discussion is to create a story about a doll who has questions about something. This is particularly effective if your students have been wondering about something themselves.

> "Elizabeth heard about a holiday called Kwanzaa. She was wondering if any of you can tell her about it, because she is really interested."

> "Mickey has been wondering and wondering about why Melly has no hair. He heard Melly's mom say that Melly has been sick and the medicine made her hair fall out. Have any of you been wondering about Melly's hair too?"

> "Ricky is curious about glasses. He wants to know what they are for and how people keep them on their faces. Does anybody know about this?"

> "When Saed visited his neighbor Mr. Spinner, he saw that Mr. Spinner had to hold onto a metal bar thing when he walked around. That made Saed wonder what that thing was and why his neighbor was using it."

This kind of "wondering story" gives the children permission to admit, "I wonder about that too. Why DOES his neighbor use one of those things?" Some children will be able to proudly show what they know about this. Many times several children will be excited to tell of their experiences with the situation you are discussing.

The discussion that will take place after you tell these basic situation setups will help your students realize it is a positive thing to have experiences with diversity. And you will have your turn to give them more information about the subject during the discussion step of the story. (We will see many examples of this in the chapter 7.)

8. To Undo Learned Stereotypes and Biased Beliefs

In their striving to make sense of the world, children categorize and try to organize everything. They often rely on stereotypes to simplify things. Adults often encourage this by expecting children to exemplify stereotypes associated with girls or boys or by labeling them as being shy or rough. And children pick up on every stereotype they hear.

The characteristics you choose for each doll's identity should contain some details that help to undo stereotypes. It is also important to tell stories designed to do the same thing. These stories give your children a chance to ask questions about stereotypes and to help each other realize how unfair and inaccurate they can be. Telling these stories will also give you an incredible amount of information about the belief systems of the children. You will see that some of the children strongly believe the stereotypes you are attempting to undo.

This is especially true of gender stereotypes. For example, many young children will state emphatically that girls have eyelashes and boys have none. Cartoons are drawn this way, and even looking at the eyelashes of the boys in the class is sometimes not enough to convince children otherwise. This belief in rigid gender differences can extend to beliefs about clothes, activities, toys, and playmates. Young children believe the stereotypes so strongly that sometimes they fear they will become the other gender if they do not adhere to them.

The fact that the children feel so absolutely certain of the truth of these stereotypes is evidence of how strongly our society insists that they learn them. Stories like the following can help free your children to play with one another and express interests and play games they might otherwise have felt were off-limits. Feeling comfortable with diversity will loosen their need to categorize the world into tight stereotypes.

> **Modeling that girls can like building things:** "Ianthe spent all day yesterday at the block center. She built a long roadway for the little cars and raced them up and down. Then she built a tall, tall rocket ship and used all the blocks in the whole block chest! She had a wonderful time. She loves blocks."

> **Modeling that kids who can't read are smart too:** "Learning to read is being really, really hard for Julio. He doesn't know what most of the English words mean. But he's a whiz in math! You should see him add and subtract! And he's even learning about times now. He loves numbers."

> **Modeling that girls and boys can play together (and girls can be engineers too!):** "Ricky saw Marcy making a train with a bunch of chairs today. She was sitting in the first chair saying, 'Whooo, whooo!' When Ricky came over and asked if he could play, Marcy said, 'Sure! All aboard!' So Ricky was the passenger and ticket taker and Marcy was the engineer. They played together all the way until lunch. It was so much fun!"

To plan this type of story, you will have to uncover your own unconscious stereotypes in order to know which ones you may have been reinforcing in your classroom. Any stereotypes that you have believed (even subconsciously) have been forcing your students into boxes that meet the terms of those stereotypes. See what pops into your mind to complete the following sentences:

> "All the girls like…"

> "My Asian students always…"

> "Kids from poor families will…"

> "I could expect a fat child to…"

Once you are aware of the unfairness of these assumptions, you are ready to present these ideas to your students. Also, a stereotype you might have unconsciously been reinforcing provides a good opportunity to tell a story that gives an example of the opposite of that stereotype. Watching your students open their minds to the wonderful variety the world contains can help you and your more inflexible adult mind do the same.

In the following story I use Elizabeth, a doll who is shaped to look like a fat child. To undo the assumption that a large child is lazy or will not want to be active, I have to know that this is a stereotype and that my acceptance of it is what might otherwise hold back the class from understanding the unfairness of such assumptions. I create a model of an active, happy, and social large child. In doing so, I show all the children that a large child can be fun to play with and, at the same time, give the large children in my class permission to run and play freely.

> "Elizabeth loves to play tag. As soon as the bell rings for recess, she is out the door and on the playground yelling, 'Who wants to play tag?' She runs back and forth and up and down the whole recess long, and when she's 'it'—watch out! She's tricky and catches everybody!"

Story lines that directly bring up the subject of stereotypes are also important. Showing the dolls going through the process of unlearning stereotypes will help your students do the same. There are several ways to use *Kids Like Us* doll stories to undo incorrect information or stereotypes. A doll can come to the circle to tell about something she used to believe and has since learned is not true. Through identifying the doll's feelings and helping the doll find a way to open her mind, your students will learn to identify their own stereotyped thinking and that of others around them and also learn strategies to break free of those beliefs.

> "Brad told the teacher he didn't want to do sewing 'cause he thought that was a girl thing to do. But then one day the sewing project was making beanbags. Brad *really* wanted one."

> "Rajit thought Mei Lin would be really good at karate because she's Asian American. Then, when they started a karate class together after school, he found out she didn't know any karate at all!"

> "Umoja really wanted to be friends with Melly. She knew Melly's family had a lot of money. So Umoja got her mom to buy her a very fancy party dress and she wore it to school. She was sure Melly would like her if she wore expensive clothes, but Melly didn't pay any attention to her dress at all."

> "Marcy thought Henry was a baby because he doesn't know how to say very many words. Then Henry had his birthday at school and Marcy found out Henry is five now. He is older than Marcy!"

If you hear your students expressing stereotyped or biased views, it is important to intervene immediately and challenge that information. This may happen as you are telling a story about something else. Once you have discussed the stereotype, you will then have to decide whether to go on with the planned story or shift focus to this new issue. Follow-up activities, discussions, or parent conferences may be needed for reinforcement. Telling a doll story on another day with a focus on undoing that stereotype could also be appropriate. It would be very effective to tell a story about a doll that used to believe a stereotype and has since learned that it is not true. At least one of your students is probably in the process of doing that very thing.

We may not hear our students express every stereotype they have come to believe. If we know the kids are being exposed to stereotypes, however, we can assume they are forming some incorrect assumptions. Luckily, we can use *Kids Like Us* dolls to counteract this. Taking a proactive approach can help keep young children from forming stereotypes in the first place and can be a first step in their learning to do some critical thinking about the information they are being given.

> "Rachel is worried that she is getting too fat. She says her waist is too big around. She was looking at her Barbie's waist and says that Barbie has a tiny little waist. Rachel wants hers to look like Barbie's. What do you think about that?"

> "Ricky thought that he would be smarter when he got his glasses. He'd seen lots of people on TV with glasses, and they were always the smartest ones. But then he got his glasses and he was just the same, except he could see better."

9. To Help Children Develop Anti-Bias Attitudes

Once your group has learned to be comfortable with diversity and is actively interested in learning more, it is time to introduce the concept of bias. Your goal will be to enable your students to recognize and reject bias and empathize with the person experiencing it. You will also explore the motivations and feelings of the one acting in a biased manner.

To facilitate discussion and begin the process of critical thinking about bias, it will be important to introduce your students to some new vocabulary.

The youngest children can learn that we must treat one another in a *fair* manner. They can learn that it is *unfair* to tell someone they can't play based on who they are or what group they belong to. They can learn the importance of

Anti-Bias Vocabulary

Stereotype: Assigning a characteristic to an entire group of people and acting as though this characteristic is shared by the whole group. *Explanation to Kids:* Saying everybody in a group has to be the same in some way.

Fair: Treating each person with equal respect, opportunity, and attention. *Explanation to Kids:* This will be explained with examples such as sharing equally, giving everyone a turn, and listening to each child's opinion.

Unfair: Treating one person better or worse than another. *Explanation to Kids:* Explained by example, such as one child getting all the markers, a child being excluded, or one child bossing others.

(continued on next page)

making sure everyone is *safe*—that no one is allowed to hurt either their bodies or their feelings. They can learn to identify stereotypes as stories that are *not true*.

> "Lucia had all the trucks. Ricky wanted some. Lucia said, 'No.' Ricky said that was *unfair.* What do you think?"

> "When the kids in the class laughed at Marcy's shoes because they had holes in them, Marcy did not feel *safe.*"

> "Lucia said Ricky couldn't make a necklace because boys don't like necklaces. Ricky said that was *not true* because he is a boy and he did want to make a necklace."

> "Mickey saw that the mean lion in the movie *Lion King* was colored darker than the nice lions. And the mean Hun in *Mulan* had skin darker than the other people in the movie too. But Mickey is smart. He knew that it's *not true* that dark is bad. They just made that up when they drew the pictures."

Children as young as five can also learn the word *stereotype* to help them identify these situations. They can learn that everyone must be treated with *respect* and without *bias*.

> "River and Ianthe were playing with the hollow blocks at recess yesterday. River insisted that he had to be the one to stack all the blocks because they are heavy. He said Ianthe was not strong enough because girls aren't as strong as boys. Ianthe said that was just a *stereotype* about girls and not true."

> "When River fell down and scraped his knee, he cried and cried. Three of the other kids called out, 'River is a baby. Cry baby! Cry baby!' Elizabeth gave River a hug and told the other kids they were not treating River with *respect.*"

These words can be introduced in doll stories and will then become tools both you and the children can use to facilitate the discussions you have about bias issues. Eventually, children will be able to use these words in their own lives to help them evaluate events and feelings they experience.

Now your students have the tools they need to actively work on understanding how bias hurts everyone and to learn to empathize with those experiencing it. The bias that children experience may take several forms. You will tell stories in which children experience name-calling, exclusion, hurtful teasing, and other biased behaviors. To develop anti-bias attitudes, you will need to tell stories that may be difficult for *you* to talk about.

> "When everyone went around the circle to tell what they want to be when they grow up, Brad said he would like to be a nurse. Then Rajit laughed and said 'You can't be a nurse, dummy. That's for girls!'"

> "When Henry went to play in the boat, two kids yelled at him, 'Go away! No black kids in here!'"

"When Ianthe was at play practice, one of the other kids told her to give up her chair. Ianthe told him no, because she was sitting in the chair. He said she should go sit on the floor because her family comes from Africa. He said everybody in Africa sits in the dirt, so Ianthe should too."

Don't be afraid to tell stories like these. Children need to experience the feelings these dolls have in order to understand how much bias hurts. They will learn by empathizing with the dolls, discussing strategies for dealing with the situations, and seeing themselves as a person who will not act in this way.

Remember that although many such situations feel heart wrenching to us, children listening to the same story may not be aware of the implications of hundreds of years of history that we feel behind such comments. And many of these situations are likely to be occurring in their everyday lives. Many times children will have even more intense experiences to relate when you bring these issues up in a story. In fact, the last two stories are real ones. The first was observed in a child care setting with four year olds, and the second was related by a ten year old.

The stories you tell will have a different meaning for each student. Some children will relate to the story as something that might or already has happened to them or the people they know. Others will recognize their own biased behavior. Both groups of children will benefit by hearing the story.

This is not to say that students will be unaffected by the feelings inherent in the stories that you are telling. As part of the planning process, you will need to prepare to support students who might relate personally to the story you are planning. (We will discuss how to do this in chapter 7.)

The main goal for all of the children when listening to these stories is the same: to learn that acting in a biased way is unfair, hurtful, and, most important, not something any of us ever want to do. They will learn to recognize common biased behaviors such as name-calling, exclusion, and hurtful teasing. As they critique these situations, all the children will practice the critical thinking skills that are essential to recognizing and rejecting bias as they experience it in their lives. This ability will make it possible for them to avoid incorporating biased ideas into their belief systems and allow them to stand up against bias when they encounter it.

To plan a story line about a bias situation, decide what bias the story will present and in what way the bias will be expressed. Determine whether the doll you use as the main character will be acting in a biased way or experiencing the bias. Then choose the doll that best fits these details.

Bias: Being unfair to someone or disliking someone because of some group they belong to.
Explanation to Kids: Being unfair to someone because of who they are.

Safety: A feeling of the absence of the possibility of coming to harm.
Explanation to Kids: Knowing no one will hurt you on purpose—either your body or your feelings.

Respect: Treatment that accords one the dignity and caring that everyone deserves.
Explanation to Kids: Treating everyone fairly and with caring about their feelings.

Subjects of Biased Behavior	Common Childhood Biased Behaviors	Motives for Biased Behavior	Types of Story Lines for Bias Situations
• appearance (body parts, clothes, size) • socioeconomic class • culture • family structure • language • religion • race • possessions • abilities and disabilities • gender • a single incident (e.g., wetting one's pants)	• asking hurtful questions • constant focus on one characteristic of another person • avoidance • insistence on conformity to one's beliefs • exclusion • name-calling • hurtful teasing • put-downs	• The fear of something new • Curiosity (usually hurtful questions or focus on one characteristic) • The desire for power over the target child, an object or a group • The desire to impress someone else • Low self-esteem (they feel bad about themselves and try to make others feel the same) • Learned behavior (they have seen other kids or adults do it) • A desire to go along with a group	• a doll experiences a new thing and rejects it • a doll acts on a stereotype she believes • a doll avoids another doll due to a bias • a doll relates how someone acted in a biased way toward her • a doll believes a stereotype about herself

It is important to deal extensively with the issue of exclusion. You can do this as part of the process of learning about the common biased behaviors. Because behavior that involves excluding others is very likely to occur among your students, you will probably find yourself needing a story about exclusion at the beginning of the year, before you have even had a chance to tell many other stories. As with any bias incident, be sure to intervene in these situations *at the time they happen.* Then you can use your *Kids Like Us* dolls in an exclusion story, even if you have not yet practiced all the preparatory skills. You can always go back and work on those later. It is more important to deal with the issue immediately.

Children often use exclusion, based on any bias that comes in handy, to wield social power. Yelling a derogatory name and insisting on making someone an outsider gives a child a sense of power and superiority if the group goes along with her. Your goal, then, in telling *Kids Like Us* doll stories about exclusion is to unmask the reasons for this behavior and turn the "kid culture" against it. This will make it impossible for anyone in your group to use this method since the others will see through the bias to this child's motivation and refuse to cooperate with the exclusion.

"The other day at recess Julio was watching a basketball game some kids were playing. He really wanted to play, but when he tried to get in the game one of the kids said, 'Man, you can't play ball with those lame shoes!' Julio ran and hid in the bathroom."

"Lucia wanted to sit with Brad at lunch time. But Brad told Lucia she couldn't sit next to him because she was a stupid girl. He said only boys can sit with him."

"Umoja and Ianthe started a doggie club with the kids on their street. Everybody got a great doggie name. But when River came by and asked to join the club, they told him, 'This club is only for us African American kids. You're white, so you can't be in it.'"

To help students understand what bias is and how hurtful it can be, you will want to tell stories about subjects common to most of your students' lives. Telling stories about things that might happen at school are easiest to create accurately and uses an environment that is familiar to the children.

Language bias; Hurtful teasing: "Julio is doing very well learning English. One thing he has a hard time with is saying the *V* sound. In Spanish that letter sounds almost like 'buh.' And then yesterday Julio told the class he was working very hard on his science project. Rajit laughed and said it sounded like Julio was working 'berry hard.' He said, "Is your project about berries, Julio?" And the whole class laughed.

Family structure bias; Insistence on conformity to another's beliefs: "One of the kids looked at Lucia's drawing of her family and said, 'Where's your mom and dad? You can't have a family with just a grandma in it!'"

Racial bias; Exclusion: "The kids were having fun up on top of the jungle gym. When Mei Lin came and tried to climb up, Rachel yelled, 'NO! ONLY AMERICANS UP HERE!'"

Single incident bias; Name-calling: "One day Rachel got the flu while she was at school. Her stomach hurt really bad and then she threw up on her desk. Melly yelled, 'Stinky! Stinky! Don't come near me, Stinky!' when Rachel walked past her. The next day Melly called her Stinky again, and so did some of the other kids."

Disability bias; Constant focus on one characteristic of another person: "Henry talks with his hands. When he first came to Saed's class, he wanted to teach Henry words with his mouth. He went to speech class to learn how to do this. But Saed would take him around the classroom and say words to him and make him try to copy him. At recess he would take his hand and make him go with him to learn more words all round the playground. But Henry wanted to play in the sandbox."

Gender bias; Name-calling: "Brad was very excited because he got to go to dance class with Elizabeth one day. But when he told Mickey about it, Mickey said, "A boy at dance class? What are you, a fag?"

Culture bias; Put-downs: "Julio could hardly wait for lunch because he had some special yummy tamales left over from the party the day before. But when he got out his lunch, Elizabeth looked at his tamales and asked, 'What's that blucky thing?'"

Remember to tailor these situations to your own class. In a class that is mostly Latino, this story might happen from the following perspective:

"Elizabeth could hardly wait for lunch because she had some special yummy potato salad left over from the party the day before. But when she got out her lunch, Julio looked at her lunch and said, 'What's that junk?'"

Each group of students has had different experiences. Your knowledge of them and the issues important to them will be the best guide as to which stories they are ready to discuss. Later you can examine biases they may not have any experience with yet.

It will be important to tell stories based on many different biases. In this way students learn that biased behavior is not really about the subject of the bias itself but about a lack of knowledge, the wielding of power, or the need to feel better than someone else. Knowing that the problem lies with the person expressing the bias helps children avoid believing in the bias themselves.

All of your students will experience bias aimed at them. This is not just an issue for the "diverse" students in your class. While some children will experience more bias throughout their lives because the bias against them is backed by the institutional power in our society, every single one of the children will feel the threat of having bias leveled against them at one time or another. If a child doesn't get teased about her race or religion, there are always other targets—a nose that is too freckled, hips that are too wide, the "dorky" shoes or the time she threw up in class. You will want your doll stories to represent this fact and not focus on a few dolls for whom bias might be "a problem." Bias is a problem for all of us.

The story line is only the beginning of the story process. With your students, you will examine the feelings of the character being treated unfairly. They will discuss the problem with the way the doll is being treated. They will brainstorm strategies to deal with the situation, and you will relate how the doll successfully handled it. Your students will take a journey through the story to the successful conclusion, right along with the doll.

Some stories should be told from the perspective of the doll that acts in a biased manner. This way you have an opportunity to discuss how a person is feeling when they do this and to help them understand the motivations behind it. An easy story line to create is one that tells about a doll who experiences something new and then rejects it.

"River had never met anyone with cerebral palsy before. When Mickey first came into River's classroom, River asked his teacher, 'How come that kid's all jerky? He gives me the creeps!'"

"Rachel's class learned a lot about what it is like to live in India. Then one day they had a special India party. Some of the kids tried on beautiful saris and jewelry from India. Everybody enjoyed a shadow puppet show. Rachel said that the saris were pretty costumes but she liked *real* clothes better."

Another story line that comes from the perspective of a doll acting in a biased way shows the doll actively avoiding other people due to its incorrect beliefs. This is a common reaction to diversity. These stories are especially good for bringing out the feelings that cause children to act in a biased way.

"Elizabeth saw a man with a missing hand at the library. He had a metal claw that could grip things. Elizabeth cried and tried to pull her mom out of the library because she thought the man was a bad man and that he would grab her with the claw."

"When Marcy first came to her child care she didn't want to hold hands with Henry. She thought his brown skin was like dirt and would rub off on her."

Dolls can also tell about a stereotype or other bias that they have come to believe. In these stories, the dolls tell about a mistake they made because of a stereotype or incorrect belief they had and how they learned from it. The feelings of *both* characters will be examined. The doll believing the stereotype will come to the circle to help the children understand that everyone acts in a biased way sometimes. The doll who has been treated unfairly will be named, to help the children begin to look at both perspectives in one situation.

"Lucia was all excited about Christmas coming. She asked Saed if he was excited too. Saed told Lucia that his family is Muslim and they don't celebrate Christmas. Lucia thought everybody celebrated Christmas."

I tell another story, usually around Thanksgiving, to counteract the stereotypes to which I know the children will be exposed.

"When River learned that Melly was Native American, he was excited. He asked her, 'Will you show me how to hunt for buffalo?' Melly said she belongs to the Siletz tribe, because her mom and dad do. She told him Siletz are water people and never hunted buffalo, even a long time ago."

Most bias stories should be told from the perspective of the doll being treated unfairly since children need much practice in putting themselves in this doll's place. To focus on how it feels to experience bias, bring a doll to circle to relate how another doll or dolls acted in a biased way toward her.

"Marcy got permission from her mom to invite Brad over to play. But when Marcy asked Brad if he could come, he said, 'Naw. I don't wanna. You don't hardly have any toys to play with at your house. Don't your parents ever buy you anything?'"

"When Lucia got mad at Mei Lin, she pulled her eyes into little slits and said, 'I don't have to do what you say. You have ugly eyes!'"

"Last week all the kids made flower vases for their mothers for Mother's Day. Rajit made two vases so he would have one to give to each of his moms. Then Umoja said, 'You can't have two moms! Everybody has only one!' When Rajit told Umoja he DID have two moms, she said Rajit was weird."

"When Umoja went to visit her grandma, she took Umoja by the arm and said, 'You're just skin and bones, child! Aren't you eating enough? You look like a bundle of sticks, you're so skinny!'"

Some stories should show how a doll used to believe in a bias against herself. This is the reality for many children (and adults too). The children really like the dolls, and so taking part in a *Kids Like Us* doll story where the entire class encourages the doll not to believe those biased ideas can help them feel better about themselves.

"Umoja hates her name. She wishes she could change it to Susan. Or maybe Hilary. When she first came to her school and the teacher told the class her name, some of the kids laughed. Now Umoja is afraid someone will laugh again."

"Mei Lin hates her straight black hair. She thinks it is ugly. She wishes she had long blond hair like River."

"Elizabeth loves dancing. Whenever she hears music, she just has to move. She even got her mom to sign her up for a dance class so she could learn more. But then one of the kids at the class said to her, 'What are you doing here? Don't you know elephants can't dance?' Now Elizabeth never dances any more. In fact, at recess time she sits on a bench and reads a book instead of running and playing tag like she did before."

"Ianthe used to think she wasn't pretty because she has dark brown skin. She used to put herself down about it. Then her class got a brown bunny for a pet. Everyone said what a beautiful brown coat the bunny had—and then Ianthe realized her skin is almost the same beautiful brown color as that bunny."

Groups of older children and children with many experiences with *Kids Like Us* doll stories can handle bias stories involving a tangle of the actions, feelings, and motivations of two or three dolls, sometimes even more. It is good to tell stories that involve multiple characters because bias incidents often happen in groups.

"River was playing Ghost Trap at recess. When he called out 'Ghost trap!' when nobody was running, all the kids laughed at him."

"Rachel and Melly were whispering together and looking over at Rajit. Elizabeth told Rajit they were telling secrets about him, so Rajit marched over to them and demanded, 'What are you two saying about me?' Rachel said, 'We're not saying anything, Nosey! Boy, you've got a big nose!' And Melly said, 'Yeah. We should call you Indian Big Nose!'"

10. To Help Children Learn to Stand Up Against Bias

Once your students have learned to be comfortable with and interested in diversity and to recognize bias and empathize with those experiencing it, the focus of your stories will shift to how the dolls stand up against bias when they encounter it.

To teach the skills needed to successfully stand up against bias, you will use the same types of story lines as in other stories about bias. You will use the same planning process, but with more careful attention to which character is telling about the incident.

Some stories will make it possible to talk about what a person might do when he is the object of bias behavior. This will most likely take place during the discussion and problem-solving step. For example, I would take Ricky to circle to have the children help him with the following situation:

> "Ricky was playing on the sidewalk, and Marcy came out to play too. She started looking at Ricky and asked him, 'How'd your ears get so big? Can you flap 'em like an elephant?'"

Other stories will center the discussion on what a person can do to make up for their hurtful and biased behavior. Both Elizabeth and Julio would attend the circle to tell the following story, and discussion would focus on what Elizabeth should do next:

> "Elizabeth laughed when Julio misspelled *from* in his reading journal. Without thinking, she said, 'Don't you even know how to spell *from*? That's a baby word!' Julio ran out of the room crying."

Stories can include a bystander who witnesses the biased behavior. The discussion would focus on what that person could do. All three dolls in the next story would come to the story circle to tell what happened. For example, if I told the following story, discussion would focus on what Ianthe could do to stand up against this bias.

> "Rajit, River and Ianthe were playing in the house corner. Rajit said he and River could be the two dads in the family and Ianthe could be their kid. But River yelled and said Rajit is weird because he has two moms. He said there can't be two dads in a house, either."

Ask the children to put themselves in the situation you have told them about in your *Kids Like Us* doll story. Ask them, "What if you saw that happen? What would you do?" or "How would you help?" The story above about Rajit and the house corner could meet this goal if, instead of having Ianthe present, the children were asked to put themselves in that place in the story. (For more on learning to stand up against bias, see chapter 7.)

6

Step Three: Identifying Feelings

At the end of the situation setup, you have completed your presentation. Except for creating a resolution at the end of the story-telling session, your job now is to facilitate the discussion. You will do this by asking questions to encourage the children's thinking and by reflecting back to the group what has been said. You will also be taking into account every one of the children's responses to the story and supporting all of them for participating and listening to each other.

● After you have presented the situation setup, you will ask a question to move the story along to a discussion of the feelings of one or more characters.

"How do you think Elizabeth felt when those kids said that to her?"

"What was he feeling right then?"

"What do you think Marcy was feeling when she screamed and kicked like that?"

"How do you think Ricky is feeling now that he can't go to Lucia's house?"

"Why do you think they sat and complained like that? How are they feeling?"

"I bet Henry was having a lot of different feelings right then. Does anybody have an idea what some of those feelings were?"

The trick to doing this step is not to say too much. For many teachers, the hardest part of the process is to remember not to *tell* but to *ask* the children how the dolls were feeling. It seems natural to provide the children with the information—"because she was really sad" or "Ricky is really upset and disappointed because he can't go to Rajit's house today."

Telling the kids the dolls' feelings takes away a perfect opportunity to work toward several goals. Instead, asking what the students think will help them to develop their feelings vocabulary, become comfortable discussing feelings, and practice understanding others' emotions.

For their first few stories, some teachers prefer to use a set phrase to begin this step that keeps them from saying more. "How do you think she feels?" or "How do you think he feels?" works in most stories to get the students thinking and discussing. Later you can vary your language according to the story.

Your students may not find it easy to identify the feelings of the characters in a story. In the beginning they may have difficulty putting themselves in a doll's place. Or they may not have the words in their vocabulary to discuss the doll's feelings. This is especially true of preschool children, but it is sometimes true of older children as well.

Once you have introduced a few dolls, you can get an idea of how "emotion savvy" your group is by telling several stories designed to spend most of the discussion on identifying feelings. Observe your students' responses. If many don't have a good feelings vocabulary, or if they find it difficult to imagine how the dolls are feeling, many storytelling sessions with identifying feelings as the main goal would be a good idea. You'll know that this is a difficult task for your group if, during a beginning story, you ask, "How do you think she feels?" and you get no response! Many times children will be able to use the words *sad, mad,* and *happy* to describe emotions. Sometimes *good* and *bad* is the extent of their feelings vocabulary.

Learning New Emotion Words

The first thing children of any age need before they can discuss emotions is a feelings vocabulary. Directly teaching the meaning of emotion words to children is very easy to do with *Kids Like Us* dolls and can help children understand the meanings of the words at a deep level because they have seen the word "in action." They have really experienced how *excited* Julio was about his new bike, how *worried* Ianthe was when her mother was sick, and how *frustrated* Henry was when he couldn't explain what he wanted.

To teach a new vocabulary word, use a situation setup designed to bring out that emotion. Then ask, "How do you think she feels?"

> "Mickey was planning to go to a horseback riding lesson. He could hardly wait! Then it rained and he couldn't go. How do you think he felt?"

You will then accept all the responses you get to this question, remembering that creative thinking and practice in thinking about another's feelings are some of the goals of a *Kids Like Us* doll story. Your first response will be a reflection of the children's contributions.

> "He might be feeling *sad* or *mad* or *ucky*. Yes. Good thinking!"

Then you will cue the children to think specifically about the targeted feeling. You will rephrase what the doll is feeling to give the children a clearer picture of the emotion.

> "Mickey was really counting on that horseback riding lesson. He was looking forward to it and all excited. Now that he can't go, he feels like a popped balloon. Do you know that feeling? What is it called when you feel like that?"

You can also help them relate to the doll's feelings by challenging them to think of times when they have experienced the same thing. Children love to do this. Often you will get more responses to this question than you will have time to explore, and hearing others' experiences might help one of the children to think of a word or words for this emotion.

> "Has this kind of thing ever happened to you? How did you feel?"

The responses to this question can also be guideposts to other issues you may want to deal with at another time, because children relate stories of things that have happened to them and the strong emotions they have experienced.

If one of the children uses the targeted vocabulary word or another good emotion word you hadn't planned on, you can immediately pick up on it.

> "So Darren says he was *disappointed* when he couldn't go to his grandma's house."

If the word is not in any of the children's vocabularies, you will have to be the one to introduce the new word to them. Its meaning will be clear because the children have already done the thinking to get inside the feeling the doll has expressed. Now they will have a new word to describe the feelings. You can help them relate the new word to their own experiences.

> "It sounds like you really know how Mickey was feeling. I think another word for the way Mickey was feeling was *disappointed.* When we are counting on something and then we don't get it, sometimes we call that being disappointed. Disappointed. That's a good word. Were you disappointed, Erin, when you didn't have a birthday party? Shanell, you were telling about that time your sister wouldn't play with you. Did you feel disappointed that time?"

Connecting the dolls' experiences and new vocabulary words to physical movement can be an effective way to ensure that every child understands and will remember the meaning of the word. This is especially important with preschool children. Stomping your feet to practice expressing *mad,* or clapping your hands and wiggling around for *excited* can be an effective way for children to learn to understand and remember the meaning of the word. It's fun too.

> "What did your face look like when you were disappointed, Shanell? Who knows what your body might do if you were feeling disappointed? Let's all try it. Look around. Do we all look disappointed?"

Remember to remain flexible. Many emotions can be described in more than one way, and each is as good as another. The goal is to broaden their emotion vocabulary, and any new words are a plus.

> "Mickey was feeling sad, upset, and let down! That's right. He felt all those ways. He was especially feeling let down, like Cam said. *Let down* means that Mickey felt so excited about his horse riding lesson it was like he was floating. Then when he found out he couldn't go, his feelings fell down like he wasn't floating any more. We call that feeling *let down.* Sometimes we call it *disappointed.* Have any of you felt let down or disappointed like Mickey did?"

Once you have told a doll story focused on teaching an emotion word, you will be able to cue the children to express their feelings by reminding them of this word and the doll story.

> "Are you feeling *disappointed* because we aren't having crackers for snack? I think you're feeling just like Mickey did when he couldn't go to his horse-riding lesson. Is that right?

For children between two and four years old, understanding and learning to talk about emotions is a major developmental goal. Stories that focus on teaching emotion words are the most appropriate ones for this age group. Since these children also need storytelling sessions to be short, as is appropriate to their attention span, these stories may not spend any time on problem solving. In this type of story the children will discuss the feelings of the characters and relate these feelings to their own experiences. Then, in a few sentences,

**Feeling Words for
Two to Four Year Olds**

upset	disappointed
mad	happy
surprised	grumpy
frustrated	bossy
excited	sad
worried	silly
loving	lonely
let down	scared
proud	friendly

the teacher will make some resolution for the doll and end the story. In this way, plenty of time is left for identifying feelings. Your goal will be to teach the children some basic words for the feelings they most commonly experience. Follow-up activities at another time can help them practice how to handle each emotion.

To get an idea of which emotions to focus on, observe the children. What emotions are they exhibiting? Also, the situations in which you observe the children experiencing these emotions make great story lines.

With this training, even two year olds can tell when they are "mad, mad, mad!" I knew one two year old who liked to do everything herself and would admit to being "fusser-a-ted" when she was unable to do something. How much more frustrated would she have been if she hadn't had that word to explain what was wrong?

Older children can expand their vocabulary to include multiple intensity levels of emotions and words for more complex emotions.

Identifying Feelings

Once children have developed a full vocabulary of emotion words, they will be able to identify the emotions of dolls in many different situations. The stories you tell to these children will be designed to help them meet some other goal than identifying feelings, but this step will always be a part of your story-telling sessions. In identifying the doll's feelings, you will

- ask how the doll is feeling
- reflect the children's responses back to the group
- ask leading questions and give new vocabulary if needed
- affirm that the doll is feeling the emotions that the children name

Here is an example of the identifying feelings step. It began with a story line about Mei Lin kicking and refusing to go to the dentist.

"How do you think Mei Lin was feeling?"

"Scared!"
"Yeah! Totally!"
"That's why she kicked. She was frightened."

"Scared or frightened. Are there any other words that describe that same feeling? [Silence.] How about afraid? Do you think the word *afraid* describes how Mei Lin was feeling?

"Yeah!"

"That's how Mei Lin was feeling, all right. She was scared, frightened, and afraid."

Feeling Words for Five to Eight Year Olds

satisfied	calm
confused	stressed
interested	jealous
anxious	bored
angry	dreamy
furious	embarrassed
outraged	grateful
irritable	curious
patient	wild
impatient	cautious
depressed	satisfied
unsure	sorry
pleased	hurt
frightened	cheated
afraid	generous
terrified	sympathetic
nervous	confident
guilty	greedy
thoughtful	

Many story lines will cause the doll to experience several emotions at once. It is excellent practice for your children to identify the doll's overlapping emotions. Most real-life situations cause people to feel complex emotions.

The following example began with Mickey's anticipation of a substitute teacher. He is not sure the new teacher will know it's his turn to pass out the snack that week.

> "What are some words that describe how Mickey is feeling?"
>
>> "I think he's scared!"
>
> "Mickey could be feeling scared. Have you ever met someone new? How did you feel?
>
>> "Nervous. I was nervous when I met you, Trisha.
>
> "Yes, I remember that day, Nick. You were nervous to meet me. Mickey could be feeling nervous about his new teacher too. How is Mickey feeling about getting his turn to pass out the snack?
>
>> "I was worried once when you weren't here. 'Member you had a sore throat?"
>> "Yeah. He's worried all right. He thinks maybe she won't know."
>
> "You have all done some very good thinking. You know, Mickey was feeling all of those things that day. He was nervous and a little scared. And he was very worried she wouldn't give him his special job."

Summarizing the dolls' feelings at the end of the step clarifies the discussion of emotions, allows you to leave out any feelings mentioned that don't really apply, and prepares the group for discussion and problem solving (step four).

Feelings of Two or More Dolls

Identifying the feelings of more than one doll is more complicated and takes more time, so it should be saved for when your children are able to identify the feelings of one doll with little prompting. You should also be experienced enough at telling the stories to discuss the feelings and actions of two characters and also manage to wrap up the story for both characters; however, you might find yourself needing to tell a story with two dolls before you have prepared to do so. For example, if you want to mirror two children in your class who are in conflict. If you need to tell this kind of story, go ahead.

If you are telling a story in which you want the children to look at a problem from two or more sides, you will start by having them identify the characters' feelings.

> "So how do you think Brad felt when Lucia said only kids who gave her candy could walk home with her?"

When Brad's feelings have been examined, you would turn to Lucia's.

"And how do you think Lucia felt when she said that to Brad? What was she wanting?"

This is usually difficult for children to do at first. They often sympathize with one side or the other and are unable to consider the other doll's feelings. This is one reason the "good guy/bad guy" scenario plays out so successfully in children's thinking. Whichever side they are on is the "good guy" side and all others are the "bad guys." This kind of thinking also keeps children from dealing with a problem fairly because they cannot évaluate what is really happening.

To help children see both sides of a problem and to be able to identify the feelings of both dolls, you will first bring both dolls to the story circle. If the children are looking at the doll, they are much more able to consider what it is feeling. Also, you may need to help them think of the motivation for the dolls' actions.

"Ianthe wanted the blocks Elizabeth was building with, so she kicked over Elizabeth's tower. Then Elizabeth hit Ianthe. How was Elizabeth feeling when all this happened?"

"She was pretty mad!"
"I think she was furious. That's why she hit Ianthe."
"I'd be mad too. I'd want to hit her."

"Yes, Elizabeth was very angry. *Furious* is a good word to describe how she felt about Ianthe knocking over her tower. Jim says he'd feel like hitting too, he'd be so mad. How do you think Ianthe was feeling?"

"She was sad she got hit."
"I bet she cried."
"I'd be mad at that girl."

"Getting hit makes everyone feel sad and mad. How was Ianthe feeling at the beginning of the story? Why did she kick over Elizabeth's tower?"

"She wanted the blocks."

"What feeling is that when you want something someone else has? Have you ever felt like that?"

"Yes! Me! I felt like that when my sister got new markers and I didn't. I felt jealous of her. I bet Ianthe felt jealous."

"Jealous. Good word! What do you call that feeling when you want something right away and you don't want to wait?"

"I know that one: not patient! My dad always tells me to be patient, but I'm not."

"I think we've got it! Ianthe was jealous that Elizabeth had all the blocks and she was impatient—she felt like she couldn't wait. When she knocked over Elizabeth's tower it made Elizabeth feel very angry—even furious. Then Ianthe got hit and felt sad and mad. They were both feeling pretty bad by that time, weren't they?"

This discussion prepares the group to examine how both of these dolls could solve their problem and, if the group's attention holds long enough, what they could do the next time so they don't hurt each other.

Teaching Empathy

If a goal of your *Kids Like Us* doll story is to have the kids practice empathy, the process will begin during this step, which asks children to identify feelings. As in all *Kids Like Us* doll stories, you will ask the children how the doll is feeling and reflect their responses. Connecting their own experiences to the doll's experiences prepares them to feel empathy for the doll. To help the children put themselves in the doll's place, you will ask, "Have you ever felt this way?" and "What made you feel this way?" and "How would you feel if this happened to you?" Children are usually quite eager to relate their own experiences.

Mirror Stories

During mirror stories, the child you are mirroring may have many reactions, from total and utter silence to yelling and sobbing and everything in between. If the child involved volunteers to speak, call on her immediately and get the group's attention for what she is saying. If she leans forward and looks as though she would like to say something but can't quite do it, call on her.

"Kelly, what did you want to say? How do you think Melly is feeling?"

Give the child a few moments to say something. If this is too difficult, let her off the hook while leaving an opening for a comment later.

"Can't quite say it? That's okay. Maybe you can tell us about it later, because I'd like to know what you think."

If the child you are mirroring watches intently but says nothing or doesn't even seem to be paying attention, go ahead with the story. This child is also experiencing the story and is as involved on some level. Leave her to listen, and she will learn from the experience. This is part of what the *Kids Like Us* doll stories are all about—exploring emotions from a safe distance.

CHAPTER 7

Step Four: Discussion and Problem Solving

The previous three steps have been preparing for this one: discussion and problem solving. This is where most of your time will be spent and where your students will learn the most. The form this step will take will vary according to the goal you have for the story and the responses of the children. ● Throughout the discussion and problem-solving step, your job will be to reflect what the children are saying, to help the children see the relationship between the doll's feelings and their actions, to ask questions that lead the children to think about different parts of the problem or different characters' points-of-view, and to pick up on contributions made by the children most affected by the situation being discussed. ● The children's responses will lead you through the discussion. Listen carefully to what your students are saying and you can use their responses as cues for what you say. Your students will learn a lot from each story, whether or not you include every possible element in the discussion.

Now, let's examine the structure that the discussion and problem-solving step will take in light of each of the ten goals.

1. To Bring Up a Subject; To Begin a Theme Study; To Give Information

In this type of story, I usually skip over the feelings step and use a simple question to create a natural lead-in to the discussion and problem-solving step. Here, for example, I wanted to introduce my three and four year olds to the theme of zoo animals.

> "Rajit went to the zoo on the weekend with his moms, and he saw a great big gray animal with a long, long nose. What animal do you think he saw?"

The main goal of this kind of story is to get the children involved and discussing the subject; there is no problem to solve. Your focus will be on three things:

- Giving the children a chance to share their own knowledge of and experiences with this subject
- Giving the children information
- Evoking excitement for learning about the subject

In response to my question about the animal Rajit saw, I received a chorus of responses.

> "Elephant! He saw an elephant!"

> "Yes! He did see an elephant. Here's a picture of an elephant Rajit brought to show you. Can we pass it around the circle? How did you all know Rajit was talking about an elephant?"

> "It's gray!"
> "And big. El'phants are biiiiig!"
> "I saw one on TV!"
> "Me, too! On Kratt's Creatures!"

> "Elephants don't live around here. They only live far away in Africa and India. That's why we bring a few of them to live in zoos—so we can go and see them at the zoo. Rajit brought more pictures of zoo animals. He wants to see if you can guess some of the animals he saw. Who wants to play Guess the Zoo Animal?"

> [A guessing game followed, giving clues describing common zoo animals, giving everyone a chance to guess at one time or another, and passing the picture of the animal around once its identity had been revealed.]

> "Wow! You all know a lot about zoo animals! You guessed the elephant, the kangaroo, the zebra, the tiger, and the panda bear. Rajit wants to know if any of you have been to the zoo like he has."

"Me! I been to the zoo."

"I want to go!"

"Curious George was in the zoo."

"My mom took me when I was a baby."

"It sounds like some of us have been to the zoo and some of us would really like to go."

"Yeah. Me. I want to go!"

"What animal would you most like to see at the zoo?"

[Everyone picks a favorite animal as we go around the circle.]

"Let's all go to the tables now and draw our favorite zoo animals. What color shall I use for the tiger I am planning?"

"Orange!"

"And black for the stripes!"

"Terrific. Rajit will sit here and watch as all of you draw. He's very glad he came to tell you about his trip to the zoo. He had fun talking with you about it." *[This last statement provides resolution, the fifth step in the* Kids Like Us *doll stories.]*

This story set up a unit study about zoo animals. It let the children share their knowledge with each other, presented information about some zoo animals and why we have zoos, and got the kids excited about the subject.

2. To Undo Incorrect Information

Undoing incorrect information will usually require more direct storytelling during the discussion and problem-solving step. The following format is one that works well for this type of story:

- Ask the children what they know.
- Problem solve briefly for where to get accurate information.
- Give correct information by adding to the story.
- Ask if there are any questions.

I told the following story because I heard some of my students saying that children who have been adopted were "thrown away" by their "real parents" because they were "bad babies." Any group would need to have this misinformation corrected, but I had several adopted children in my group and needed to deal with this misinformation *immediately.*

That afternoon I told a mirror story about Rachel, one of my *Kids Like Us* dolls who is adopted. Two classmates told her that she had been thrown away by her real parents because she was a bad baby. We explored Rachel's feelings of hurt, sorrow, guilt, and anger. One of the kids said Rachel might feel afraid that she would be "thrown away" again if she did something bad.

I started the discussion and problem-solving step by asking what my students knew about adoption. This is a good way to get the group talking and find out which students believe the incorrect information.

"What do you think? Were those kids right about being adopted? Were they thrown away because they were bad babies?"

"Yes. My brother told me."
"No, I was adopted because my birth parents couldn't keep a baby."
"I think all babies cry and stuff."
"It was mean to say that to Rachel. She's a neat kid. I like her."
"But why did she get given away?"

If many of the children in the group seem to have some correct information about the subject, the teacher can encourage them to share what they know. In this case, only one child knew something (and that child was the one the story was mirroring). I decided not to make her try to educate all the rest, so I added to the story. I made sure to acknowledge the student's information and reassure her before we went on.

"Barbara knows some real information about adoption. That's right, Barbara."

Once you have a good idea of what misperceptions exist, you are ready to give the group some real information. First, have them do some problem solving about where to get the correct information. This helps children understand that everything they are told may not be true. It also lets them practice finding sources of information they can trust.

"It sounds like we all have different ideas about this subject. And Rachel is feeling some pretty strong emotions about this. She needs to find out the truth about it right away. How do you think she can get real information about being adopted? Who could she ask?"

"Her mom!"
"She could ask her Bubbe." [A grandmother of whom I had reminded the children in the introduction to the story.]
"Maybe her teacher knows."
"I have a book about being adopted. You can read my book, Rachel."

"Good thinking! She could ask her mom or her Bubbe or her teacher. Books are a good way to learn things, Kim. She had a lot of places to go for information."

Then I added to the story line, telling how the doll got the real information and what that information was. Before you do this, however, you may need to do some research to be sure you are giving them the correct information and that you will have the answers to whatever questions come up.

I did not write out this story and memorize each sentence. I planned five points I wanted to be sure to include and then let the details weave together informally with other parts of the story, such as lots of love from Rachel's mom. The five points I wanted to include were that all babies are good, birth parents can't always take care of a baby, when birth parents can't take care of a baby they can make an adoption plan, Rachel "came home" at six weeks, and that Rachel has a birth mom who is not a part of her life and a life mom she loves. Here is how I wove these points together into a story:

> "So as soon as Rachel's mom picked her up after school, Rachel threw herself in her mother's arms and got a great big hug. That made her feel better. Then she told her mom all the things the kids had said to her. She asked her mom if she had been a bad baby.

> "Rachel's mom told her that all babies are good babies, and Rachel had been the most wonderful bundle of love she had ever seen. She reassured Rachel that when kids get adopted, it is not because of anything the kids did. It is because the birth parents weren't able to take care of a child right then. Sometimes birth parents aren't old enough. Or sometimes they are sick. Or sometimes they don't have a home and clothes and all the other things a baby needs. So instead they make an adoption plan to find a home and parents who can really take care of that child.

> "And that's what happened to Rachel. Her birth parents couldn't take care of her so they made an adoption plan for her with an adoption agency. That's how Rachel got to come home to her mom when she was only six weeks old. So Rachel has a birth mother who isn't part of her life and a life mom she lives with and loves. And her mom and her Bubbe and Zaide will be her family forever and always, even if she does something wrong sometimes."

In this type of story, the teacher acts as the correct source of information, countering the incorrect information the children may believe. I also gave them some words to use when talking about adoption—for example, *birth parents* instead of *real parents, making an adoption plan* instead of *throwing away* or *giving away* the child. I would then continue the discussion to be sure the children have a chance to ask all their questions about this subject.

> "Are there other things you would like to know about adoption? Who has a question?"

> *"How come some kids get adopted from far away, like Rajit?"*

> "That's a good question, Lerryn. Rajit came all the way from India when he was two years old. He needed a good home, just like Rachel did, and they didn't have one for him in India. Rajit's moms very much wanted a child in their family, so they sent for him to come to our country, the United States of America. Now Rajit is Indian American because he came from India and now he lives here. Kids get adopted all over the world. Sometimes they find a home in their birth country and sometimes they find a family somewhere else."

> *"My brother says my parents will give me away if I don't clean my room."*

QUESTION #11

Q: *Are the dolls always having problems? Don't the kids get tired of that?*

A: I did wonder about this once when I brought a couple of dolls to my circle and one of my kids said, "What problem are they having *now?*" Since that time I have made an effort to remember to tell some stories about a wonderful event in a doll's life. This is especially important when working on teaching emotion vocabulary, so the children don't get the impression that all emotions are negative.

But the other side of this issue is the children's proud assertions, "Whatever problem she's having, *we* can help her. We're good at that!" Many of my students eagerly anticipate helping the dolls with a sticky problem when they see me bringing them out.

"That's not true. Your brother made that up. People don't give away their kids because they do the wrong thing. We all make mistakes! You can tell your brother you know that is not true."

"How come some kids get adopted really old?"

"Another good question. You kids are really thinking! Sometimes something happens to a child's family and they can't take care of a child anymore. It's not because of the child, but because of what the parents are able to do. Children need safe homes with parents who can take care of them. If their parents can't give them a safe home, sometimes older kids go to live with foster families for a while. Sometimes kids get adopted when they are older when they find a family to love them forever."

When telling a *Kids Like Us* doll story to undo incorrect information, you will encourage the children who know the correct information to share it with the group. You will then confirm this information in the life of your doll during the resolution step. If none of the children have the correct information, you will give it to them in the process of narrating the story and then spending some of the discussion time encouraging the children to ask questions.

Occasionally you will need to give the children this information in the middle of a story you have designed for some other purpose. *Never hesitate* to correct children's incorrect assumptions. Just add that information onto the discussion you are having, unless the children seem to have concerns about something that requires a lot of discussion. In this case, drop the plans you had and focus on the children's questions and concerns. You can always tell another *Kids Like Us* doll story another day on the subject you had intended to present.

3. To Learn a New Emotional Vocabulary Word; To Teach Skills for Handling Emotions

When the story is being told that is designed to help children learn a new emotions vocabulary word, identifying feelings will take up most of the story-telling session. The children will think about the feelings of the doll, learn the vocabulary word, and discuss their experiences with the particular emotion. The teacher will skip the problem-solving step by telling the solution that the doll came up with. This usually occurs during the final step in *Kids Like Us* stories, the resolution step.

Stories that intend to help children learn skills to handle emotions will also spend quite a bit of time on identifying feelings. Often the children will relate their own experiences to the feelings they have identified in the story. Then, during the discussion and problem-solving step, they will discuss how to handle the emotions they have identified. Again, this is usually done by relating the situation in the story to their own experiences. Also, the teacher may suggest appropriate and inappropriate ways to deal with these emotions and then ask for feedback.

In the following story, I summarized what the group had discussed so far. This served as a transition from identifying feelings to problem solving. Next I asked the children to think of ways for the dolls to handle their feelings. I responded to the children's ideas through active listening, or reflecting back to the group what has been said. You will use this technique of active listening during all types of discussions. It helps to focus the children's attention and assures them that their ideas have been heard and understood. It also helps you keep track of the discussion because you summarize what has been said as you go along.

> "So Henry and Ianthe were feeling disappointed, grumpy, and bored because their car is broken and they can't go to the beach like they were planning. Alma says she felt disappointed once when she thought her grandma was coming and then she couldn't come. And Brian was grumpy and bored during spring break. It seems like a lot of you have felt these feelings before. What could Henry and Ianthe do with these feelings?"

>> "Maybe they would sit around. They're pretty disappointed."

> "Yes. They might need some time to just sit around and feel those feelings. What about when they want to feel better—when they are done feeling grumpy and bored?"

>> "They could find something else to do."
>> "They could play together. That's what me and my brother do."

The teacher now offers her own inappropriate choices. This technique emphasizes that there are happy and sad choices to make when dealing with emotions. Kids love to tell you these are not good ideas!

> "They could find something to do. Maybe doing it together would make them feel better. How about drawing big, ugly pictures all over the walls? Would that make them feel better?"

>> "No! That would make them feel worse 'cause they'd get punished."

> "Maybe going to their mom or dad and whining [the teacher puts on an incredibly whiny voice], 'We are soooooo bored!' Would that be a good idea?"

>> "No!"

> "Why not?"

>> "The mom would be mad."

> "Yes. Then they'd all be grumpy, I guess. You all are so smart! I can't fool you! Who has some better ideas? What could Henry and Ianthe do to help themselves feel better? José said they could play together."

> *"They could make up stories."*
>
> *"Maybe they could think of another day to go."*

> "Ah! Now we're getting somewhere! They could make up stories. Maybe planning the trip for another time would help. Who has another idea?"

As this example shows, thinking about the feelings involved and problem solving for how to deal with them go hand in hand.

When strong emotions take over children's actions, children are unable to think clearly about a response. So the appropriate behaviors need to be easy to access. Stories about anger and other very strong feelings sometimes will be more effective if you include a short role-play. This will allow the children to practice emotion-releasing activity, and young children remember things better if they can use their bodies in addition to their minds. Telling several stories with the goal of discussing anger management skills can also be a helpful way to discuss and practice appropriate responses to emotional situations, as are books and activities that reinforce what has been learned. (See the resources section for more suggestions on anger management skills.)

Some stories that have the goal of practicing ways to deal with anger involve only one doll and the anger she feels. Others should be told about two or more dolls involved in a conflict. This situation is very common in child care or school settings, so children need to practice seeing both sides of a situation. Let's look at an example of each type of discussion.

In the following story, the children are told that Ricky (a three year old) dropped his flashlight and broke it. The group decides that he felt mad, angry, and sad. Since my goal was to help the children learn to deal with anger, most of the discussion and problem-solving step focused on dealing with these feelings (discussion), rather than on what to do about the broken flashlight (problem solving).

> "Ricky was feeling really mad, angry, and sad about his flashlight. What would be good things for him to do with those feelings he's having?"

> *"Don't be mad."*

> "Maybe he could stop being mad. But, you know, there's nothing wrong with being mad, and Ricky was feeling a whole lot of mad. It was filling up his body from his toes all the way to his head. He's got to do something with all that mad. What can he do?"

> *"He could throw the flashlight really far."*

> "Maybe throwing the flashlight would feel good. He'd have to be careful not to hit something with it. It's hard to be careful when you're that mad! Have any of you ever been that mad? What did *you* do with all that mad?"

"I growled like a bear. Then I laughed."

"I hitted my sister when she made me mad."

"Maybe Ricky cry?"

"Hey! Growling like a bear makes a good mad sound! Let's try it! *[Lots of growls.]* Do you think that would help you get your mad out? What about hitting someone? Would that make things better?"

"No! They might hit back!"

"I had to sit out when I hitted my sister."

"Yes. Hitting just makes everyone feel worse. When you're mad you have to get your mad out without hurting anything. How about stomping your feet? Would that help? Or Alex suggested crying. Maybe those things would be good when you are mad. What do you think?"

The discussion would continue as long as the children are involved and interested. Skills that are presented can be practiced. In the story above, this is done when the children practice growling. The younger your children are, the more you need to use active participation.

Stories involving two dolls are discussed in a similar way, spending some of the discussion time on the feelings and choices of each doll. If this is too much for your group to handle, bring only one doll to the circle and discuss the situation from this doll's perspective. In this example, Rachel was cleaning paintbrushes at the sink when Saed shoved her away from it. The children identified Rachel's feelings as mad and furious. They thought Saed was feeling bossy, impatient, and happy.

Throughout the story I acknowledged the children's strong feelings and encourage them to deal with these feelings before approaching the other person. Too often angry children strike out at the first thing in their path. Having problem-solving skills and knowing to first take a few moments to cool off helps them handle these situations.

"So Rachel is standing beside the sink with a paintbrush in her hands, totally mad and furious. And Saed is washing his hands, feeling bossy and impatient and a little happy too because he got what he wanted. What do you think Rachel should do now?"

"I think she should shove Saed back!"

"She could shove him back. Would that make her feel better?"

"Maybe, if she got the sink back from him."

"What would Saed do then, do you think?"

"Shove Rachel again. They'd just start shoving back and forth."

"And which one of them would have done the wrong thing?"

"Both. And they'd both be mad."

"Hmmm. Sounds like a mess to me. That doesn't seem to work well. I'll bet Rachel has mad coming out all over her. How could she get some space to deal with her anger before she tries to work things out with Saed?"

"I know! Back up three steps, like we practiced before!"
"Yea. Then she could stomp her feet and she wouldn't stomp Saed."
"She could huff and puff."
"She could go tell the teacher. Or get a hug."
"Sometimes I go to my bed when I'm mad. I yell at pillows."

"Good thinking. When you are feeling mad it's important to find something you can do to let that feeling out without hurting anyone. Stomping your feet, doing some big breathing, or yelling at pillows can get your mad out. And it can really help to get a hug anytime, don't you think?"

"That's what I'd do."

"Now, what about Saed? What did he want?"

"He wanted to wash his hands."
"Maybe he had paint on 'em."

"Why do you think he pushed Rachel? How was he feeling?"

"He was not patient."
"Yeah. Remember? He was feeling like he didn't want to wait."

"Yes, he was feeling impatient. Is it fair to push someone out of the way because you are feeling impatient?"

"No. That's not respect."

"What could Saed have done when he was feeling impatient to wash his hands? Something that would not hurt someone else but would help him deal with his feelings?"

"My mom taps her foot when she waits at the grocery store."

Once we had fully explored Saed's options for dealing with his impatience, I would change the goal of the discussion to problem solving. I would pick up on the children's suggestions that the two dolls talk about their problem, have both of them tell what they wanted, and then come up with a way to take turns at the sink. (We will examine specifically how to teach these problem-solving skills later in this chapter.)

4. To Teach a Pro-Social Skill; To Teach a Classroom Skill

Stories for teaching pro-social or classroom skills can take three forms. One models the right behavior, the second gives the children the opportunity to think of the correct behavior, and the third explores what happens when the incorrect behavior is chosen. All of the stories will encourage children to tell of their own successful attempts at using these skills and encourage them to admit mistakes. They will also learn to see themselves as people who try to do the right thing.

Discussions that teach pro-social and classroom skills have three parts: (1) examining why the main character acted as she did, (2) listening to children's experiences with this same behavior, and (3) giving the children a chance to affirm that they would use the target skill in the same situation.

When *Kids Like Us* dolls model successfully using the skill you would like your students to learn, the discussion will focus on the positive feelings the doll receives through this behavior. This will allow the children to identify with these feelings and relate them to their own experiences. For example, in one story, Umoja's mom was tired, so Umoja took care of her little sister, Imani, while her mom took a nap.

"Why do you think Umoja took care of Imani like that?"

> "Her mom was tired."
> "She wanted to help out."

"Yes. She knew her mom had a problem and she wanted to help. We call that feeling 'caring.' When you have caring in your heart, you help the people you care about. Have any of you ever acted in a caring way? Have you helped someone you care about?"

> "I helped Roger pick up the books he dropped today."
> "Yeah! He did! And I helped him get his shoelaces tied."

"I hear some very caring behaviors happening right here in this school! You can tell that Roger and Xiaodon know how to act in a caring way. Who else has done this?"

After more children had told of their caring behaviors, I asked the last question:

"What would you have done if you were Umoja? Would you have offered to help your mom, or would you have gone off to play instead?"

By this time all the children were eager to identify with the caring behavior and to be as much like Umoja as possible. During this type of story, the students will want to convince you they would be the most caring children ever.

"Me! I would help!"
"I could play with my little sister all day!"
"I'd fix dinner too!"

This part of the discussion gives the children who didn't have any instances of caring to share a chance to brag about what they *would* do as soon as the opportunity arises! This, of course, is exactly what you have been working toward.

The second type of story is much like the first, except that the story stops sooner and does not tell what the correct behavior is. The students will discuss this first, coming up with the behavior themselves (with a bit of help from you). Then, as they did in the earlier story, they will relate their own experiences.

This story is designed to help children learn about empathy. Rachel and Lucia were in the bathroom when Lucia slipped and fell on her arm. The students would identify Lucia's feelings as hurt and scared and Rachel's as scared and worried. Then the discussion would begin with an exploration of the target skill—feeling empathy.

"Yes. Lucia was just scared as could be because she was hurting very badly. Why was Rachel scared too? She wasn't hurt."

"She was scared for Lucia. Lucia was hurt."
"Rachel knew how much Lucia was hurting."

"So, it was kind of like Rachel felt how much Lucia's arm hurt, even though she wasn't hurt herself. She was putting herself in Lucia's place to understand that, wasn't she?"

"Yeah. She cares about Lucia."

"Yes. When we care about people, and if we think about it, we can understand how they are feeling sometimes. That's called 'empathy.' Have any of you ever felt empathy for someone, when you really put yourself in their place and understood how they were feeling?"

"I empathyed with my sister when she lost her dollar."

"Good example! You felt empathy for your sister when she lost her money. How did she feel right then?"

"Real sad. And disappointed, because she was going to the movies but she didn't have enough."

The group would continue to explore the concept of empathy by relating their own experiences. The teacher could then cue the group to do some problem solving for Rachel.

"Well, knowing how hurt and scared Lucia is feeling, what should Rachel do to help her?"

A third type of story that helps teach pro-social or classroom skills starts with a mistake. The children identify the mistake and then offer alternative behavior. The rest of the story follows the same pattern as the others. This type of story allows children to tell about making similar mistakes, since the dolls have been so forthcoming about their own. The discussion also can include how the doll could make up for the mistake. If this is too much to cover, you could supply this information in the resolution step. For example, when working with a group of five year olds on the classroom skill of sharing, I tell this story of Elizabeth and Ricky. Both wanted the jump rope, so they started pulling on it and yelling at each other.

"So both Elizabeth and Ricky want the rope, and they are both hopping mad. What made them feel so mad?"

"They both pulled on it at the same time."
"They both think they should get it."

"Yes. They both want the rope. The first thing they both did was to run, grab the rope, and start trying to tug it away from the other one. Was that a good way to work out the problem?"

"No."
"Unh-unh."
"That made it worse."

"What other mistake did they make?"

"They yelled at each other."

"Yelling just made things worse, too, don't you think? *[Many children nod their heads.]* Have any of you had this problem with a friend or a brother or sister?"

"Me and my sister argue about the TV box all the time."
"At quiet time I got in a tug-o-war with Carrie about that mouse book."
"I always want the swing, but May's always on it."

"So you have this happen to you a lot too, it sounds like. This will be a good thing to figure out, then. If we come up with some good ideas for Ricky and Elizabeth, all of you can use them. What could they do that would help them work it out fairly?"

"They could put the jump rope away. That's what my dad does when my brother and I argue over a toy."

"They could put the jump rope away and neither of them could have it. That's one idea. How do you feel about it when your dad does that? Is it a happy choice for both you and your brother?"

"We don't either of us like it. Then no one can play with it. It's totally bogus."

"That doesn't sound like the solution we want, then. What do you think would be a *happy* choice for them both?"

"They could take turns. Ali and me take turns with the shovel in the sandbox."

"Yeah. They could share it. We have to share the markers at the drawing table."

"They could get another kid and do big jump rope with two holders. Three kids can play that."

"They could take turns or even play three-person jump rope. Helen said they could share the rope. What does *share* mean?"

"Like, they use it together. Or take turns or something."

"Yeah. So both of them get it."

"Sharing is a way for two or more kids to use something together?"

"That's right! They could share it, like, first me and then you."

"Who knows a fair way to choose who goes first?"

"The one that got there first."

"Does that work?"

"Sometimes."

"Sometimes it makes everybody grab."

"Does anyone know a choosing game, like 'One Potato, Two Potato?'"

"No."

"Well, that's how Elizabeth and Ricky decided who got to jump first. They decided taking turns was a good idea. So first they did 'One Potato, Two Potato' and then they took turns. Here, I'll show you just how they did it."

In this case the story leads the children to come up with ideas and discard solutions that will not work. The teacher can move the discussion along by suggesting possible actions, both appropriate and inappropriate, and then asking the children to evaluate them.

Next, during that resolution step, I told how they shared the rope and also how they used "One Potato, Two Potato" to decide which one of the dolls would go first. We practiced this rhyme. The next week I told another story that gave the children a chance to problem solve for the dolls by suggesting they use "One Potato, Two Potato." This time many children were eager to suggest this turn-taking game, and a couple had learned a new one from older siblings. By this time it was common to hear on the playground, "Hey, we gotta share this. I'll do 'One Potato' to see who's first."

5. To Practice Problem-Solving Skills

Many discussion sessions will devote some time to helping the *Kids Like Us* dolls solve their problems. These stories will be designed to focus on these four steps in the problem-solving process:

- Describe the problem.
- Find many possible solutions.
- Evaluate the solutions.
- Choose the ones that have the greatest chance of success and meet the needs of everyone involved.

Your job will be to ask questions that lead the conversation through these stages and encourage the children to think about all aspects of the situation.

Some groups will not be ready to spend the time it takes to discuss all four of these aspects of problem solving. The storyteller can step in and finish the story at any time by explaining how the dolls evaluated the possible solutions and chose the one they all felt best about. For example, when discussing Rajit's problem with his baby sister getting into his things (especially his colored pencils), the five-year-old children in the group identified Rajit's feelings as frustrated, mad, angry, and sad. I then guided the discussion through a description of the problem and thinking of multiple solutions.

"Who can tell me what Rajit's problem is?"

> "He can't draw."
> "Yeah, 'cause his sister chews his pencils."
> "She's too little. She could get sick that way."

"So his little sister gets into his pencils. Do you think she gets into anything else of his, or are pencils his only problem?"

> "Little kids get into everything. My baby does."
> "I bet he has to put away his Legos too."

"So how would you describe Rajit's problem?"

> "He has to keep his sister away from everything."
> "Yeah, everything small."
> "So he can't do the things he wants to do, 'cause she gets into it."

"Now we really know what the whole problem is. Can anyone think of some solutions?"

> "What's a solution?"

"A solution is an idea that might help fix the problem. What could help Rajit fix this problem he has? We need to think of lots of possible solutions first."

"I know! He could do those things at a friend's house."

"I play with my trains when my baby is taking a nap."

"No, that's not right. I think he should play in his room and close the door."

"Everybody's thinking is helpful here. We'll help Rajit decide later which solutions he wants to try. But to help us think, let's be open to all kinds of ideas. Who has another one?"

Because these students were new to problem solving, I focused this story mainly on thinking of multiple solutions, and I moved to the resolution step once this had been accomplished. I left practice on evaluating and choosing solutions for other stories. After a few more solutions were proposed I said,

"You have thought of a lot of possible solutions! Rajit is amazed to hear he had so many choices of ways to solve his problem. And he thought of some of those solutions himself. The last time he had to put his things away because his sister was grabbing them he cuddled up in the big chair in his living room and thought about how to solve the problem, just like you just did. He thought about yelling at his sister, but decided that would not help and wouldn't be nice to his sister either.

"I knew that, Rajit!"

"Then he thought maybe he would try going in his room and shutting the door when he wants to draw."

"That was MY idea!"

"Yes. You two had the same idea. Rajit talked to Momma Betty about his idea and she agreed to try to distract his sister if she gets upset that he is in his room. He tried his plan yesterday and it worked! He drew and drew in his room and then came out to show his pictures to his sister. He had to remember to keep the door to his room closed, though. He wants to thank all of you for helping him to think of good solutions. He's going to remember your other ideas too. He may need those sometime as well."

6. To Support a Child or All the Children by Mirroring a Situation

Your major concern during mirror stories is the child or children the stories are based upon. You will need to subtly watch their reactions to what is being said, call on them immediately if they indicate they want to take part in the discussion, and lead the discussion in the way that will be most helpful for them. You will need to be careful to maintain the child's anonymity, if necessary, and, if the child speaks up about the situation, express interest without making a big deal of it.

Common goals for a mirror story are

- to provide support for a child by showing someone else who is experiencing the same situation
- to help the child find solutions
- to change the child's perception of herself or her problem
- to change the child's perception of the group's feelings about her or her situation
- to change the group's perception of the child or the child's situation

All of these goals can be met without the active participation of the child who is being mirrored. By being there and experiencing the story, the child can feel supported and hear possible solutions. It can be a relief just to know that the problem can be talked about with friends.

The following story is told with two children in mind—one has recently started bullying the other children, and the other has been the main target of the bullying. The child who has been bullying will see clearly the group's feelings about this behavior. The child who has been a target will have the support of seeing someone else with the same problem. Both children will learn some possible solutions to their problems.

Rajit and Ianthe, the main characters in this story, will both come to the story-telling session because the discussion will involve the feelings and choices of both dolls. Rajit and Ianthe were chosen because they have quite different identity characteristics from the children in this situation.

The situation setup told that Rajit had a problem. When he is eating his lunch with Julio, Saed, and Elizabeth, Ianthe comes along and makes him give up his place at the table. She threatens to hit him if he doesn't move. The kids identify Rajit's feelings as mad and scared and Ianthe's as bossy and satisfied.

I started the discussion with a focus on Ianthe as the one with the problem. Too often the victim is seen as being responsible for the situation.

"Why do you think Ianthe did that to Rajit?"

"She wanted to sit with her friends. It was the only seat."

"So Ianthe had a problem. She wanted to sit and be friends with Julio, Saed, and Elizabeth, but there wasn't room at the table. What solution did Ianthe choose to this problem?"

"She was mean to Rajit. She kicked Rajit out."

"What did Rajit do to make Ianthe be mean to him like that?"

"He didn't do anything. Ianthe just picked on him."
"Maybe she thought she couldn't make Elizabeth go, but Rajit would."

The next part of the story speaks directly to the child who has begun to exhibit this behavior. Many times such a child thinks the others admire his strength and ability to push kids around. I wanted him to hear the opposite directly from his peers.

> "So it really had nothing to do with Rajit. Ianthe had a problem and just picked Rajit because she thought she could scare him. Was that a good solution to Ianthe's problem?"

>> *"No! That's not fair!"*
>> *"That's not nice to Rajit!"*
>> *"Just because she's bigger doesn't mean she gets it."*

> "So having a stronger body than somebody else doesn't mean you just get your own way? Is that what you're saying?" *[General nods.]*

>> *"No!"*
>> *"I had a big bully push me down on the playground at the park. He laughed at me. I didn't like it."*
>> *"I did that once to my sister. I took her candy and ate it. I was happy about the candy. But my sister cried. She didn't like it at all."*

It is important to acknowledge children's bravery in admitting to mistakes. The child who admitted to taking his sister's candy was not the one being mirrored; however, the child who *was* being mirrored was watching closely and now had seen another child model admitting to mistakes. Also, it is always a good idea to look for a glimmer of empathy. Although the child has related an incident in which he acted incorrectly, he also related his understanding of how his sister felt. This is the first step in gaining the ability to refrain from a behavior because it will hurt someone else.

> "Yes. It must be tempting to take power over somebody when you're bigger than them and you can. Don't you think that's true?"

>> *"Yeah."*

> "You could see how upset your sister was. It's good that you noticed that. Thanks for telling us about that. Do you agree, Ivan? Were you upset when you got pushed down at the park?"

>> *"Yes. I was mad too."*

At this point I felt that we needed to summarize what had been said. I also wanted to repeat the basic principle that I wanted the child who was being mirrored to hear.

> "So even if Ianthe *could* get Rajit to move out of his seat, she shouldn't do that because it's not fair and makes people upset and mad. Is that right?"

>> *"Yes! She shouldn't do things like that."*

" Okay. Let's see how Ianthe's solution to her problem would work. She got a seat at the table. That made her feel a bit satisfied to get what she wanted. Why did she want to sit there?"

> " To be with the other kids."

" Yes. But if *you* were at that table and Ianthe pushed Rajit out, how would you be feeling about Ianthe right now?"

> " Yucky."
> " Really mad."
> " I would leave the table and not talk to her."

" Yes. I've noticed that people don't want to have anything to do with someone who is acting like a bully. They stay away. How would it feel to you if you were Ianthe and the kids all stayed away from you?"

> " Oh, that would be soooo lonely."

I took the opportunity to once again summarize the situation for the child who was being mirrored before moving on to a focus on the other child.

" It sounds like Ianthe's bully solution was not a good one for two reasons. First, it's not right to push people around just to get what you want. Second, other kids will stay away from someone who does that. What about Rajit's solution? He just got up and left. Was that the best solution for him?"

> " No. He could stand up to Ianthe."
> " He could say 'NO!'"
> " He might be afraid Ianthe would hit him. She said she would."
> " Owwwww!"

So many times children feel alone with their problems. Encouraging them to get help can really make a difference. The child who has been a target of a bully will see the support the children gladly give Rajit and will know that support is available for her too. I also wanted the group to take responsibility for not letting this go on around them.

" Is there any way Rajit could get help with his problem? We can't always do things all by ourselves. Who could Rajit count on to help him?"

> " Me! I'd help you, Rajit!"
> " His friends could help."
> " Maybe the teacher."
> " Or his parents. Maybe they could tell him what to do."

" He could get help from friends, a teacher, or his parents. Those are great ideas. It's good to know you are not alone. What if you were one of the friends at the table and you saw Ianthe threaten Rajit. Would you just watch or would you try to help?"

> " I'd never let him do it!"
> " I'd say, 'No bullies here!'"

The child who made this blanket statement banishing bullies from the classroom was the child who had been bullying the other kids in my classroom. I picked up on this child's contribution immediately and took the opportunity to let him tell about his own problems without having to admit he was talking about himself. I was careful to use the same tone of voice and level of interest as I had with the other children's comments. I ignored all the other waving hands and side comments so that I could focus on what Joel had to say. Listening to Joel helped the whole group to see that the bullying child is someone who wants something and has just chosen the wrong way to get it.

> "Good thinking, Joel. You wouldn't want someone acting like a bully around you, would you?"

> *"No way!"*

> "Why do you think Ianthe pushes Rajit around, Joel?"

> *" 'Cause she can, I guess. It works pretty good, doesn't it?"*

> "What do you think Rajit could do, Joel, to stop Ianthe from pushing him around?"

> *"He should stand up to her and not move, I guess."*

After a few exchanges with Joel, I took the focus off of him to keep him from feeling under too much pressure and to get back to the solutions we were seeking for the other child and the group.

> "Thanks for helping. Rajit thinks that's a good idea, especially if his friends will be there with him. Would any of you help Rajit if you were there with him?"

> *"I could hit Ianthe myself. That would stop her!"*

> "You'd want to help Rajit stand up against Ianthe's threats. That's terrific, Dawn. What about hitting, though? We know it was wrong of Ianthe to threaten to hit Rajit. Would it be okay for Rajit to hit Ianthe?"

> *"No. That's the same as Ianthe."*

> "Then they'd both be wrong. What a mess! So working together to help a friend stand up against threats is a good idea, but hitting is not. Instead, Rajit could tell his friends about his problem, or he could tell his teacher or his parents. He could tell Ianthe he is not going to move. These are all great ideas."

I ended the discussion on a positive note for Joel, to let him know the children were willing to change their feelings if he changed his behavior.

> "The kids are all pretty mad at Ianthe right now because of her bullying behavior. Do you think they could ever feel good about her again?"

> *"Yes. If she stopped shoving people around."*
> *"I like Ianthe. And so do lots of the kids. We just don't like what she did to Rajit."*

"That's great. It's a great relief to Ianthe to know she doesn't have to be a bully and all alone. All she has to do is stop acting that way and let the kids know she'll be friendlier now. And Rajit feels better, too, to know there are things he can do and other people to help him."

The resolution step of this story would show all the dolls standing up against the bully and not allowing her to chase Rajit away. It would also show Ianthe admitting that she just wanted to sit with the kids and didn't know another way to do that.

It is common for the child who has been acting inappropriately to take an active part in the discussion. In fact, it is not uncommon for this child to be the most vehement in stating, "I'd never do that!" At that moment, I think the child really believes this statement. And if taking the positive role in a *Kids Like Us* doll story helps this child to see herself in a more positive light, it could help her act more appropriately in the future. To really believe that she has a choice of how to behave is the first crucial step. And it is likely that the child who is being bullied will just listen to the story and not make a sound, although some children in this situation will take the opportunity to unburden themselves.

If one child is being bullied, the other children are usually aware and passively accepting of it. Sometimes one of them will draw a parallel between the story and this real-life relationship. This could happen in any story, but it is most common in mirror stories. The teacher can give the child who is being mirrored a chance to tell her feelings about the situation but should change the focus if the child obviously doesn't want to be part of the discussion. For example, in the following story my goal was to mirror Rosario's feelings about his cat's death two weeks earlier. I created a story about Melly, whose canary died yesterday. Her feelings were identified as sad and lonely. I introduced the feeling of grief and explained it meant a strong feeling of having lost something and being sad about it.

"That's just like Rosario! His cat died last week. He told me! Huh, Rosario?!"

Since Rosario's loss had been brought into the story, I focused on him for a moment, to let him know I understood how important this was to him. Since he looked at me and was willing to talk a bit about his cat, I gave him the opportunity to do so.

"Did your kitty die, too, Rosario? Just like Melly's bird?"

[Rosario nods sadly, looking directly at me, but says nothing.]

"What was your kitty's name?"

"Jake."

"I bet you are really sad about Jake dying. Are you grieving for Jake?"

   [Rosario nods.]
   "He used to sleep with me."

"It's really hard when a special pet like Jake or Melly's canary dies. I'll bet you miss Jake very much. Have any of you had a pet die?"

   [Many children raise their hands, eager to tell of losses from the more distant past.]

Although I hadn't planned on bringing the child who was being mirrored into the spotlight this directly, I got Rosario to talk a bit about his feelings, and I was able to support his grief. Then, by asking a redirecting question, I took the focus off of Rosario. Hearing about Melly losing her canary as well as his peers' accounts of lost pets, Rosario also got the support of knowing that he was not alone.

So, although mirror stories can be tricky to facilitate, they are very powerful tools to help the children deal with their own problems from a safe distance. Just keep an eye on each child's feelings and manage the conversation with your goals in mind, both for the child who is being mirrored and for the whole group.

7. To Help Children Become Comfortable with Diversity

To bring in stories designed to help children become comfortable with diversity, have a doll model this comfort. Two ways to model this comfort is to tell a fact about the doll's own life or tell about a new thing a doll has learned. Most of the important learning in these stories is done simply by having the children experience the comfort the dolls model. There is no problem that needs a solution. As a result, the discussion and problem-solving step of these stories will be brief. This will not be true, however, if one or more of your children has a negative reaction to the information you present. If this happens, you will address it during the discussion step.

The main goals of this step will be

- to introduce new diversities to your group
- to model interest in and acceptance of diversity
- to be a calm, encouraging source of information
- to encourage the children to relate their own experiences to those of the doll

For example, after a story about birthday traditions in Ricky and Brad's family, the discussion step will begin with a question.

"How are birthdays celebrated in *your* family?"

As children tell about their traditions, their own family cultures are affirmed. At the same time, asking this question assumes that each family has its own customs. Hearing of other family's traditions or the fact that they don't have any birthday traditions helps to work against young children's assumption that their way of living is the only right way. As they listen to one another proudly tell of their personal experiences, they learn to be comfortable with diversity.

Some students may have a negative reaction to these discussions. If some of your children are not yet comfortable with diversity, they may make disparaging remarks about either the doll's story or other children's comments. Some students will have a difficult time letting go of their "center of the universe" belief system. Comments like these are not uncommon at first:

> "Her family doesn't have a TV?"
>
> "River's weird. Boys are supposed to have short hair."

Disparaging comments may also be directed at an actual child.

> "You eat rice for breakfast? Gross!"

When these remarks are made, you will need to be the clear, direct voice of reassurance. Remind yourself that this is a learning opportunity, and respond calmly. The conversation might go like this:

> "That's right. Elizabeth's family has decided they don't want a TV. You sound surprised, Jack. Do you know that there are many people in this world that don't have a TV?"
>
> > "I didn't know that. I wouldn't want to be one of them!"
>
> "So Jack really likes having a television at *his* house, and Elizabeth likes *not* having one at hers."

If a child's identity is being put down, your first focus must be on supporting that child's right to be herself.

> "Emily's family eats rice for breakfast, and so do *millions* of other families. It's a nice warm food to start the day. Did you know that, Josh? *[I leaned over at this point and gave Emily's hand a squeeze.]* Let's not have put-downs here, because they make people feel bad."

Comparing different feelings and opinions and making a point that no one viewpoint is the "right" one can help children learn to accept their own individuality and allow others theirs.

"Joan says she thinks purple is the prettiest color there is. Nancy likes red better. Graciela likes black and gold together. Which one of them is right?"

The children love to catch on to this "trick" question. It usually takes one experience of me "fooling" them before they learn to call out with great glee,

"ALL OF THEM!"
"It's their opinion!"
"Everybody has their own idea!"

When questions arise or comments are made that make you realize information is needed, you need to be prepared to answer these questions and concerns with correct information. If you need to, do some research. Many times this kind of discussion is needed when the children are first being introduced to a doll, especially when the doll has a personal or physical characteristic that your children are not familiar with.

When meeting Mickey, my doll that has cerebral palsy and gets around in a wheelchair, it is common for one of the children to ask questions.

"How come he's in that funny chair?"

"Mickey has cerebral palsy. That just means his muscles have a hard time doing what his brain tells them to. Mickey has to work very hard to do things that are simple for many of you. He can sit up a bit, but his leg muscles won't hold him up, so he uses a wheelchair to get around. This is his wheelchair. He likes to call it his race car."

Nonvisible characteristics may also need to be discussed in depth.

"Henry does not know how to say words with his voice yet."

"I don't get it. I'm four like him, and I can talk."

"That's very true, Leslie, but not everyone learns the same way. Henry can't hear what people are saying very well, so learning to say words is very, very difficult for him. His eyes work great, though, so he's learning to talk with his hands and to listen with his eyes."

Understanding about Henry's method of communication was essential to understanding other stories about Henry, so this detail was presented when I first introduced the doll to the children. Many adults have a difficult time with the questions children ask.

"How come Mickey's lookin' all sideways?"

Often children are told not to speak of these issues, but asking questions is the best way to learn. If the children feel free to ask questions, it means they trust you to give them honest answers and not to "shush" them. If you are able to have a calm discussion with the kids about these issues, it will set the stage for many more such open discussions. Just put yourself in the role of information source and answer whatever comes up.

"Mickey's head leans to the side because his neck has a hard time holding it up. He can see you just fine with his head a bit tilted. You can try it yourself and see."

Encourage children to get all the information they want. You can present information yourself, but it is also good to get the kids to think for themselves.

"If you were going to play with Mickey, what game would you play?"

"Who has tried really, really hard to learn how to do something?"

"Does anybody have a question they'd like to ask Mickey?"

Often children will have strong emotions about difference, especially if it is something they don't have any experience with or have previously had anxious reactions about from adults. Your job will be to model calm acceptance of diversity and present the correct information the children are missing.

"Oohh. Don't let him touch me! I don't want to get that yucky thing!"

"You can't catch cerebral palsy. This happened to Mickey when he was born. He's not sick, so touching him is okay, as long as he says you may."

These information sessions spare children the experience of having to hear this said about them, and it helps relieve the scared child's anxiety around this subject.

Another kind of story designed to encourage comfort with diversity and give information shows a doll learning something about diversity herself. In one story, Ianthe is surprised when River's dad says River's hair is too oily and should be washed. She tells the group that her hair always needs oil put *into* it.

"Ianthe is really surprised to learn that some people have too much oil in their hair and some people need to add oil to their hair. What about your hair?"

With this simple question, the conversation is open to children's comments about the hair oil they use, how they wash their hair every Saturday, or that they never noticed one way or the other but will ask their parents. The goal of this story was simply to open the children's eyes to the fact that we all have hair, but we all have our own kind and our own ways of caring for it.

In the story about Umoja visiting church with Julio, I tell some of what Umoja liked about her experience; then I can ask, "Do any of your families go someplace special to pray?" This creates an opportunity for the children to relate the story to their own lives and to take pride in this aspect of their own lives while also listening to their classmates' customs. It is important as well to validate lifestyles that do not include prayer. The teacher's responses to the children's information model interest and respect.

"So your family goes to Temple every Saturday as well as on special holidays. What's your favorite thing you do there?"

Another way dolls can present information is to come to the circle with a book they would like the group to learn from, or they could ask a question about something they want to know about. In both of these types of stories, you will have three goals:

- To give the children information
- To give the children an opportunity to show what they know
- To have all the children see that knowing about everyone is a good thing

When a doll introduces a book, most of the information will come from the book. After the book is read to the children, the discussion should be short.

"That's a great book. I learned a lot. I think we should thank Julio for bringing it to share with us."

"Thank you, Julio!"
"I like your book, Julio!"

"Who can tell me something they learned about skin from Julio's book?"

"I know we all have different colors."
"That's 'cause of melon."

"That's right! We all have different skin colors because we have different amounts of melanin in our skin. That's what Julio wanted to know when he got this book, remember? Who else can tell us something they learned from the book?"

"I like the picture on the front."

"Oh, yes. Look at all the faces on the front of Julio's book. I'm glad you noticed, Jacques. How many people in this picture look exactly like another person? Hmmm?"

"NONE!" [General chorus.]
"Everybody is unique!"

"I just can't fool all of you. Each person is different from each other person. That's right. It's the way the world is."

If the doll comes to the group with a question—a "wondering story"—the kids, with your help, come up with the information that the doll needs. This is an easy method to encourage children to proudly show how much they know. For example, Elizabeth is interested in Kwanzaa and hopes the children can tell her about it. This story would work well in a class where several children celebrate Kwanzaa or where some children have learned about this holiday in previous years at school. Before the discussion began, the children would identify Elizabeth's feelings as curious and interested. Then the teacher would open the discussion with a question.

"Who can tell Elizabeth something about Kwanzaa?"

"It's a holiday about Africa. My family has a party."

"So it's a special holiday when people learn about Africa. Denicia's family has a party for Kwanzaa. What else is Kwanzaa about? Does anybody know about the seven days?"

"Me! Me! Each day has a special thing, like working together."

"Yes! Each day has a special principle that is celebrated and practiced. Each one is named in Swahili. That's one of the languages of Africa. The days celebrate things like working together, like Sean said, unity, and being creative. Who knows some special symbols of Kwanzaa? Elizabeth would especially like to know about a candleholder she saw."

"Oh! That's the kinara!"

By asking questions, the teacher keeps the exchange of information moving, adding bits and pieces to the information the children already know. Don't worry if your students draw a blank on the subject, however. If this happens, as it sometimes does, the discussion will center on ways to find the information. Then the doll will tell how she used some of these methods to find the information and what she found out. This gives the story a double purpose—it gives the children information about a subject, and it shows them *how* to gather information.

"When Saed went to visit his neighbor, Mr. Spinner, he saw that Mr. Spinner had to hold onto a metal bar thing when he walked around. That made Saed wonder what that thing was and why his neighbor was using it."

My purpose in telling this story is to give the children information about walking aids. If none of the children know about this subject, the conversation would go like this:

"That made Saed wonder what that thing was and why his neighbor was using it. Can anybody tell her about it?"

"I never seen one."

"It seems like none of us know about this. How can Saed find out what he wants to know?"

"He could ask his neighbor."
"Or his mom."
"Or in a book."

"Three good ideas! Do you know what Saed did? He used Ebony's idea. He asked Mr. Spinner about it. Who knows a good way to ask him?"

Respectful ways to ask for information could then be practiced, and Saed could relate what his neighbor told him about walkers and other ways to help people get around. This type of story can be a good way to let children admit that they have been wondering about the same subject. It is important that they learn to feel comfortable asking questions and discussing diversity.

One of my dolls, Melly, has no hair. I needed a doll for a story one day and had not yet glued Melly's hair on. While at first I thought I could not use her that day, after a moment I remembered that one of the children had an aunt who had lost her hair due to cancer treatment. I decided it would be good to represent a child going through chemotherapy to help the children become comfortable with this condition. So now I tell a "wondering story" about Mickey, who would like to know why Melly has no hair. At the end of the situation setup I ask, "Have any of you been wondering too?" Although I mentioned that Melly has been sick and taking some medicine that made her hair fall out when I first introduced her, this story gives me a chance to give the children more information and to help them think about what support Melly could use to get through her illness.

"Have any of you been wondering too?"

  "She's sick, huh?"

"Yes, that's right. Good remembering, Abram. Melly has an illness—not a catching kind—called leukemia. She has been very sick, but she's feeling better now. Her blood hasn't been growing right, and she had to take medicine to try to fix it."

  "Is she better now?"

"Yes, she is better now. She might get sick again, but right now her blood is doing very well. Who knows why she doesn't have any hair?"

  "The medicine did it."

"Uh huh. Most medicine doesn't make your hair fall out, but this was very strong medicine just for leukemia. It made all her hair come right out. Now that she's done with the medicine, what do you think will happen to her hair?"

  "It'll grow back! I know 'cause that happened to my Aunt Laurie. Her hair fell out too, but then it growed back."

"Right! That's just what will happen to Melly too. Well, Mickey wants to know how he can help Melly when she's sick. Do you know any ways?"

  "He could go play with her."
  "I'd draw her a picture to feel better."

"I can see that you know how to be good friends to someone when they are sick. What would you say to Melly about her hair?"

  "I'd say 'You have a nice bald head.'"
  "I'd tell her I liked it."

"Do you like her bald head?"

  "Yea. Now that I'm used to it. It's nice and round."

"Then that would be a good thing to say. Does anybody have questions about Melly's illness or her hair that they have been wondering about like Mickey? This is a good time to ask. Maybe one of us knows the answer. We know an awful lot!"

Although our goal here is to help children become comfortable with diversity in general, it is also true that they will be comfortable when any of these children meet a person who has lost her hair. Everything we introduce our children to means one more thing they understand about the people in the world around them.

8. To Undo Learned Stereotypes and Biased Beliefs

To help children to undo learned stereotypes and biased beliefs, you may tell stories in which the dolls model the opposite of the stereotype, have a mistaken belief challenged, or believe a stereotype about themselves. Each discussion session will be unique, depending on the form your situation setup takes and your students' reactions to it. While facilitating these discussions, remember these three points:

- Find as many opportunities to state clearly and with certainty that the stereotype is not true and is unfair.
- Watch for the children's reactions to what is being said, and lead the discussion wherever necessary to undo the incorrect beliefs that they express.
- Ask questions to help the children think past the stereotype.

Some of the stories you tell to help children undo learned stereotypes or biased beliefs will be simple modeling stories. You will be modeling the opposite of a known stereotype. These stories follow a similar pattern to the stories told to model comfort with diversity. There will be little discussion needed, and there is no problem to solve, unless one or more of your students has a problem believing the story because it goes against a biased belief they have learned.

I tell a story where Ianthe spends all day building things with blocks. The purpose of this story is to model a girl who is free to be interested in building things. By their responses to your story, you will know if any of your students have categorized blocks as a male activity. If this happens, have patience, but be clear that stereotypes are unfair and not true. Here is how the discussion might go:

"Ianthe loves blocks. Who else here loves to build with blocks?"

"Ianthe's a girl! Girls don't like blocks."

Rather than just telling this child that he was wrong, I turned his statement into a question for the group.

"Really, Dylan? Did someone tell you that was true? All girls don't like blocks? Let's check that out. Are there any girls here who like to build with blocks?"

"Yes! Me!" [Many hands waving.]
"I like to build with blocks."
"Yeah, me too! It's the best!"

"Sunnie, what kind of blocks do you like best?"

"I like Lego blocks. I like to make cars."
"My brother always says our blocks are for boys, but I don't believe him."
"Yeah. I'm a girl and I like blocks."

To involve the boys in the discussion, I address the next question to them.

"How about you, boys? Have you seen girls enjoying building with blocks?"

"Jo Ellen and I made a house with the big bricks yesterday."

"I remember that, Allan. You two sure had a good time building together! So it seems like a lot of girls like blocks. You know, that's the problem with those stereotypes. They try to make everybody be the same. Some boys like blocks. Some don't. And some girls like blocks, and some don't. That stereotype sure had you fooled, huh, Dylan?"

"Yeah. I guess so."

In this way I bring up the concept and even the word *stereotype*. It is a new word to the children, but it is important to know. If children hear statements like "All those Asian kids are good at math," they will recognize them as stereotypes and reject them as untrue. This knowledge can be an important tool for children to use to fend off the bias they encounter.

It is also important to note that, without the intervention of this story, Dylan's attitude could very well have spread (and probably had) among the boys and been forced on the girls, especially when boys wanted a space in the block center. After this discussion, it is unlikely that the boys would repeat this stereotype, and the girls would know that they are free to spend time in the block center.

Discussions about gender stereotypes often uncover issues affecting the children in a very personal way, since these stereotypes are commonly used by children and adults alike. You will have to be prepared to deal with the real-life issues as well as the dolls' issues during these discussions. This is an excellent learning opportunity that helps the children gain a personal understanding of how stereotypes hurt everyone.

In a simple situation setup, I told about a time when River told Ianthe she couldn't read as well as he does because she is a girl and boys are smarter than girls. After the children identified each doll's feelings I asked

"Have any of you ever heard someone say girls can't do something? Or girls don't like something?"

When I opened up the discussion with a simple question, the situation at the computer came right out, in the new atmosphere of gender equality.

> *"Yes! Kenny said that to me at the computer! He said I had to go away because girls don't like the computer. But I DO like the computer!"*
>
> *"Yeah. He said that to me, too. I didn't like it. And that's not fair. Because girls can do anything."*

> *"Yes, that's right. Every girl is different, just like every boy is different, so we can't say what someone will like or not like if that's all we know about them. But I'll bet Kenny didn't know that, huh, Kenny?"*

> *"Unh, uhn. I didn't know that. But I do now."*

> *"Hey, that's great! He just learned something new! Terrific. I am also wondering if maybe this came up because lots of kids are wanting more time on the computer. Is that true?"*

The story went on to include problem solving for a fair way to share computer time in our classroom.

Another type of story brings incorrect information directly to the group. A doll tells about an experience in which a belief is challenged. In the discussion step, you will lead your students to help the doll understand that her information is incorrect. After hearing a lot of boasting going on about toys, I decided this boasting was an attempt to say, "I'm better than you because I have more than you." I decided to tell a story to undo the bias that material possessions make you a better person.

I used Lucia and Marcy for the story. Marcy had all the kids trailing after her outside because she was telling a wonderful story. Marcy was the butterfly queen. She was wearing wings that she made with paper and paint, and all the other kids were butterflies too. Marcy used her imagination to think of all kinds of adventures for the butterflies to get into. Lucia, seeing how much everybody liked Marcy, wanted the kids to like her like that too. So she got her grandma to buy her a fancy set of real-looking butterfly wings from a catalog. She went to school with her wings, sure that the other kids would think she was better than Marcy now!

> *"What do you think the kids did when they saw Lucia's wings?"*

> *"Ran to see 'em."*
>
> *"I would ask to wear 'em."*
>
> *"Me too! I would tell Lucia I liked the wings."*

> *"That's exactly what happened! The kids all gathered around her and admired her wings. How do you think that made Lucia feel?"*

> *"Great!"*
>
> *"Everybody liked her."*

"It's a happy feeling to have people like you, isn't it? We all need that. But was everyone liking Lucia, or were they liking the wings?"

"The wings."

"Yep. In fact, when everybody looked at the wings, they ran off to hear what new adventure Marcy had thought up for that day. How do you think Lucia felt then?"

"Sad."

"Upset."

"Why did all the kids enjoy being Marcy's friend so much? She didn't have any fancy toys or costumes or clothes."

"She made good stories."

"She let everyone play."

"She liked adventures, like me."

"Yes. A friend is someone who is fun to be with. And someone who treats you kindly and cares about you. Do fancy clothes or toys help you be kind?"

"No, I guess not."

"What would happen if someone who was very mean to you and called you names suddenly got some fancy clothes and the latest rad shoes. Would you want to play with them?"

"No way!"

"So Lucia's not better than the other kids because she got fancy butterfly wings? Does she need to be better than the other kids in order to have friends?"

"I think she just needs to play."

"Yeah. Like, she could invite someone over to her house. I did that with Tamar."

"Yes! She could invite somebody to play. What are other good ways to make new friends? Could she play the butterfly game with the others?"

"Yeah. If she liked it."

"She could play blocks with someone."

"She'll have to think about that. Thanks for talking it over with her. She has some hard thinking to do now. You have all really helped her to straighten out some of her ideas. Shall we send her around again for one last hug?"

If a child has been exposed to a stereotype about herself, she may be unwilling to discuss it, but she also may welcome the chance to talk it over with the people she trusts. Your modeling comfort with discussing these issues is important in developing that trust. Your strong and clear stance against stereotypes and all other forms of bias will help children know they do not have to believe them—either about others or about themselves.

Stereotypes are insidious. Children believe what they are told. It's likely that the children believe negative stereotypes about themselves. While the work you are doing to teach children to be comfortable with diversity and to gain an anti-bias attitude will help to keep this from happening, sometimes a child needs the reassurance of seeing her peers, her teacher, and a doll friend affirm that she is okay.

This will be the goal when you tell a story about a doll that believes a stereotype about herself. That doll will learn that the negative view she had of herself is just a stereotype, and the child in your group will be learning the same thing. For example, it's common for young girls to believe that their hair is ugly. Long, flowing blonde hair is seen as the ideal, and everything else is lacking. In one classroom, I had seen Dawn, who had lots of little black cornrows, combing a blonde doll's hair and crooning over and over, "You're so pretty." I used Mei Lin, who has long, straight black hair, to tell a story the day after I saw Dawn with the doll. The story line said, "Mei Lin hates her straight black hair. She thinks it is ugly. She wishes she had long blond hair like River." The kids identified Mei Lin's feelings as sad and jealous. I began the discussion with a question I knew the answer to—the children loved Mei Lin already.

"What do you think of Mei Lin's hair. Do you think it is ugly?"

"No."
"It's pretty."
"I like your hair, Mei Lin!"

Children can be amazingly perceptive when given the opportunity to think about what they have seen. I give them a chance to explain where these stereotypes come from, if they can.

"Kelly thinks Mei Lin's hair is pretty. So do I. Why does Mei Lin think hair has to be yellow to be pretty?"

"She saw Barbie. Barbie always has long, blonde hair."

"Barbie might make her think blonde is best. What else?"

"Eve always says her hair is prettiest. Maybe Mei Lin knows somebody like that."

"Other kids might have told her only blonde hair is pretty. What kind of hair do you all think is best?"

Now the children will use the knowledge gained in earlier stories in which they practiced respecting and being interested in diversity.

"All kinds of hair is pretty."
"Yeah. We all have our own kind."

"Who can tell me something they like about their own hair?"

"I have black hair like Mei Lin. I like how it shines."

"Just like a beautiful night sky! I like your hair too. Who else can tell us something they like about their hair?"

"Mine is curly all over. My mom calls me Curly Top."
"I like my braids."
"Mine is just the color of cimanon toast! My dad said so."
"I like Sylvie's hair 'cause she has lots of beads at the ends."

"That's true, then. People like lots of different kinds of hair. Every kind has something great about it."

Since the mirrored child had not said anything she liked about her hair, I next gave her an opportunity to talk. When she didn't speak, I did it for her. Then I immediately took the focus off of her so she did not have to either accept or deny that her hair was nice. At the same time I modeled needing to hear something nice about myself.

"Dawn, how about you? What do you like about your hair? Can't think? Well, I love the neat patterns of cornrows your hair can make. Your hair sure is perfect for making cornrows. I wish my hair would do that, but it's too wispy. Who can tell me something nice about my hair?"

9. To Help Children Develop Anti-Bias Attitudes

Your first stories that directly address bias should be designed to teach the vocabulary necessary to discuss this subject. The discussion will focus on exploring the meaning of the anti-bias vocabulary you are presenting.

The following story was told to three year olds. The goal is for the children to learn about the word *safe*. I led the discussion directly to the meaning of this word.

"When Ricky shoved Lucia and called her stupid, Lucia did not feel *safe*. How do you think Lucia was feeling when Ricky shoved her and called her stupid?

"Sad."
"She fall down?"

"Good thinking! She was sad. George wants to know if Lucia fell down. She almost did! How would you feel if you got shoved like that?"

"That's scary!"

"Yes, that can be scary. Do you think she was scared?" *[Nods.]* Yes, I think she was scared and sad. That's why I said she didn't feel safe. Feeling safe means you know nothing will hurt you.

"Don't push!"

"That's right! We don't push here, Helen. And we don't call names like *stupid,* either. You know, everyone needs to feel safe. One of my jobs is to be sure everyone can feel safe here. That means nobody hurts your body or your feelings. Who likes feeling safe at school?"

"Me! Me!" [Everyone joins in.]

"Lucia says she feels safe here with all of you. She likes that!"

With children ages five and older, more of the discussion can be left to them. Stories will model a type of biased behavior, and you will guide the discussion to the use of one or more vocabulary words you would like the children to understand.

In the story about River crying because he scraped his knee, three kids laughed and called him *cry-baby* and Elizabeth told them they were not treating River with *respect.*

"What did Elizabeth mean when she said *respect?* What does *respect* mean?"

"Like, they weren't being nice to him."

"Yeah. They called him names."

"Those kids were acting like he was wrong to cry. But boys can cry too!"

"I cried once when I skinned my knee. It bled all over the place."

"So calling names is not treating someone with respect. What would the kids do if they were treating River with respect?"

"They wouldn't call him names."

"They'd be nice to him."

"Elizabeth did it. She was kind to River when he got hurt."

"Yeah. Not picking on somebody is more like respect, I think."

"That's exactly right, Tracy, and good thinking too! Respect means not picking on somebody, treating them fairly, and caring about them and their feelings. Elizabeth did treat River with respect, just like Ibrahim said. Which of you in this class would like to be treated with respect too? Everybody? Well, count me in! I think everyone deserves respect, don't you?"

If the group seemed ready for more, I could have picked up on the child's comment that boys can cry too as an opportunity to discuss the word *stereotype,* a concept we had already practiced. When this came up in the middle of the story, I remembered my goal of working on the concept of respect and decided not to discuss stereotypes at that time.

Once your group has the basic vocabulary to discuss bias, you will be free to tell many stories with the goal of turning everyone in your group away from believing bias they experience and stopping them from acting in a biased manner. Your focus during the discussion and problem-solving step will be to turn the group attitude against such behaviors as exclusion, name-calling, put-downs, and hurtful teasing.

To create this anti-bias attitude in the children, you will need to help them to do three things:

- To recognize bias
- To empathize with the person experiencing the bias
- To consider the motivations and feelings of the person acting in a biased way

To encourage the empathy that is crucial to forming an anti-bias attitude, most of these stories will be told from the perspective of the doll that has experienced bias.

In the following story, a child looks at Lucia's drawing of her family and tells her it that can't be her family with only a grandma in it. The teacher's goals are to have the children learn to recognize insistence on conformity as a form of bias, to empathize with Lucia, and to validate many kinds of families. Lucia's feelings are identified as *upset, mad,* and *confused.* Then the discussion begins.

"Why is Lucia so upset, mad, and confused?"

" 'Cause of what that kid said."
" He said her gramma's not her family."
" Did Lucia cry?"

"She might have been upset enough to cry. *Is* her grandma her family?"

" Yes. That's right. She told us before."
" That's why she drew her grandma."

"It seems like that other kid wanted everybody's family to be the same. But it's not true that all families are the same, is it?"

" No. I live with just my mom and my brother."

"Yes. That's your family, Han Eul. A family is the people who love and take care of each other. There are many different ways to be a family. How would it feel if someone told you your family isn't right?"

" I'd be mad."
" I'd say that's not true!"
" That would hurt my feelings."

"I'll bet you would! That's just how Lucia felt. Now we know that it's not right to try to tell someone they have to be the same as someone else. And we know how much that hurts, don't we?"

Another example involves a story about bias against a physical characteristic using hurtful teasing and exclusion. In the story, Ricky is taunted about his ears. The kids laughed at him, flapping their hands up by their heads, saying, "Look! I'm Ricky! I can fly with my elephant ears!" Then the kids run away from him. Identifying Ricky's feelings will be a very important step in this story. Encouraging the children to put themselves in Ricky's place will help the children identify his feelings.

> " Oh, that would hurt Ricky's feelings awful."
> " What a mean thing to do!"
> " I think he'd be really sad."
> " He'd be embarrassed too."
> " It might make him feel bad about his ears."
> " He'd probably want to fall in a hole and disappear. I would."

" Wow. That's a lot of feelings all brought up because of teasing. Would all of you feel this way if this happened to you?"

> " Yes. I would."
> " I wouldn't believe it. I'd tell them to shove off."

" Are Ricky's ears awful? That's what the kids were saying to him."

> " They're not awful. They help him hear better. That kid was just picking on him. He shouldn't believe that."

" Yes. They wanted to make Ricky feel bad so they put him down by teasing him. There is nothing wrong with Ricky's ears. It's great that all of you realize that. Would you act in this biased way against Ricky because he has ears that stick out?"

> " No!"
> " Not me!"
> " Never!"

" That's terrific. I'm glad to see this group knows how to treat each other with respect."

Once your students have discussed several bias stories with their *Kids Like Us* friends, they will be able to easily recognize the different forms bias can take among children. You can simply ask what happened at the beginning of the discussion, and you will get the immediate response from several children:

> " They're doing name-calling."
> " That was a hurtful question she asked Rajit."
> " They are excluding her on purpose. They shouldn't do that."

When your students are skilled at this, they are ready to focus on putting themselves in the place of the person experiencing the bias. To help them, you will encourage them to relate their own experiences to that of the doll. They may tell stories of very different experiences, but this is all right because we are trying to get them to experience a common *feeling* with the doll.

In a story told to help students practice this skill, I tell about some kids yelling, "Hey, Brownie. Get off our street!" at Ianthe when she was riding her bike near her home. The children identify her feelings as *mad, put down,* and *embarrassed.*

> "She was really feeling mad, put down, and embarrassed. How did this happen? A minute before she was feeling happy on her bike."
>
> > *"That's because they used name calling, and they told her to go away. That's excluding too."*
>
> "Wow. Two kinds of bias at a time. No wonder she feels awful. Have you ever felt like this?"
>
> > *"My brother called me 'Piglet.' I got red in the face 'cause I was embarrassed and I was soooo mad, but I didn't let him see."*
>
> "I'm sorry that happened, Jeanne. You shouldn't have to listen to things like that. I bet you understand how Ianthe felt. Who else has felt this way?"

Discussions beginning from this same type of story can focus on how any biased behavior feels to the recipients of that bias.

> **Put-downs:** "Do you remember a time when someone put you down just for who you are, like they did to Melly because she's Native American?"
>
> **Hurtful teasing:** "Marcy was so hurt when they teased her about not having a lunch box. It made her feel like something was wrong with her. Have you ever felt like that because of what someone said?"
>
> **Constant focus on one characteristic of a person:** "River kept going on and on about Ianthe being African American. Has that kind of thing ever happened to you?"
>
> **Avoidance:** "Have you ever felt like Mickey did when none of the kids would hold his hand in the circle?"

All of these stories will go past empathizing with the dolls to problem solving with them, so children will learn strategies for dealing with bias. In the following story about exclusion, we will look at the entire discussion. The problem-solving skills practiced in other stories will now help the children cope with bias. These problem-solving sessions will follow the same steps used in previous stories, except that the focus will be entirely on the doll who was a target of bias.

Brad and some other kids have made a fort in a jungle gym. When Ianthe comes along to play, Brad yells to her, "You can't play here. Only white kids are allowed in this fort!" The kids identify Ianthe's feelings as hurt, sad, furious, and embarrassed.

> "Ianthe is very hurt, isn't she? And furious too! She's even a bit sad and embarrassed. How did this happen? What was Brad doing when he said that to her?"

"He wanted Ianthe to feel bad."

"He was excluding her. That's not nice."

"I don't like excluding."

"Yes, he definitely was using exclusion to direct things, wasn't he? Has this ever happened to you?"

"My brother always does that to me. He says, 'No girls!'"

"Jaime said I couldn't be in the butterfly club once."

"I did not!"

"Yes you did!"

"Jaime feels like it would be wrong to exclude someone. He wouldn't do that now that he knows how much it hurts. Right, Jaime? *[Jaime nods.]* What was Brad saying was the reason he could exclude Ianthe?"

"He said only white kids."

"What does he mean by that?"

"Ianthe is African American."

"Is it wrong for Ianthe to be African American?"

"No! She is."

"Brad just said that."

"That's right. Ianthe is African American, and that's something she can feel good about. Brad just said that because he felt like stopping Ianthe from getting into the fort. He just picked something to say. What should Ianthe do now?"

"She should yell at Brad."

"She should tell Brad that he hurt her feelings."

"I would climb into that fort anyway and shove Brad out!"

"I'd go find someone else."

"Wow! You have a lot of good ideas! There are many choices of things Ianthe could do now. It depends on how she feels. She could try to work it out with Brad, or force them to let her in, or she could go find someone else to play with. What could she say to Brad if she wanted to try to work it out with him?"

"Don't exclude."

"African Americans can too!"

"How would he like it?"

"She could remind him that excluding someone is not okay. She could tell him that African Americans can be in the fort if they want. She could try to get him to think about how he would feel if he was excluded. Those are all great ideas. What if she wanted some help in dealing with it? Where could she find help?"

"Her friends. She could go get 'em."

"What about the other kids in the fort?"

"Maybe the teacher?"

"Yes. She has lots of places she could look for help. What if she's feeling bad about what Brad said?"

> "I'd give her a hug."
> "Me too. Don't listen to Brad, Ianthe. He's wrong."

"You would be good support for Ianthe. She could even talk to her parents about it when she gets home if it is still bothering her. It helps to tell someone, you know? Well, what if she just wanted to do something else to help her feel better? What could she do?"

> "She could join another game."
> "Make her own fort."
> "She could find a friend to play with."
> "I'd play with you, Ianthe. I like you."

"You think finding something else fun to do would make her feel better. Or maybe just being with friends. I'm sure telling all of you about it has helped her feel better too. She's glad to hear that you like her just the way she is!"

Some stories will also include the point of view and feelings of the child acting in a biased way. The main goal of these stories will be to uncover some of the motivations that cause bias (a list of these motivations can be found in chapter 5). Understanding these motivations will allow children to realize that the person acting in a biased way has a problem that has nothing to do with the person they are treating badly. Let's look at an example of a story in which we explore motivation for bias.

At the library, Elizabeth cried when she saw a man with a metal claw for a hand. The kids knew immediately that Elizabeth felt scared.

"Why do you think Elizabeth was so scared that she cried and tried to get away?"

> "She never saw a hand like that."

"So she was scared of something new. Have any of you seen a person with a metal claw for picking things up?"

> "No. I never."

I give some information the children are lacking.

"Sometimes when a person doesn't have a hand or an arm, doctors make a special pretend arm and hand for them. They make them out of metal because metal is strong. Then they make it like a thumb and a finger so the new hand can pick things up, like this." [I demonstrate using one finger and thumb to pick up an item.]

> "I saw one on TV once."
> "I saw Captain Hook. He was mean."

"Many children have seen pictures of Captain Hook. Do you think everybody with a hook is mean like Captain Hook?"

"No. That's a stereotype!"
"Captain Hook is just a story."

"How do you think it felt to that man in the library when Elizabeth screamed and cried when she saw him?"

"That hurt his feelings, I bet."
"Maybe he was embarrassed. I bet everybody looked."
"It was mean that Elizabeth did that."

"I think it probably did hurt his feelings. Nobody wants to be scary. Did Elizabeth mean to hurt him?"

"No. She was just freaked out."
"It's okay, Elizabeth.
"She didn't know it's okay to see something new."

"Yes, now Elizabeth knows there is nothing to be afraid of because she has learned about artificial arms. She is also beginning to understand she doesn't need to be afraid of something just because it's new to her. I'm glad you all explained that to her."

Fear of something new and curiosity are the most common reasons very young children act in a way that hurts others. Let's examine one of the most common motivations of older children—power.

In this story, the kids start a game of hide-and-seek and discover that both Julio and Henry want to be "it." Julio says to Henry, "You can't be 'it.' You're too dumb to even count right!" Then he mocks Henry's speech and laughs. Henry's feelings of shame and anger are explored, and then the discussion begins. We will get right to the motivation for the biased action.

"Why did Julio do that? He must have known it would make Henry feel really bad."

"He wanted to be first."
"I don't think he was thinking about Henry's feelings."
"He thought the kids would laugh and they would like it."
"That was definitely a put-down."

"Good thinking. Julio put down Henry because he wanted to be first at hide-and-seek. Do you think Henry is stupid?"

"No! He's as smart as me."
"He just can't hear good. He's not dumb."

"So Henry is okay and Julio is the one with a problem. What does Julio need to learn?"

"Put-downs hurt!"
"Other kids don't like that."
"You have to take turns if you're gonna play."

If a group of dolls is involved, the storytelling will be more complicated because of all the emotions and motivations involved. To keep track of each doll, you will choose a point or two to remember about each as you reflect what the children say about them. Then you will have these ideas ready for use in the resolution.

For example, in the following story, the identifying feelings step and the discussion step are combined, dealing with one character at a time. Rachel, Melly, Elizabeth, and Rajit will all be present as the story takes place.

"On the school bus one morning, Rachel and Melly were whispering. Elizabeth told Rajit they were whispering secrets about him. So Rajit went over to them and asked what they were saying about him. Then Melly called him 'Nosey' and told him he had a big nose. Rachel chimed in with, 'We should call you Indian Big Nose!' How do you think Rajit was feeling?"

"Awful."

"He felt sad his friends said that."

"I bet he was angry too. I would be if they said that to me."

"He might be embarrassed about his nose."

"Lonely, 'cause they are all against him."

"That's a lot of feelings all at once. He probably was angry, sad, embarrassed, and even lonely. Did you know you can feel lonely even when you are surrounded by people? I think Rajit did. How about Rachel and Melly? How were they feeling?"

"I think they were just being silly."

"And they were sharing secrets. They felt, like, together."

"Yeah. They were being friends. But not with Rajit."

"So Rachel and Melly were feeling silly and friendly together. What were they feeling about Rajit?"

"They were mean to him. I think they were feeling mean."

"I think they were just being goofy. That's how they were feeling."

"So they were feeling friendly to each other, and maybe a little goofy and mean. Do you think they hurt Rajit? Were his feelings hurt?"

"They sure were! They called him names about his nose."

"Yeah. And because he's Indian American."

"They were using name-calling weren't they? Is there anything wrong with Rajit's nose?"

"No!"

"Rajit, you have a nice nose."

"Those kids just said that to be funny."

"That's right. Rajit's nose is just fine. Rachel just picked that to make up a name about. The same with Rajit's heritage. He's proud to be from India, but that day they made it sound bad. When Melly made up that name, what did Rachel do?"

"She made one up too."

"Uh huh, wanted to say something like Melly."

"Do you think maybe Melly said something mean to Rajit so Rachel would like her?"

"Yeah! And then Rachel said something mean to Rajit so Melly would like her!"

"Wow. So it was all really about the two of them and not about Rajit at all. Remember that Elizabeth was there? She told Rajit the other two were whispering secrets about him. Why did Elizabeth do that? You know, when they called Rajit names, Elizabeth laughed really loudly and tried to get Rachel's attention. What do you think Elizabeth was feeling?"

"I think she wanted to be whispering with Rachel and Melly."

"She thought they'd like her better."

"Maybe she felt left out?"

"Yes. Sometimes people think that by putting down one person, another person will think they are really neat or smart or something. That's called 'trying to impress someone.' Do you like someone more when you see them acting biased like this?"

"No!"

"I don't like that."

"I would think they were being jerks."

"You know, I think a lot of kids would know that what they said to Rajit was not okay. But when Rachel and Melly said those things on the bus, you know what the other kids did?"

"No. What?"

"They laughed."

"Why'd they do that?"

"Was it funny?"

"No. They just wanted to laugh."

"And get in on the joke."

"Like Elizabeth did."

"Sometimes people in a group want to feel like they are together. That can be good. But sometimes they try to get together by keeping someone else out."

"Like Rajit."

Discussions like these can go on to help the children problem solve for both dolls. They also can be used to encourage children to put themselves in the scene to practice how to stand up against bias.

10. To Help Children Learn to Stand Up Against Bias

By now the children are comfortable with diversity and interested in new experiences. They understand and can recognize bias and will reject it because they know how it hurts. They empathize with someone experiencing it, and they have the vocabulary to discuss these issues.

You will judge when your group is ready to discuss standing up against bias. In teaching these skills, you'll use many of the same bias stories already discussed. The children have already learned that in any situation a person has choices as to how to respond. You will encourage the children to think of several choices of action in each situation. You will discuss which choices make the most sense in different situations. You will also show the children that each person must choose for themselves which course of action to take.

You will turn the topic of the discussion to standing up against bias by asking four questions:

- What do you think the doll could do to stand up against the bias?
- What would you do if that incident happened to you?
- What would you do if you were with the child being targeted for bias?
- What would you do if you were in a group that was acting biased?

To help the children think of appropriate actions, you will turn their attention to the motivation for the biased action as demonstrated in the previous section. Many times uncovering the reason the person acted this way makes the best response clear.

You will be encouraging the children to think of *constructive* ways to deal with bias, to support the person experiencing it, and to take action to keep it from happening again. Don't encourage the children to shame the person who acted in a biased way. This response shuts down the thinking process and makes eliminating biased beliefs impossible.

Let's look at discussion and problem-solving sessions for stories of bias to see how this works. In the discussion of Rajit and his experience on the bus, we know that the dolls were motivated by wanting to impress someone else and by wanting to go along with the group.

"What are Rajit's choices now that this has happened? What if he wants to stand up against the bias?"

> *"He could yell at all of them—but that won't help, I guess."*
> *"He could tell them they are being biased."*
> *"He could tell Melly and Rachel they are just trying to make everybody laugh and he's proud to be from India. Nothing is wrong with his nose, either."*

"What if he didn't feel like dealing with those kids. What if he wants to be done with it?"

> "He could ignore them."
>
> "He could look for someone being friendly to him and talk to them."

"So he has several choices—some for standing up against the bias and some for just taking care of himself. He will have to choose what to do because he's the one stuck in the middle of it. But what if you were there too? How could you make things better?"

> "I'd tell Rajit he could sit with me."
>
> "I'd tell him not to listen to those kids."
>
> "I'd sure not laugh when everybody else did!"
>
> "I'd stand up and tell them all they were biased idiots!"
>
> "Then you'd be calling names!"
>
> "Oh, yeah. Well, I'd tell them I'm not going along with laughing at somebody."

"Wow. That would take courage. You have to be really strong to go against a whole group because you think it's the right thing to do! Who thinks they could be that strong?"

> "ME!" [Everyone responds enthusiastically.]

I take the opportunity to emphasize moral strength and how important it is. Because our society emphasizes physical strength as a source of pride, children tend to think that whoever is physically stronger is better. I use the word *strong* here to mean having the strength to stand up for what is right. Acquiring this skill is really much harder than working out in the gym to make your muscles bigger—and much more important.

In the following discussion, I pick up on the children's desire to educate their peers. Mickey says his friend Elizabeth can't sit next to him at lunch because she's a stupid girl. He says he only sits with boys. The kids decided Elizabeth's feelings were hurt and rejected. They said Mickey did that because he learned it from other kids.

> "That's the way it was at my old school. Boys always sat together."
>
> "Mickey probably thought he had to or the other kids would laugh."
>
> "Boys always say girls are stupid."
>
> "Not me. I don't say that."

"So Mickey learned a bias against boys and girls being friends from the other kids, and he went along with it because that was what the group was doing?"

> "Yeah. That's right. Because they were all doing it."

"Well, is there anything Elizabeth can do about this, if she wants to, to change it?"

> "It would be hard, 'cause they all agree with it."

QUESTION #12

Q: *What if my children don't respond to my questions during the discussion step?*

A: The first thing to consider if you have a group that is reluctant to participate is what's holding them back. It may be that they are afraid of what the other children's reactions will be. This is sometimes the case with six to eight year olds, especially if one or two in the group loudly put the others down. They have to trust each other to open up about their feelings or mistakes they have made.

The solution to this problem? A *Kids Like Us* doll story, of course! Bring this problem out in the open by showing a doll in the same situation.

"River really wanted to tell about the time he was scared of the dark, but he thought the other kids would laugh at him."

(continued on next page)

"Is it true that they all agree with it? Maybe they all want to be friends, but they're just going along with the group."

"*Yeah! Maybe nobody is brave enough to say it's wrong.*"

"What would you do if you were Elizabeth and this happened to you?"

"*I'd stand on a table and yell to everybody to stop dividing up!*"
"*Kids would only laugh at you and you'd get in trouble.*"
"*You could talk to each one after school.*"

"Talking to each one after school or getting everyone's attention and talking about it right there are both possibilities. Who else has an idea?"

"*I would write a note and pass it around.*"

"That's an interesting idea. What would the note say?"

"*I think girls and boys should be able to be friends and sit together at lunch.*"
"*And say there's nothing wrong with being friends.*"
"*And you could even have people sign their name if they agree.*"
"*That's a petition. You could make a petition!*"
"*I bet a lot of kids would sign it.*"

"Writing a note or even a petition are possibilities too. We have lots of choices of how to stand up against this bias. Good thinking, everyone. What if you were there in the lunchroom, standing next to Elizabeth? What would you say to Elizabeth?"

"*I'd say, 'Don't listen to him, Elizabeth. He's wrong.'*"
"*I'd push right in next to Mickey and tell him we're sitting with him.*"
"*Yeah. And tell him we don't care what everybody else says.*"

"What if *Elizabeth* doesn't feel like pushing in? Remember, she was feeling pretty hurt and rejected."

"*I'd tell her she could sit with me.*"
"*I'd tell her I'm a boy and I'd like to sit with her. I'd tell her not everybody goes along with that stuff.*"

This story examined a few strategies for dealing with learned biased behavior and group-reinforced bias. Both of these require some group education, and the children thought of a couple of interesting ways to bring this about.

Now let's look at bias caused by a doll's low self-esteem. In this story, Rajit and Mei Lin went to a karate class together. Then, during class, Rajit tried a move and fell down. When Mei Lin's turn came, she fell down too. Rajit said to Mei Lin, "That was really lame. You Chinese kids are supposed to know all the karate moves." The kids knew Mei Lin felt put down, embarrassed, and mad. Rajit was feeling angry and embarrassed that he fell down.

"Why do you think Rajit said that to Mei Lin?"

> *"He wanted to make her feel bad. Put-downs always make people feel bad. Everyone knows that."*
>
> *"He was embarrassed 'cause he fell."*
>
> *"I think he wanted Mei Lin to be embarrassed too."*
>
> *"Or try to make everybody look at her instead of him."*

"You think Rajit was feeling bad about what he did, so he tried to make Mei Lin feel bad too? Hmm…. What do you think Mei Lin could do when he said that to her? What would you do if you were Mei Lin?"

> *"I'd tell him off!"*
>
> *"I'd tell him not to try to make me feel bad."*
>
> *"I'd ignore him."*

"Those are all good possibilities. You know, Rajit and Mei Lin have been friends. I think Mei Lin is pretty mad and upset at Rajit right now. Is there anything they can do to get to feel like friends again?"

> *"She should tell him how she feels."*
>
> *"Yeah. Maybe he'd say he was sorry. Maybe he would understand if she told him."*

"What would she say to him?"

> *"Do not tease me about how I do in karate."*
>
> *"Don't try to make me feel bad just 'cause you do."*
>
> *"I'd say, 'Don't say stereotypes about me.'"*
>
> *"Yeah! I'd tell him that's just a stereotype. How would I know karate before I took a class and learned it?"*

"So you would let him know he was using a stereotype right away, Carl. And Jean would tell him, 'Do not tease me!' Tallish thinks she would say it's not all right to use stereotypes. I heard a lot of good suggestions. What about Rajit? I know you wouldn't do this, but if you were Rajit and said that to Mei Lin, is there any way you could make up for that mistake?"

> *"I'd have to say a really big sorry!"*
>
> *"I'd tell her I was just feeling bad and I was wrong."*
>
> *"I'd never say something like that again, even if I fell a million times."*

"What if you were there, right next to Mei Lin in the class. What would you do?"

> *"I'd tell Mei Lin she's doing okay."*
>
> *"I'd say everybody falls when they're first learning. I did."*
>
> *"I'd tell her to ignore what Rajit said."*

Also, require that everyone in your classroom be treated with respect (at all times, not just during *Kids Like Us* stories). A doll story about the meaning of respect is helpful in explaining this. Rule out put-downs and name-calling, and remind kids that they want to be listened to, so they must listen to others. *Then* try to have a good *Kids Like Us* discussion, and be sure all answers are listened to and treated with respect. Call on a few good talkers at first if nobody volunteers. Once they get started talking, you won't have time to call on everyone who wants to talk. And if you can successfully establish trust, your students will be more willing to share their writing, show their artwork, and explain how they solved that math problem to the group as well.

"What if Mei Lin wanted to talk to Rajit about it, but she was scared to do it? How could you help her then?"

> *"I'd go with her."*
> *"I'd tell her I could hold her hand."*
> *"We could get all the kids in the class to go talk to him together, if she wanted."*

"You could go with her, offer to hold her hand, or even get all the kids to talk to him. You would all know how to be a good friend to Mei Lin. You would have to let Mei Lin decide which way she wanted to handle it, because it was happening to her. That's important. But it sounds like you would be right there with her. That's what a friend would do. What do you think you could do if Rajit kept on saying things like that to Mei Lin?"

> *"I'd stand next to him instead so he couldn't bother her."*
> *"I'd tell her to tell the teacher about it so the teacher would make him stop."*

"Yes. Sometimes it's important to get help. You know, nobody should have to put up with bias. And sometimes it takes some work to make it stop. I'm glad to see you all thinking of ways you could do that."

When facilitating the children's learning about standing up against bias, it is also a good idea to tell a story or two that involve bias on an institutional level. They will need to deal with this too. For example, to start the following discussion, I told a story in which Mickey went to the toy store one day. He wanted a little raccoon pet like Ianthe had. But then he saw they had put up big signs at the ends of the aisles. One aisle had a big pink sign that read, "Girls' Toys" and the other had a sign marked, "Boys' Toys." The little raccoons were in the girls' section.

"How do you think Mickey felt?"

> *"I'll bet he felt very upset."*
> *"If I was there I'd a felt hopping mad!"*
> *"Yeah! They can't tell us which toys to play with, can they?"*
> *"Could a boy get a girl's toy?"*

"All the little cars were in the boys' section. And the Lego blocks and the Playmobil sets. How would you girls feel about that?"

> *"I love little cars!"*
> *"We get to play with whatever we want!"*

"That's what Mickey thought. If you were Mickey, would you have bought that raccoon you wanted?"

> *"Yes. Those signs are wrong."*
> *"If I wanted the toy, I wouldn't let a stereotype stop me."*

"Mickey did buy that toy. He was strong and didn't let those signs tell him what he should or shouldn't like. If you were friends with Mickey and he told you about those signs, could you find any way to do something about them?"

"We could all go to the store and tell them to take the signs down."

"Or write a letter."

"Yeah! And we could all sign it."

"Then they'd know lots of us agree."

Each situation is different and will call for different solutions. When planning the discussion and problem-solving section of the story, you can make a note of the most likely reasons for the bias that has occurred and think of a couple of appropriate responses based on that information. Then you will be ready to ask questions that lead the children to think about the variables that will help them come up with strategies themselves. Just remember, whenever possible, ask questions that get the students to think instead of telling them the information.

Other examples of institutional bias that affects children's lives can be seen in movies (for instance, "bad guys" depicted as unkempt poor people), books (boys are the majority of characters and take the active roles), television shows (jokes made at the expense of the "funny" fat character), action figures ("bad guys" painted dark), and toys (blue boxes for "boy toys" and pink for "girl toys").

Once you become aware of it, you will be able to find examples of bias everywhere. With the help of the *Kids Like Us* dolls, your students will be aware of the bias, too, and will be able to say, "That's unfair and I don't believe it," instead of drinking it in as the truth.

8

Step Five:
Resolving
the Story

ow you have met your goal for your *Kids Like Us* doll story and need only to conclude it by wrapping up loose ends, telling how the dolls dealt with the situation you presented in the situation setup, and giving the children a sense of closure. ● The resolution step will be brief. Six or seven sentences are all you will need in most cases. The goals of the resolution step are to make some conclusion of story elements, to reinforce the goals of the story, to show how characters dealt with strong emotions, to use children's ideas whenever possible, and to reinforce the group's participation (thinking, helping the doll, problem solving, and caring). We'll look at each of these goals.

Make Some Conclusion of Story Elements

Just as the situation setup brought up a scene to get the children thinking, the resolution step will conclude the scene, wrapping up the main elements of the situation and giving closure to the dolls' lives. You will do this so the children are not left wondering, "What ever happened to Umoja?"

> "So Melly went to the slumber party and she had a really great time. She missed her mom right about bedtime, but she closed her eyes and thought of her mom giving her a big hug, like Ginnie suggested, and that made her feel better. She's really glad she was brave enough to go, and she can hardly wait for the next slumber party!"

Do not confuse making a conclusion with "everyone lived happily ever after." Things do not always work out perfectly, and it is important not to make the resolution step represent this idyllic view of the world. Here's an example of a resolution that is unrealistic:

> "And so then all the children hugged and kissed and promised to be friends forever and they all went out for ice cream."

You will occasionally want a resolution like that after a story about a happy incident. But this kind of resolution would not be appropriate at the end of every story or at the end of a story about a bias incident.

For many stories, a more appropriate resolution might be something like this:

> "Umoja felt better when she told those kids to stop yelling stuff at her and that she wasn't listening to them anymore, no matter what they said. She used Moon's suggestion, too, and called some friends on the phone, so she could talk to some people who treated her with respect. Then she turned around and ignored those kids any time they came by her house."

Children need to know the best thing to do in any situation. They also need to know that things don't always work out the way we want, but we can feel okay about it because we did the best we could.

> "So the kids *did* write a letter and they all signed it. It was a good letter that told three reasons why the signs in the toy aisles should come down, like Hans suggested. They said boys and girls should be able to play with any toys they like, that the signs would make kids think they could only go in a certain aisle, and that kids could find the toys they wanted without those signs telling them where to go. They mailed the letter, and the manager wrote them back and thanked them for writing. He said he couldn't take the signs down because all

the stores had to have them and it wasn't up to him. The kids were disappointed, but they knew they had done the right thing when they wrote that letter. And they all agreed that they would ignore those signs."

This type of resolution is sometimes most realistic for a conflict story as well. In conflicts, children often continue to disagree but find some way to work out the conflict. It is good to show a doll or dolls changing their minds about an issue because of the discussion they have had, but it is also important to show how situations can be worked out when the dolls continue to disagree.

> "Ianthe still felt she shouldn't have to take Henry to the park with her, but she understood that her mother needed some peace and quiet to get her work done. Once Henry agreed to stick near Ianthe instead of running off, Ianthe felt better about it and went off to the park with him. She had to remind Henry once to come back, but they had an okay time together."

The goal is to conclude the situations you set up at the beginning, whether or not everything worked out perfectly.

Reinforce the Goal of the Story

In the resolution, you also can show the dolls using the skills you wanted your students to learn. For example, for the story in which Melly's canary died (see page 125), my goals were to support Rosario if he wanted to talk about his cat, to make death a subject that can be discussed, and to allow the children to ask questions. I also wanted to give the children the emotion word *grief,* to give them permission to miss someone who has died, and to know the loved one is never gone because good memories keep them with you. I reached my goal of supporting Rosario during the discussion step. I introduced *grief* during the identifying feelings step. We accomplished all the other goals during the discussion step, when the children told of pets they had lost. The resolution step was then my opportunity to show Melly using this information to reinforce those goals.

> "Melly is really glad to hear about all of your experiences with pets that have died. You know, when her canary died she felt like she was all alone in the world and that she would never be happy again. She was really grieving. So she went to see Grandma Lynn the next day, and she told Grandma Lynn all about her canary—how much she loved him and how he had just died. She hugged her grandma and cried for the longest time. Then she drew a picture of her canary to put up on the wall of her room. She felt a little better after that, but she knows she'll love her canary and miss him for a long, long time."

Show How Characters Dealt with Strong Emotions

Whenever the situation setup creates a scene in which a doll experiences strong emotions (such as anger, fear, worry, excitement, sadness), it's important to show the character successfully dealing with those emotions. Children really care about the dolls and need to know that they are all right at the end of the story. They also need the modeling of how to handle these feelings themselves. During some stories, your main goal will be to help the children learn skills to deal with the emotions the doll experiences. In this case, most of the resolution step may focus on how the doll accomplishes this.

Remember the story in which Ricky got advice from the group on how to deal with his anger when his flashlight broke? During the resolution, I used just a few sentences to model taking some space to yourself to deal with strong emotions, letting anger out in a way that does not hurt someone or something, and working on a solution to the problem once you are calmer.

> "Well, Ricky was so mad. He thought about throwing his flashlight right across the room, but he remembered just in time that he might break something else. So he stomped his feet and growled, just like a really angry bear. Then he threw himself on his soft bed and cried for a little. He felt better then and went to tell Brad to see if maybe he could fix the flashlight."

Even when learning to deal with strong emotions has not been one of your main goals, the resolution step should contain a sentence or two about how these feelings were handled. In the story about Mei Lin feeling her hair was not pretty, my main objective was to mirror a child who felt the same way about her hair. I had supported this child directly during the discussion. In the resolution I continued that process by having Mei Lin find ways to feel better about herself.

> "Thanks for talking to Mei Lin about this. She says she feels better just hearing what you all had to say. She wants me to tell you something else that happened that helped her feel better about her own hair. She decided to think about something she really likes about herself to help her feel better. She realized she is a really good bike rider, and she likes the way she smiles. Later that day, when she met River, who was out on his bike, she told him that she always wished she could have hair like his. River laughed and said he always wished for shining black hair like Mei Lin's! They both had to laugh about that, and Mei Lin realized just what you all said—all kinds of hair can be beautiful."

Use Children's Ideas Whenever Possible

Many stories will encourage children to tell their ideas about how the dolls can deal with their feelings effectively or solve their problems. When telling the resolution to the story, you will include a few of these ideas as the ones the doll used. For instance, during a discussion about a doll that has trouble getting to school on time, the children might suggest that he could set his clock ahead, set his alarm earlier, go to bed sooner, skip breakfast, take a shower to get moving more quickly, enlist the aid of a parent, lay out his clothes before going to bed, and move to a house closer to the school.

All you will need to do is to choose which of these ideas will best exemplify the goal of the story. I usually choose the ideas as I reflect them back to the group. When I reach the resolution step, I have my ideas planned and just have to put them into sentences. In this example, I would leave out moving and skipping breakfast as unrealistic and unhealthy. Then I would pick a couple of the other ideas and tell this resolution:

> "River is really pleased that you have taken time to help him. He decided to try setting his alarm fifteen minutes earlier to give him more time to get ready. And when all the people he lives with had a group meeting, he told them what he was trying to do. He asked them to be sure not to spend a bunch of time talking with him in the morning. They agreed to help. Then he laid out his clothes each night so he wouldn't have to find them in the morning. And guess what?"
>
> *"What?"*
>
> "He started being on time! Isn't that great?"

When Ianthe was told by Brad that she couldn't come into the fort because only white kids were allowed in, my students suggested many solutions for this problem, including finding another game to play and telling Brad, "African Americans can too!" I chose a couple of their ideas for Ianthe to use during the resolution. I also added reinforcement of my main goals: to help the children understand that excluding someone because of who they are is unfair and painful to the one who is excluded. I managed to include a little bit about how we can help each other stand up against bias.

> "At first Ianthe was so mad and embarrassed she stomped her feet and cried as she walked away from the fort. Her feelings were really hurt. Then she went to find her friend, Julio. She told him all about what Brad said, and he told her he would go back to help her talk to Brad if she wanted to."
>
> *"I said she could find a friend!"*

"Yes, Ravi, you did. And Ianthe liked your idea. She found a good friend too, because Julio listened to her problem and offered to help. That's what good friends do for each other. So Ianthe and Julio went back to the fort and Ianthe told Brad, 'It's not fair to exclude people.' She got that idea from Joe. Then she said, 'African Americans can be in forts too.' She asked all the kids in the fort if they wanted to be fair to everyone, and they said they did. So Brad said he did, too, but the fort was getting crowded. They worked out a way to take turns and had a great time."

Reinforce the Group for Thinking, Caring, Problem Solving, and Helping the Doll

Either at the beginning or the end of the resolution, I usually take the opportunity to positively reinforce students for the work they do during the *Kids Like Us* story. The dolls can easily and truthfully be grateful to the students for their help in working out their problems and for caring enough to do so.

"Rajit is glad to hear all your ideas about how to deal with Ianthe trying to bully him. He realized it wasn't fair for him to have to move and that he should get some help to deal with the problem. He agreed with Haley that Ianthe only picked him because she thought he would do what she said. So he talked to her friends after school, like Thomas suggested, and they agreed to help him stand up to Ianthe. The next day Rajit told Ianthe, 'NO! I will NOT move. Find another chair.' And all the other kids told Ianthe they would not let her hit Rajit, no matter what. And Ianthe went and found another chair! She grumbled about it, but she quit picking on Rajit. Rajit thinks you kids are really great problem solvers, and he wants me to tell you 'Thanks for helping!'"

• • •

"Saed is glad he had this chance to talk to all of you. He says you are good friends to care about his problem and help him think about how to feel less scared. He says he likes Melissa's idea. He thinks that taking a picture of his mom to keep in his cubby will make him feel less scared. He's going to try it tomorrow. And he is going to try the fun things they have at preschool too. He thinks Yoshi is right and doing things will make him feel happy. He's going to do painting the very first thing!"

• • •

"Well, you know what River did to solve his problem? He went right up to his brother and told him, 'I won't try to scare you if you don't try to scare me. Okay?'"

"*That was my idea!*"

"Yes, River got the idea from Kimmie. And it worked! His brother said he thought River liked being scared, so River told him he definitely did NOT! And he also tried Barbara's idea and found a time to have fun with his brother—they made cookies together—instead of just arguing with him all the time. Sometimes his brother still bugs him, but they get along better now. River says you kids are great thinkers and know how to help out a friend."

Don't worry about the physical impossibility of the doll using your students' ideas for a problem that happened in the past. It is all part of the magic of the *Kids Like Us* dolls, and your students won't mind a bit.

Of course, some resolutions will be much shorter than this. Don't feel a need to go on and on if there aren't elements that need to be wrapped up.

"Well, Rachel had fun showing you her solar system poster. She's going to let us borrow it for a while so we can all look at it. Shall we put it on the wall over here?"

"Umoja understands a lot more about the plus symbol now. She's going to add things together all afternoon and even in her dreams! She says she's glad she told you about her problem. You really helped her with it."

"So now Brad really understands all the things police officers do to help his town. He still wants to be one when he grows up, but not to shoot bad guys. He wants to help lost kids get home!"

When the story is done, I often put the doll or dolls in our special chair "to be with us today." The kids see this as a kind of reward for the doll for coming to the circle to talk. They often say hi to the doll as they pass by during the day. After school I put the doll back up on the shelf to watch with the others.

If I feel a child or several children have had a strong emotional reaction to a story or if I have told an especially difficult mirror story, I will invite the children to spend some special time with the doll. I remind them the doll is not for playing with but say that they would like to spend some quiet time talking in the pillow pit with anyone that would like to do this. It is usually the children most affected by the story who take me up on this offer.

After a Kids Like Us Doll Story

. . . .

It can be a good idea to do some follow-up activities after the story. These activities can be directly about the story itself or just related to the subject discussed in the story.

Having the children draw a scene from the story can be an excellent way to review the information, to gauge the children's understanding of the concepts, or to create a display of the learning that happens during *Kids Like Us* stories. Be sure to have "skin color" marker sets available so children are able to draw the dolls the way they really look. It is interesting to see what the children do when instructed to draw one of the dolls and you add their dictation of what the doll is saying.

Other activities to further reinforce the skills you presented during a *Kids Like Us* doll story can occur throughout the week. Making a two-sided puppet from paper plates and Popsicle sticks can be fun and reinforce the skill of identifying emotions. The teacher tells something that happened to the children and they turn their masks to show a mad or excited face, depending on the event. Dancing to "The Mad Mad Polka" on Josh Greenberg's tape *Rhythm and Rhymes* can encourage appropriate responses to anger. There are many possible ways to build on the learning that began in a *Kids Like Us* doll story.

CHAPTER

9

Telling Stories
for Different
Age Groups

Now that you have learned how to use all five steps to tell a *Kids Like Us* doll story, let's examine some whole stories. These stories were designed for three different age groups using a Five-Step Planning Sheet.

Ricky's Disappointing Snack: A Story for Two and Three Year Olds

Two and three year olds often have difficulty with transitions and not getting what they want. This story is designed to introduce the word *disappointed*. The story is only the first step in their learning process— it introduces the concept, and real-life practice follows. ● Before I told this story I filled in a Five-Step Planning Sheet. You'll find it on the next page.

Kids Like Us Five-Step Planning Sheet

Main goals: introduce and define the word <u>disappointed</u>; practice use of word

Children who may need support: Lizzie—disappointed at end of recess; Seneca—tell her feelings

Doll(s) to use: Ricky

1. Introduction:
basic facts about the doll (reminders)
- age 3
- likes sandbox

facts to prepare for this story
- likes bananas

2. Situation Setup (keep it short!)
Ricky saw bananas on the counter. He said, "Yummy! Bananas for snack." But when snack time came, they had crackers! No bananas for Ricky.

3. Identify Feelings (ask, don't tell!)
Note a few feelings appropriate to the story; circle new vocabulary you will present.
<u>disappointed</u>, sad, mad

4. Discussion/Problem Solving (ask questions to make them think)
List questions you can ask to help children think about each important issue.
- Who likes bananas?

5. Resolution (use children's ideas)
List important elements of story you will need to be sure to conclude.
- what Ricky does

This is the story I would tell based on this plan. I would gather between three and eight children into a circle and then bring Ricky to see them.

"Here comes Ricky to join us in circle! I'm going to bring him round for a quick hug. Oh, he's so glad to see you, Danielle! And he gives a big hug to Brady. He's smiling at you, Leroy! Yes, that's a nice hug for Ricky, Lizzie. Ricky says hi to Seneca. He's coming around to see each of you. Then he can begin his story."

◀ *I begin with a general greeting. I carry the doll around to each for a quick touch or hug and a greeting to focus them on the doll. I hold the doll, presenting him briefly to each child. This helps to keep the greetings short but gives each child a chance to be greeted personally by the doll.*

"You all know Ricky. Remember when he came to circle to meet you before?

"I know Ricky."
"I 'member him."
"He's my friend."

"Yes, he wants to be friends with all of you. Do you remember that Ricky is three years old?

"Me too!"
"Me! I'm three!"
"I'm this many." [The child holds up two fingers.]

◀ Step One—Introduction. *I begin by reminding the children that they know this doll.*

◀ *Age is a very important personal characteristic for young children. This makes it a good characteristic to encourage the children to relate to the doll.*

"Danielle is two and so is Seneca. And Brady, Leroy, and Lizzie are three years old. Ricky is three too. Ricky likes to play in the sandbox every day at day care. Remember he told us about the sandbox when he came to see us before?"

"I like the sandbox."
"I dig."
"I go swing."
"Ricky play with me."
"No, me!"
"Yes!"
"Me! Me!"

"Everybody wants to play with Ricky. Right?"

[General head nodding.]

◀ *I acknowledge what the children have told me. Then I tell a reminder detail of Ricky's life. This has nothing to do with the subject of the story but is part of the introduction step, which involves reminding the children about their previous experience with him.*

◀ *Sometimes the children need to be reassured that they can all be part of the story and part of the doll's circle of friends.*

Step Two— ▶
Situation Setup. This is the lead-in. I have brought up the subject of the story and asked a question that will help the children relate the story to their own lives.

It is very common for children of this age—beginning conversationalists—to make comments that are totally off topic. Don't worry about this. Part of what these young children are learning during these doll stories is how to have a back-and-forth conversation.

I try to bring the topic ▶ *back to bananas. I encourage a quiet child, Seneca, to contribute and reinforce her for speaking.*

This is the rest of the ▶ *situation setup.*

Step Three— ▶
Identifying Feelings. This is the step I plan to focus on in this story. I begin by simply asking questions so children can practice identifying feelings and I can gauge what they already know.

"Well, Ricky asked to come to circle today to tell you all about something that happened at snack time. Ricky saw bananas in the kitchen. He thought they would have bananas for snack. Ricky loves bananas. Who else likes bananas like Ricky?"

"Me!"
"Bananas!"
"We have bananas at my house."
"Oatmeal!"
"I have a kitty."

"Do we have bananas for snack at our school sometimes?"

"Uh, huh."
"We have 'nanas?"

"Yes. Sometimes we do eat bananas. Do you like bananas for snack, Seneca?"

"Yummy!"

"Seneca likes bananas."

"Yum, yum!"
"Snack time?"

"It will be snack time soon! You know what happened to Ricky? Yesterday he saw bananas on the counter. He said, 'Yummy! Bananas for snack.' But when snack time came, they had crackers! No bananas for Ricky."

"How was Ricky feeling?"

"Sad."
"Hungry."
"No bananas?"
"Where's the bananas?"
"Did Ricky cry?"

"I think Ricky *was* sad, Danielle. And hungry too! Leroy wonders where the bananas went. I'll bet Ricky is curious about that too. Do you cry when you're sad, Seneca?"

"Mmm hmm."

"Me, too. I think Ricky did cry."

◄ *I summarize and reflect to the students what they have said. I take the opportunity to introduce the word* curious. *I won't have time to explore this word in this story, but it's a good introduction.*

"He was feeling something else too. I think he was feeling *disappointed.* Disappointed means you wanted something to happen, but then it didn't. Can you say that word, *disappointed?*"

"Disappointed!" [A general chorus arises as they try to say this word.]

◄ *I bring up the emotion word, which is my goal for the story. I explain the word as simply as possible and direct the students to try saying it. This will help them to make this word part of their knowledge.*

"Ricky was disappointed because they didn't have bananas for snack. He wanted bananas. Now he's disappointed."

◄ *I use the word as many times as possible and will continue to do so throughout the story.*

"But Ricky knows what to do when he's disappointed. He ran to his teacher and got a big hug. He told her, 'I'm disappointed.' Then he asked her, 'Where's the bananas?' And she told him they would have bananas for lunch. Then he felt better. Do you think that was a good thing to do when he was disappointed?"

"Yeah!"
"Uh huh."
"Hugs fix everything!"

◄ Step Five—Resolution. *Note that we skipped step four—the discussion and problem-solving step. I will jump to the resolution of Ricky's problem because the story has already gone on long enough for this young group. I reinforce the new vocabulary word one more time by having Ricky use it. Ricky models going to a trusted person for comfort, using words to tell how he feels, and asking for information.*

"That's right. Yay for Ricky! *[I move the doll as if it is dancing around.]* Will you tell me when you are really disappointed about something? I'd like to know."

"Uh huh." [A general chorus arises from all of the children.]

◄ *I create a little celebration to reinforce the idea that expressing your feelings is a good thing.*

I'm glad that I realized ▶
this story needed to be told
right before snack time,
and that I planned to serve
bananas.

" And now I think it's time for us to have snack! Shall we have bananas?"

" Yeah!!!"

I conclude the story, ▶
then reinforce the children's
good thinking, their caring
about Ricky, and group
feeling and then move on
to our next activity.

" Thanks for listening to his story! He likes talking to you. And Ricky's going to watch us as we wash our hands and go to snack. Who's the snack helper today?"

Now that I have introduced this word, I will be watching for chances to help children express their disappointment when it occurs. I also send a note to the children's parents that explains the doll story to parents. I encourage them to cue their children to use the word *disappointed* when this emotion occurs at home.

Lucia's Elephant: A Story for Four and Five Year Olds

This story is for four and five year olds who have already worked on emotions and appropriate ways to handle them. You will hear them repeat what they have already learned from other stories, such as what to do when you are really mad. This story will help the children discuss problem solving and practice how to react to an accident.

I brought both Rajit and Lucia to the circle because I wanted the children to relate to this story from both sides of the conflict.

We do our greeting ▶
ritual to focus the children
on the dolls. I remind them
to give a quick hug so this
doesn't take too long. I will
remind any child who holds
onto the doll. Since we
have practiced this routine
many times before, this is
rarely a problem.

" Look! Rajit and Lucia have both come to talk to us today. I'll send Rajit this way around the circle and Lucia this way. Give them a quick hug and send them on to greet your neighbor. When they come all the way around to my place in the circle I'll begin telling you their story."

Kids Like Us Five-Step Planning Sheet

Main goals: meaning of <u>accident</u>—how to handle an accident (both sides) handling quick anger reaction—review

Children who may need support: Tracy and Linh

Doll(s) to use: Rajit, Lucia

1. Introduction:
basic facts about the doll (reminders)   **facts to prepare for this story**
- Rajit: 5, 2 moms, new sister, karate class
- Lucia: 4, lives w/ Grandma, speaks Spanish at home, plays little kitties

2. Situation Setup (keep it short!)
When the teacher said it was time to clean up, Rajit went to the blue table and started squishing the colored dough and putting it back in the container. Then Lucia came back from the bathroom and screamed, "You wrecked my elephant!" and pushed Rajit so hard he fell down.

3. Identify Feelings (ask, don't tell!)
Note a few feelings appropriate to the story; circle new vocabulary you will present.
- Lucia: sad, shocked, upset, mad, furious, disappointed
- Rajit: shocked, scared, hurt, mad, surprised, sad—helpful at first

4. Discussion/Problem Solving (ask questions to make them think)
List questions you can ask to help children think about each important issue.
- Did Rajit mean to hurt Lucia? What is it called when someone hurts someone by mistake?
- Why was Lucia sad? Why was Rajit sad?
- Why did Lucia push? (mad) What would be a better way? (practice it)
- What could Rajit say then? (make up for mistake?)

5. Resolution (use children's ideas)
List important elements of story you will need to be sure to conclude.
- the two talk and do something (use kids' ideas)
- will remember to get mad out first
- practice "It was an accident."

I included these facts in the introduction because they are things that have already been discussed about Rajit and Lucia in other stories. It is amazing to see how much the children remember of previous stories.

" Here's Rajit. He enjoyed those hugs. Do you remember that Rajit is five years old?"

   " I'm five!"

" Yes, Rajit is the same as you in that way, Chuck. Rajit wants to be a nurse when he grows up. He likes helping people."

   " I 'member that. Somebody laughed at him."

The children comment ▶ on what I have said, which is great, but it makes the introduction take longer than anticipated. To get to the situation setup sooner, I skip some of the introduction I had planned.

" Yes, we had a story where the dolls learned that boys can do any job they really like. Good remembering, Ursula. And another thing I remember about Rajit is that there are two moms in his family—Momma Betty and Momma Asha. And do you remember who is new in his family?"

   " His baby sister!" [General chorus.]

" That's right! She just came from India last month. Rajit likes to play with her. And here's Lucia too. She and Rajit are in the same room at school, you know. Lucia lives with her grandma. She is four years old."

   " I remember your birthday. I sang 'Happy Birthday' to you, Lucia."

Step Two— ▶
Situation Setup. This is the lead-in to the story. I prepare the children for a difficult situation and encourage them to see themselves as good thinkers who will be able to help their "friends."

" Lucia did come to the circle on her birthday. That was fun for her when you sang to her. Well, today she and Rajit have come to tell you about something that happened that wasn't at all fun. Will you listen to their story and help them think about it?"

   " Yes!"
   ": We can help you."

"Terrific! This happened on Monday after center time. It was time to clean up for lunch, so Rajit went to the blue table and started squishing the colored dough and putting it back in the container. Then Lucia came back from the bathroom and screamed, "You wrecked my elephant!" And she pushed Rajit so hard he fell down!

◄ This is the story line. I was careful not to tell how either doll was feeling, leaving this for the children to think about. I also took this opportunity to portray a boy feeling helpful and a girl feeling angry. This kind of modeling, which is just incidental to this story, can give girls and boys permission to break away from gender stereotypes.

"How do you think Rajit felt when that happened?"

"Sad."
"He cried."
"Rajit was mad."
"That scared him when she pushed."

◄ Step Three—Identifying Feelings. These children have practiced identifying feelings in previous stories. This is now an easy task for most of them.

"Rajit would have been sad or mad, all right. It would be scary to get pushed down like that, wouldn't it, Tracy? Good thinking."

◄ I reflect the children's answers back so the whole group hears what was said and each child's contribution is acknowledged. I give extra attention to Tracy's idea since she is a quiet child who rarely speaks up. I marked her on my plan sheet as one to keep an eye on because I had seen her get pushed around by another child when she hurt them by accident.

"How about Lucia? How was Lucia feeling?"

"She was mad at Rajit."
"Lucia wanted her elfanant back."
"She was sad it got squished."
"Lucia pushed."

"Lucia was mad because she wanted her elephant back. But it was already squished, and that made her sad."

◄ With this question I move the group on to consideration of the other doll's feelings. Then I repeat the ideas to the group.

Telling Stories for Different Age Groups   **173**

Step Four—Discussion ▶
and Problem Solving.
Since my main goal is to
work on an understanding
of the word accident, I ask
a question that will lead us
to that issue.

"Why did Rajit squish her elephant? Was he trying to make her mad and sad?

The children are quite ▶
earnest about Rajit's inno-
cence! One child has the
word I am looking for. If
none of them had come up
with it, I would have contributed it to the discussion.

"No! He didn't mean it."
"He was cleanin' up."
"He had to squish it."
"It was a accident."

I define the term I want ▶
them to understand and
relate it to the story line.

"An accident! That's what happened, all right. Rajit was just trying to clean up.
He didn't know Lucia wanted the elephant. That's called an accident. When you
hurt somebody or something by mistake. Did Lucia know it was an accident?"

Some children will not ▶
understand everything the
first time. I use the word or
get the children to say it
many times. I let the "yes?"
go by without comment,
but I stay aware of this child
as I continue to explain
the story.

"Yes?"
"No. She was in the bathroom."
"She pushed fast."

I tie the feelings in the ▶
story to the child's actions
to remind them that what
we feel affects what we do.
Then I give them a chance
to show off what they have
learned in earlier stories
about how to handle anger.

"She did push fast, didn't she? Before she could find out it was an accident.
Remember how she was feeling then?"

"Mad. Real mad."

"Yep. She was furious! Can you help Lucia so she'll know a good thing to do
the next time she feels that mad?

"Back up!"
"Back up 1-2-3!"
"I know! Take a big breath!"
"Or shake all over."
"I can growl like a doggie."
"I can say, 'Mad, mad, mad!'"

"Wow! You all know LOTS of good things to do when you are mad. Backing up is a good idea. It gives you room to let your mad out without hurting someone. Lucia wishes she had thought of that. Then what could she do to work things out with Rajit?"

> "Talk to him."
> "Ask Rajit, 'Why did you do that?'"
> "Where's my elephant?"

"It sounds like she needed to do some talking with Rajit. How could Rajit explain what happened to Lucia, to tell her he squished her elephant by accident?"

> "He could say sorry."
> "He didn't know."

"That's right. He hurt her, but he didn't mean to. What is that called?"

> "Accident!"

"Yes! Rajit could tell Lucia, 'It was an accident. I didn't know you wanted that elephant.' Rajit and Lucia think these are great ideas! 'It was an accident'— Can everybody say this?"

> "It was an accident." [All the children try saying the phrase.]

"Let's try those ideas and see how they work. Who will pretend to be Lucia? Okay, Linh, you be Lucia. Who will pretend to be Rajit? Michelle. Great! Michelle, you pretend to put away the colored dough at the table here. Linh, start at the bathroom and come see what Michelle is doing."

"You are going to be very mad in a minute, Linh. What are you going to do?"

> "Back up and say, 'Mad, mad, mad!'"

◀ Now that we have reviewed how to handle anger, I move the discussion on to problem solving.

◀ The children are extremely pleased with themselves to know this answer. I am extremely pleased too!

◀ I model the exact words the children can use in these situations. For young children, having a patterned response memorized can help them know how to respond quickly during a real situation.

◀ I set up a role-play situation. I choose Linh to play Lucia because he has a quick temper and frequently reacts with anger to small accidents. I want him to get this lesson into his whole being by going through the motions physically.

◀ I review what he is supposed to say so I am sure he will practice doing the correct thing.

"Okay. You're ready. Go to the table." *[Linh goes to the table, then backs up.]*

"One, two, three. Mad, mad, mad."

"Michelle, what would you ask Linh?"

"What's wrong?"
"You wrecked my elephant and I am very mad at you."
"It was a accident. I didn't know."
"Oh."

► Michelle doesn't seem to know what to do. I help her by asking a question rather than stepping in and saying it for her. If she really could not come up with what to say, I would probably whisper it to her so she would still have the opportunity to be the one to say it out loud.

"Hey! That was terrific! Let's give them a round of applause!"

► I quickly cue the group to give the two actors some encouragement. Role-plays of two to four exchanges are the most effective for kids this age. I might also give several other children a chance to act out the same scene if the story was short enough to allow time for this. Or we could do more role-playing of this and similar scenes at another time.

► I ask some questions to bring out the fact that this new solution to the problem is a happier choice than the one the dolls chose in the story.

"It seems that taking some space and then talking it over worked very well. Did Michelle and Linh end up crying like Rajit and Lucia did?"

"No."

"Is anyone hurt?"

"No."
"Only the elephant."

► I pick up on this statement about the elephant because it concerns the last detail we need to discuss.

"What about the elephant? Rajit still feels bad about that. What could Lucia to do help him feel better?"

"Give him a present."
"Say sorry."
"Make an elephant for him."
"Or help fix it."

"Well, you are all so smart. And you know what? That's just what they did. After Rajit got up and they both cried a bit, *then* they remembered to talk about it. Rajit asked, 'Why did you push me?' And *then* Lucia told him, 'You squished my elephant.' And she asked, 'Why did you do that?'"

"That was my idea! I thought of that, Lucia!"

◀ Step Five—Resolution. *I move the conversation back to what Lucia and Rajit did in the story. I do not have Lucia say she is sorry because a real child would probably not feel sorry at this point in the story. We must be careful to use "I'm sorry" only when the meaning of the statement is true. I use the children's ideas to form the specific sentences the dolls say to one another.*

"Yes, you did, Linh. Thank you for helping them think of the right thing to do. And you know what Rajit said to Lucia when she asked him why he squished her elephant?"

"Accident!"
"It was an accident."

"Exactly. He told her, 'It was an accident.' He explained he was just cleaning up. Then Lucia understood what happened, and she knew Rajit did not mean to hurt her. She said she was sorry that she pushed him down. She really did wish she hadn't pushed. Then Rajit got the squished elephant back out of the container and together they tried to fix it. Lucia says next time she will remember not to push. And Rajit will remember to tell somebody it was an accident if he hurts them by mistake. Thanks for helping them learn that!"

◀ *I notice Linh's contribution, making sure he gets a good feeling from helping someone and knowing the right thing to do. Then I create one last chance to practice the key phrase of this story.*

Kids Like Us Five-Step Planning Sheet

Main goals: recognize size bias and reject it; undo incorrect belief (such as that it's okay to make fat jokes)
empathy, stand up against bias for yourself and others
respect—right of all to live a full life without harassment

Children who may need support: Aggie—thinks of herself as being fat

Doll(s) to use: Elizabeth

1. Introduction:
basic facts about the doll (reminders)

- six years old
- loves tag, soccer, wild horse
- loves computer, insects

facts to prepare for this story
- loves dancing

2. Situation Setup (keep it short!)
Elizabeth got her mom to sign her up for a dance class so she could learn more. But then one of the kids at the class said to her, "Look! An elephant at dance class. Watch out! It's gonna be an earthquake!" And some of the other kids laughed and started falling around yelling, "Help! Elephant! Earthquake!" Now Elizabeth never dances anymore. In fact, she has been sitting on a bench and reading a book instead of running and playing tag like she did before.

3. Identify Feelings (ask, don't tell!)
Note a few feelings appropriate to the story; circle new vocabulary you will present.
embarrassed, hurt, lonely, <u>depressed</u>, put down, mad, guilty

4. Discussion/Problem Solving (ask questions to make them think)
List questions you can ask to help children think about each important issue.
- Why does Elizabeth feel embarrassed? —Did she do something wrong? (No, reinforce this.)
- Would you feel this way if it happened to you?
- Why do you think a kid said that? (jokes)
- Was Elizabeth treated with respect?
- Is it all right to make someone feel bad about their size?
- What would you do if you were there? What if all laughed?
- What would you tell Elizabeth now? Should she stop dancing?

5. Resolution (use children's ideas)
List important elements of story you will need to be sure to conclude.
Change Elizabeth's mind about dancing because...She will have to be strong to not believe...

Elizabeth Loves to Dance:
A Story for Six to Eight Year Olds

I like to tell this story each year when my older group has some experience with recognizing bias and the motives that cause it. This story is important because it involves a common type of harassment, and it makes the children aware of the hurt harassment causes and the consequences it can have in a person's life.

"Here's Elizabeth. She hasn't been here to see you in a while. Say hi and pass her around the circle. She's happy to see all of you."

"Hi, Elizabeth."
"Hi, Elizabeth. Did your cocoon hatch?"

◄ The cocoon is a detail from an earlier story I told about Elizabeth.

"Oh, Bethany remembers that Elizabeth has an insect collection. Last time we talked with her she was waiting for a cocoon to hatch. Guess what?"

"What?"

"It did! A beautiful green moth came out!"

"Wow!"

"So, you all remember Elizabeth. You know she loves to play tag and computers. Who knows her favorite game?"

"Soccer!"

◄ Step One—Introduction. I hadn't planned to talk about the cocoon, but since it has come up I work it into the introduction.

◄ The children are so familiar with Elizabeth that I do not tell some of the basic identity details that I have included in previous introductions. Instead, I focus on what Elizabeth likes to play, which will lead us to the subject of today's story.

"That's right. She loves to play goalie. Remember the wild horses club she made? Remember what fun she had galloping across the playground with the others?"

"Yeah. And she told everybody they could be in it."

◄ In earlier stories I have been sure to break the stereotype that fat children are lazy, so I have already shown Elizabeth to be an active and happy child. These facts about her have been told as details in other stories and in other introductions.

Elizabeth's enjoyment ▶
of dancing is a detail I need
to establish so I can use it
during the story. To help the
children relate to it, I show
Elizabeth enjoying a com-
mon activity at our school.

"Uh huh, and they all had so much fun. You know, there's something else Elizabeth just loves to do. She likes to dance. When she hears music she just feels like she has to move. Sometimes at school they put on music and dance any way they want."

Children love to ▶
recognize themselves in
stories. It also puts them
in the position to empa-
thize with the character in
the story, which is one of
my goals.

"Just like us!"
"We do that!"
"I like to dance, too, Elizabeth!"

Step Two— ▶
Situation Setup.

"Elizabeth really loves to dance, just like Hexane does. Well, dancing is what Elizabeth wants to talk to you about. You see, Elizabeth got her mom to sign her up for a dance class so she could learn more about it and because she thought it would be really fun.

I leave a bit of silence ▶
here to let the impact of
this settle in. If anyone
laughs, I will appear to
ignore it but will take note
of who found this funny
and who felt the need for
nervous laughter. Some
might also laugh after others do. This tells me something about each student's
feelings about this subject.

"But then, when she walked in, one of the kids in the class laughed and said, 'Look! an elephant at dance class. Watch out! It's gonna be an earthquake!'

By this time, anyone ▶
who was laughing has
stopped and is contem-
plating this.

"And some of the other kids in the class thought this was a funny joke. They started falling over laughing and yelling, 'Help! Elephant! It's an earthquake!' After that, Elizabeth didn't enjoy the class at all. [Pause.] Elizabeth doesn't dance anymore. In fact, since this happened she has been sitting on a bench watching everyone at recess instead of running and playing with the other kids like she did before.

Step Three— ▶
Identifying Feelings.

"How do you think Elizabeth is feeling?"

" Sad."

" Oh, her feelings were hurt awful."

" I bet she was embarrassed those kids did that."

" She was hurt. I think she still is."

" Yeah. That would hurt me, inside, you know?"

" In her heart. I bet she felt lonely, too."

" She'd be mad too. I would."

" I'm hearing sad, hurt, embarrassed, lonely, and mad. Wow. What a lot of awful feelings from one joke.

" Did you know making a joke about someone could make them feel so bad?"

" She didn't care. That kid wanted to make Elizabeth feel bad."

" That's like name-calling."

" That's not funny."

" I think people just laugh."

" They don't know."

" It's exactly like name-calling. Good thinking. It does seem the kid who made the joke wanted to hurt Elizabeth, but we don't know why. Sometimes other people just laugh at such things without thinking, just to go along with the group."

" Is it okay to laugh at a joke about someone if other kids are laughing?"

" No."

" It doesn't matter."

" That's not respect."

◄ These children have had a lot of practice at identifying feelings, so this step is short but crucial.

◄ I reflect back to the group what has been said so that everyone hears it and the children's responses are recognized.

◄ Step Four—Discussion. I open the discussion with a question about the effect of jokes on others' feelings.

◄ The last two comments came from the two who laughed when the joke was told. It is good that they are analyzing their actions.

◄ I acknowledge the desire to go along with the group. This is a very important concept. As they get older, being part of a group will become a major motivation for biased behavior. I make a mental note to tell a story about this another day. Right now I add a question to clarify that bias is not okay for any reason.

This is the core of the ▶ *problem. Many people believe that because they think people should not be fat it is all right to make jokes about them. Asking this question leads the children to separate their feelings about how someone "ought to be" from how they deserve to be treated.*

By openly ▶ acknowledging the fact the Elizabeth is large and modeling my comfort with this, I take the shame out of it. Then I ask the children to put themselves in Elizabeth's place. This is active practice in empathy.

I show the children how ▶ good it feels to have someone understand your feelings. I also show how bias can affect someone for a long time.

I ignore the use of the ▶ word fat for the moment so I don't directly criticize this child, but I keep it in the back of my mind to weave it into the resolution. I reinforce that people of all sizes make good friends.

The kids are glad to ▶ acknowledge their friendship with Elizabeth.

" So these kids did the wrong thing when they told the joke about Elizabeth and then laughed. Why was Elizabeth embarrassed? Did she do something wrong?"

" She's big."
" They called her elephant because she's big."
" She ate too much."

" Elizabeth *is* much bigger than some of the other kids. Her parents are big people too. That's why Elizabeth is big—not because of what she ate. Her size is just a part of who she is. If you were bigger than some other kids, like Elizabeth, would it be okay for other kids to make fun of you?"

" No!"
" Name-calling hurts."
" It's not funny at all."
" Ohhh, I wouldn't like that."
" That's not respect."
" I'd tell them to stop it."

" Oh, she is sooo glad to hear you say that, because what those kids did really made her feel bad about herself. She *believed* that joke."

" Why did that kid make a joke about Elizabeth's size?"

" Maybe she thought it was funny."
" She thought the kids would laugh."
" I don't think it was funny."
" It wasn't funny to Elizabeth."
" I'm sorry, Elizabeth."
" Yea. That was wrong, Elizabeth. They shouldn't make fun of you 'cause you're fat."

" We know she's a wonderful person! Size is not what tells you who will be a good friend. Sometimes friends are small. Sometimes they are big. Remember how Elizabeth invited everyone into her wild horse club and then made up grand adventures for them? Would YOU like to be Elizabeth's friend?"

" Yeah!"
" Yes, I'd like to be her friend."
" Be my friend, Elizabeth."

"What do you think *you* would do if you were there in that dance class? Would you laugh at that joke?"

"*NO!*"

"*I'd never laugh.*"

"*I'd tell them stop saying that.*"

"*I'd say that's not respect.*"

"*I'd tell them name-calling hurts.*"

"Wow. We have some strong people in here. You have to be strong to stand up for someone like that. Raise your hand if you are really strong—strong enough to stand up against this size bias. Look at that! Everybody! That is so terrific.

"What would you do to support Elizabeth?"

"*I'd hold her hand.*"

"*Tell her, 'Don't listen to them.'*"

"*I'd call them all stupid heads.*"

"*I'd tell Elizabeth she can too dance.*"

"*I'd tell her to come over and dance with me.*"

"Those are lots of good ideas. You could hold her hand or have her come dance with you. That would feel friendly, so she would not feel so lonely. You could tell Elizabeth she can dance if she wants to. You'd say, 'Don't listen to them. People of all sizes love to dance and no one should stop you.' How about calling them dummies or something?"

"*No, that's name calling too.*"

"Right. Then *you* would have done something hurtful too."

"*Oh, yeah.*"

◀ *Now we move on to the goal of learning to stand up against bias. First we look at it from the perspective of a person who is observing the action take place.*

◀ *I use the word* strong *here to emphasize the importance of moral strength, as opposed to the physical strength that our violence-prone society tends to reinforce.*

◀ *This is practice in problem solving how to be a friend to someone who is experiencing bias. When children go through this exercise in a doll story, dramatic changes occur in the way they treat each other in real life.*

◀ *I reflect back their ideas. Then, in a slightly different form, I bring up one suggestion that I want to discuss.*

◀ *This is often a difficult concept. Many children have internalized the "good guy/bad guy" philosophy which says, "If someone does something wrong, she is the 'bad guy.' The 'good guy' can then do anything to the 'bad guy,' including the thing the 'bad guy' just did wrong." When one child realizes the connection, I use this opportunity to remind the children that all bias hurts, no matter what the motivation.*

I ask a question to ▶
help the children relate
Elizabeth's feelings and the
bias she has experienced
with her current behavior.

"Well, Elizabeth is glad to hear all this. She's been pretty depressed since this happened. You know, I told you she has been staying by herself at recess, reading a book. Why do you think she is doing that instead of running and playing all her favorite games? How do you think she is feeling?"

"Maybe she thinks she shouldn't go."
"She's really down."
"I think she's afraid of jokes now."
"Yeah. I would be afraid."
"Sad."
"She is afraid. I would be."

I acknowledge how ▶
frightening bias can be.
I also acknowledge the reality that Elizabeth, and many
other children, live in a society where they will con-
tinue to experience bias.
Learning how to stand up
against this bias for yourself
is the goal of this section of
the story. This is for all the
children because, at some
time or another, they will all
have to deal with these
issues themselves.

"I would be afraid too. And pretty down. It's sad to not feel free to do things. People do make biased jokes, though. Do you think Elizabeth should let those jokes stop her from doing what she likes to do? Tell Elizabeth what you think."

"Elizabeth, you can do what you want."
"Elizabeth, I will be your friend. I will never call you names."
"Those jokes are wrong. Don't be afraid."
"Just go play. If you like to run, you should."
"Find friends to play with."
"Yeah. You have to ignore those other kids."
"I agree with what Emma said. Friends don't do bias."

Step Five—Resolution. ▶
I incorporate some of the
children's ideas into
Elizabeth's plans so the kids
can see that they helped
her and that they can find
good solutions to problems.
This also reinforces their
belief that it is right to
stand up against bias.

"Elizabeth says thank you for all your good ideas and support. She has decided to run and play no matter what anyone says, like Kelsey said. And she has good friends like Julio and Ianthe who won't tease her about her size. She'll play with them."

I add this detail, which ▶
I saved from a comment
a child made earlier in
the story.

"And she wants to tell you one more thing. Elizabeth doesn't like to be called *fat* because people make it such a mean word. Will you all remember not to call her that?"

"Okay." [General nodding of heads.]

"You know, Elizabeth is going to have to be strong to keep herself from believing the biased things people say about her. It sure helps to have some friends you can count on. She feels safe and respected here in this classroom.

"And you have really changed her mind about dancing. She *does* love dancing, and she's not letting some laughing kids stop her. What do you think about that?"

"Yeah!" *[Cheers—I hold Elizabeth up in the air and make her jump up and down.]*

"And she's going to run across the playground playing tag and wild horses. If somebody laughs, she is going to ignore them. What do you think about that?"

"Yeah!"

"In fact, Elizabeth feels like dancing right now. Who will dance with Elizabeth?"

[We take turns holding Elizabeth as we dance to some rock and roll.]

◄ *I use some of the important anti-bias language we have learned recently while I reinforce once again that the children can make a difference in someone's life by their words and actions.*

◄ *I dance Elizabeth around a bit to make this exciting.*

◄ *In the beginning of this story, we saw a group working together to make someone feel bad. Here we have a celebration because a group can also work together to support someone—and it feels so good!*

◄ *We celebrate Elizabeth's freedom to dance. This was not planned—it just felt right.*

CHAPTER 10

Planning and Researching Kids Like Us Doll Stories

Kids *Like Us* doll stories can be told with minimal planning. When you are beginning to tell stories, you will spend more time and write down more of what you will say than you will when you have been telling stories for a few months. Even when you are an old hand at this, it's a good idea to take some time to think through the important details of each of the five steps before you tell a story.

● Two planning sheets—one for first introduction stories and one for basic five-step stories—can help you think through a story and organize your thoughts. You can put the sheet beside you as you tell the story and refer to it as needed. When children have asked me about the sheet, I tell them I have taken some notes about what the doll has told me so I will remember how to tell the story correctly. Sometimes I say, "Now, let's see...what did Ianthe tell me about that?" while looking at my planning sheet.

First Introduction Planning Sheet

Kids Like Us **First Introduction Planning Sheet**

Doll(s) to be introduced:

Children who may need support:

1. Greeting the children

2. Basic facts

Name:
Age:
Gender:
Family structure:

3. Important characteristics to be introduced (one or two most important – plan the details)
languages, race, religion, special abilities, disabilities, parent's jobs, family history, home, some detail of the family's culture, issues central to the child's personality

4. Favorite activities and foods (choose one or two to tell a bit about)

5. Other dolls that are close friends (if any – plan what they do together)

This sheet will help you consider which details to bring into your first introduction of any doll. First you'll choose which doll you would like to introduce. Then think about this doll's personal characteristics. If the doll shares any special issues or physical disabilities with one of the children, put that child's name in the "children who may need support" category. Children are usually excited and happy to see their lives reflected in the doll stories. But if a child does not feel good about herself, she may initially reject the doll for this very reason. Also, other children may initially have a negative reaction to the doll, which may be difficult for the child who is being mirrored. You may want to discreetly arrange for this child to sit next to you for a touch of reassurance if needed. Having another adult available to join any child who needs reassurance is another way to be sure that support is available.

The "greeting the children" space is a reminder to connect the children to the doll in some way before beginning to tell about her. I usually send the doll around to let each child say hello and give the doll a hug if they would like. When you are telling your first stories, you may want to write down how you will do this and even what you will say as you do it.

The "basic facts" are the details you will tell in every first introduction story, and often in reminder introductions as well. If you have created a Biography Page for the doll, you will be able to take these facts right off of it. Name, age, gender, and family structure should be included here.

"Important characteristics to be introduced" include many different possibilities. Any of the details that are key to the doll you are introducing should be introduced immediately. Julio's first introduction, for instance, included the fact that he had just recently moved to our town from Guatemala and knew very little English. The children could not understand what was going on in Julio's life without knowing this, so I made it part of his first introduction. Include any physical conditions that the children are likely to notice and ask about as well.

You may need to do some research before introducing the doll. If you are planning a doll who is from a culture or has a physical condition you are unfamiliar with, do some research about it before introducing the doll. Then choose a couple of details to include in the doll's first introduction. Only tell the children the most important facts about a doll in the first introduction. Leave the rest to unfold over time as you use your dolls in other stories.

In the "favorite activities and foods" category you will add the fun details that give the children a sense of the doll's personality. Plan to tell one or two details from this section. You may want to make some support networks for the dolls, identifying one as a special friend of another or a group of three or four that like to play a specific game together. Plan this in the "other dolls that are close friends" category.

Now you are ready to tell a first introduction! The following is an example of planning for a first introduction story for Rachel.

Kids Like Us First Introduction Planning Sheet

Doll(s) to be introduced: Rachel

Children who may need support: Hilary (only Jewish child in class)

1. **Greeting the children** send her around for a hug; remind not to pull hair (fragile)

2. **Basic facts**

Name: Rachel Kahn
Age: 5
Gender: girl
Family structure: single mom, very close to Bubbe and Zaide

3. **Important characteristics to be introduced** (one or two most important – plan the details)
languages, race, religion, special abilities, disabilities, parent's job, family history, home, some detail of the family's culture, issues central to the child's personality
- just moved: little house—to be close to Bubbe and Zaide—visits them Thurs. after school
- Jewish: go to temple on Sabbath (Saturday)—a special day for her family

4. **Favorite activities and foods** (choose one or two to tell a bit about)
- likes robots—wants to be a robot scientist
- just learned to blow bubbles with gum—very proud
- loves building with big blocks—made a zoo

5. **Other dolls that are close friends** (if any – plan what they do together)

Here is the first introduction story that I told using the information from this planning sheet.

"Here's a doll that has come to meet all of you! Her name is Rachel, and she'd like to come round to say hello to each of you. Give her a quick greeting and send her on to the next person.

"So, this is Rachel Kahn. She is five years old and she is a girl. She is new to her school because she and her mom just moved here a little bit ago. Rachel lives with her mom in a little house, just the two of them. They moved here because they wanted to live closer to Rachel's Bubbe and Zaide. They are her mom's parents and Rachel loves them very much. Now that they live in the same town, Rachel goes to their house every Thursday after school to visit them. And because Rachel's family is Jewish, they also go to temple together on Shabbos—that's on Saturday. It's a very special day in Rachel's family.

"Rachel's all-time favorite thing is robots. She draws them all the time. She wants to be a robot scientist when she grows up.

"Rachel loves building with the big blocks. She made a whole zoo with them the other day and put the zoo animals in it.

"Rachel told me to be sure to let you all know that she has just learned how to blow bubbles with bubble gum. She is very proud, because it wasn't easy to learn and she didn't give up. Now she's practicing to blow really big ones— with sugarless gum, of course.

"Does anyone want to ask Rachel anything or tell her something about yourself?"

Main goals:

Children who may need support:

Doll(s) to use:

1. Introduction:
basic facts about the doll (reminders)   **facts to prepare for this story**

2. Situation Setup (keep it short!)

3. Identify Feelings (ask, don't tell!)
Note a few feelings appropriate to the story; circle new vocabulary you will present.

4. Discussion/Problem Solving (ask questions to make them think)
List questions you can ask to help children think about each important issue.

5. Resolution (use children's ideas)
List important elements of story you will need to be sure to conclude.

Five-Step Planning Sheet

To help you plan your stories, I have created a Five-Step Planning Sheet. This is a tool to help you organize your decisions and plan the story you will tell. Some teachers even keep this sheet beside them as they are telling the story. The Five-Step Planning Sheet has spaces to make notes about what you will say during each of the five steps of a regular *Kids Like Us* doll story.

You have seen examples of completed five-step planning sheets at the beginning of each story in chapter 9. "Main goals" for a basic five-step story should be your first consideration. "Children who may need support" are those children for whom the story might have special significance. *"Doll(s) to use"* is a section to make a note of which doll or dolls you intend to use.

Note two to four basic facts to remind the children of the doll's identity in the "Introduction" section. If you will need to introduce the children to any other aspects of the doll's life before you tell the story, note them under the "facts to prepare for this story" section.

If you are a new *Kids Like Us* storyteller, it is sometimes best to write the whole situation setup on your planning sheet. This will force you to keep it to a few sentences and help you feel confident that you know exactly what you want to say in the main portion of the story.

In the "identify feelings" section, write down the emotion vocabulary words that would be appropriate to describe the emotions of the doll or dolls during the story. If you think there are several words that your students do not know, circle one or two to introduce during this step.

There is no way to plan exactly what will be said during the discussion and problem-solving step. So in this section of the sheet make short notes of each issue you hope to discuss or a question you might ask to get the students thinking about that issue.

Much of the resolution will also come from the students' ideas. You can list the important elements of the story that will need to be concluded. Then, during the story, you can match these elements to some of the children's ideas to form the resolution.

Biography Pages

It is a good idea to create a Biography Page for each of your dolls once they have been introduced to your group. This will make reviewing the details of each doll's life as simple as taking a look at their Biography Pages. It will also give you a place to record the basics of the stories you have told about each doll. This can give you a way of looking back at which dolls you have used frequently and which you have not used that much. It will help you to tell a balanced set of stories about each doll. It will also be a record of all the stories you have told to your group.

Take a look at a Biography Page I assembled about Elizabeth one year. I filled in the top of the page at the beginning of the year from information I planned for Elizabeth's identity. I circled details as I presented them in stories during the year. The rest got filled in over time as I told stories in which she was involved.

_____Elizabeth_____'s Biography Page

Full Name: Elizabeth Ann Henry   **Age:** 6   **Gender:** Girl

Race/Ethnicity:
African American, Native American

Physical Characteristics/Challenges:
Very large child

Family Structure:
mom and dad

Language(s):

Class/Home/Parent Occupations:

Family History/Culture/Religion:
grandparents moved here from Texas;
family food = fried chicken, potato salad;
family sings together at holidays;
celebrates Juneteenth with relatives

Favorite Activities/Foods/Friends:
soccer, tag, Lego blocks, insects,
dance, Julio

Special Behaviors:

Date	Stories Told	New Details
9/17	Introduction—family, soccer, insects, dancing	
9/25	painted with Mickey	
9/28	conflict with Ricky—jump rope	loves jump rope, tag
10/18	didn't do laundry as mom asked	
10/30	makes own dragon costume	many books at home
11/30	called "elephant" at dance class	
12/10	wants to know about Kwanzaa	
2/1	on bus tells Rajit others are whispering abt. him	
	wanted to be friends with Rachel and Melly	
3/25	sat out for talking to Julio during quiet work	
4/3	went to art museum	no TV at her house
6/1	celebrated Juneteenth with family	

If you make one Biography Page for each of your dolls, you can easily refer to them to find out which dolls you have used recently or to find a doll with characteristics appropriate for a story you want to tell. They also provide a way to review what you have said about a specific doll before telling a story about her.

You might also find it helpful to keep the Identity Planning Chart you created when forming your dolls' life histories as an overview of your doll collection.

When to Tell a Story and Which Ones to Tell

Now that you have a method for planning stories and a way to record the stories you have told, you need to decide which stories to tell and when to tell them. There is no magic formula or planning sheet for these decisions since each group has different needs. But a few guidelines can help you form a schedule and sequence of storytelling.

You will begin, of course, with introduction stories. Some teachers like to introduce one doll every day at the beginning of their school year or in the fall when they are likely to have many new children in their group and not too many away on vacation. Some introduce a doll or two each week. The reason to get the children acquainted with some dolls immediately is that you will soon find yourself in need of a doll story about the conflicts the children are having or the classroom skills you need them to learn.

Once several dolls have been introduced, your story sequence will have three branches: more introductions, stories told to meet a specific classroom need, and stories told in sequence to teach social and emotional skills.

More Introductions

You will introduce three or four dolls at first, and then begin to use these dolls in five-step stories. After that you will introduce a new doll every once in a while.

One of the reasons not to introduce all the dolls at one time is that this does not allow your children to get to know the dolls individually and become fond of each one. Introducing several dolls in the beginning allows you to begin telling five-step stories sooner. Especially when beginning with a new group or when getting to know many new children, you will soon have a need for a story about sharing materials or how much exclusion hurts. Once your group has met some dolls, you will not have to wait to tell these stories.

The first dolls you introduce should be ones that share many characteristics with your students. By introducing a few dolls at the beginning you will be able to represent the diversity present in your group and then introduce dolls with characteristics new to your children. For instance, if your group of children includes a child with a prosthesis but not a child with a hearing impairment, you will introduce your doll with a prosthesis as one of the first dolls.

Stories Told to Meet a Specific Classroom Need

Once your students have become familiar with a few of your *Kids Like Us* dolls, you will be free to use them in stories any time you have a need for them.

For example, you may notice that your students push and shove each other at the drinking fountain. Or you may notice one child frequently watching the group from the corner, afraid to join the others. You may see a child is being teased about his freckles. Or you are about to begin a theme study about penguins. Or you are worried about the children rushing out in front of the cars when their parents come to pick them up. Each of these situations can be discussed and taught by designing a *Kids Like Us* doll story.

In fact, once your *Kids Like Us* dolls become a part of your classroom, you will often find yourself thinking, "That could be a doll story." Part of the strength of this method is its flexibility. Another strength is the small amount of preparation required and, therefore, the possibility of using *Kids Like Us* doll stories whenever needed. Many times I have noticed a conflict or bias incident on the playground and presented a doll story to the children on that subject as soon as they returned to the classroom. When you know the dolls and the storytelling method, you will be able to use them in this impromptu way whenever your class would benefit from it.

Each teacher will also have to create a schedule for presenting *Kids Like Us* doll stories. Some teachers tell one every day, as part of their daily routine. Some use them only occasionally, as a special need arises.

Age Groups

A large part of the decision of what stories to tell, when to tell them, and what goals to focus on will rest on what age your children are and how much time you have to devote to developing social and emotional skills.

Two and Three Year Olds

Stories for these children must be kept very short. These children do not need complicated storylines and will not attend to or understand long, drawn-out discussions. They will be very fond of the dolls, though, and happy to see them every day, if you wish to use them that often.

QUESTION #13

Q: *What do I do if my children seem restless during the discussion?*

A: This is a signal that the story has gone on too long. If the group's attention is beginning to wander or several children are needing to move, guide the discussion quickly to the resolution and end the story as quickly as possible.

If this happens often, you may be telling stories that are too involved and that require complicated discussions that are beyond your group's ability. Try simple storylines that involve only one doll with only one problem that lends itself to several simple solutions. Evaluate how the group responds to these simpler stories to determine what they are ready to learn next.

(continued on next page)

Goals best suited to this young age group are to bring up a subject or give information, to learn a classroom skill, to learn to identify and deal with emotions, and to become comfortable with diversity. This is just the right age to turn many stories into active practice of the skill the doll has learned—for example, going directly to the table to share the juice pitcher or stamping feet to "let out some mad." Learning simple emotion vocabulary at this stage can be very helpful to the child and everyone around her because she will be able to express herself with words ("mad, mad, mad!") instead of with a tantrum. And learning from the dolls how much hitting hurts can go a long way toward curbing this common expression of anger.

Helping these young students to become comfortable with diversity is also an important goal. Rather than doing this through stories about bias incidents or stereotypes, it will be more appropriate for these young children to learn by getting to know the dolls themselves. Becoming a friend to a doll in a wheelchair or a doll of a different skin tone will go a long way toward helping them grow up without the discomfort around diversity that so many adults have because they have never had these experiences.

If bias does enter your room through the children's behavior, however, this specific bias may be a good candidate for a doll story, especially if many of your children have already been exposed to the behavior. For instance, if one child has corralled most of the others into excluding another child because of her skin color, all of the children need to understand how much this hurts and learn that everyone needs to feel safe at school. In this case, a doll story in which a doll cries and is feeling lonely because the others are excluding her would be appropriate.

A focused sequence of doll stories for twos and threes, then, will begin with introductions. Then many stories will be told to introduce and reinforce emotion vocabulary words. Once the children have a good emotion vocabulary, stories will help them practice identifying emotions in different situations and focus on skills to help them deal with strong emotions. Pro-social and problem-solving skills can also be introduced through stories toward the later part of the year. And throughout the year, dolls representing identity characteristics new to your children will be introduced to help them remain comfortable with diversity.

The following diagram is a rough guideline of how these skills might be presented to two and three year olds beginning in September and ending in June. You will have to judge how fast to move ahead by how the children are responding to the stories. And regardless of how far you get in this progression of skills, just meeting and getting to know your diverse population of *Kids Like Us* dolls will benefit the kids.

If you have one or two children who have difficulty paying attention no matter what activity you are doing, try to seat them next to you or near a parent volunteer or aide during the stories. Often a hand on a back can be a steadying influence.

When you tell a story in response to an immediate classroom need, you may also feel the students are a little at sea because they have not practiced all the skills that the type of story you are telling is designed to teach. In this case it is very easy to find yourself dragging out each step, trying to coax the children through each one. Remember that your students haven't yet practiced, for example, problem solving, so you will have to take a larger part in the discussion to help them along. It's okay to suggest some feelings yourself if the children are unable to come up with anything close. Your own idea for a solution can be suggested in the form of a question for the children to consider. Remember to get their ideas first, then help them along if they need it.

TWO AND THREE YEAR OLDS				
Sept.	Nov.	Jan.	March	June

Introductions --- Introductions -- Introductions

Theme Studies ---

Emotion Vocab. ---------------------------- Identify & Deal with Emotions ----------- Pro-social Skills &
Problem Solving

Four and Five Year Olds

Children of this age are inquisitive and ready to be social. Their social skills do not always match their eagerness to be a part of everything. Their increased maturity, however, makes them ready to learn skills such as empathy and fairness.

Kids Like Us doll stories will need to remain short for this age group too. Stories with one doll to consider (maybe two in conflict situations) and only one issue to deal with will be the most effective at engaging their attention and reaching a satisfactory conclusion before their interest wanders.

Activities connected to the stories will be a big hit with these children and will serve to cement the information they receive and the understandings they reach during the *Kids Like Us* doll stories. Drawing is becoming an important skill for these children and can be an excellent way for them to communicate what they learned from the stories. Other activities are also recommended, like playing a cooperative "we all win together" game after a story in which the dolls learn to include everyone. (Sources of these games and activities that reinforce the *Kids Like Us* goals are listed in the resources section at the back of the book.)

All the goals in the *Kids Like Us* doll sequence will be appropriate for these children. Like the two and three year olds, they will need quite a bit of practice with new emotion vocabulary and dealing with feelings at the beginning of the year, along with classroom skills. These children will then be ready to work on understanding and beginning to use pro-social and problem-solving skills. It will be important to carry this work over into your everyday life in the classroom, reminding the students of the skills the dolls used and encouraging them to use the skills themselves.

Being introduced to and becoming familiar with dolls representing a diverse set of identities is a good, concrete way to bring diversity to their lives, and it should be continued for several months. These children will also benefit from many stories designed to help them become comfortable with diversity. They will enjoy and remember information discussed during stories about doll's interests and backgrounds. They will enthusiastically join in to tell about their own experiences and knowledge of the subject being discussed. These stories will have a great effect on children of this age.

The vocabulary needed to discuss bias can be presented at any time. Some preschool teachers like to establish safety as a right and expectation in their classrooms at the beginning of the year so they can refer to it when children are having conflicts or acting in a biased way. These stories can be told earlier, to establish the "everyone has a right to be safe here" rule. The stories help the children understand what the rule means and bring their attention to its importance.

Comfort with diversity will begin for these children as they meet and come to know the dolls. It will be good for them, over the span of the year, to meet dolls representing new diversities. Situation setups to help these children develop anti-bias attitudes should be based on issues common to your class. This age group is still quite concrete in their thinking and will best relate to familiar issues. It is the same with stories about learning to stand up against bias. Children this age can easily relate to and discuss ways to stand up for a fair turn at the computer for everyone, for instance. They can begin to analyze books, television shows, and movies for bias and to discuss this with their peers.

The following is a rough guideline for the sequence of skills that can be presented to four and five year olds. Remember that stories designed to meet any of these goals should be told any time there is a direct need in the classroom, regardless of what skills the class is working on.

FOUR AND FIVE YEAR OLDS				
Sept.	Nov.	Jan.	March	June
Introductions -- Introductions -------------------------------				
Theme Studies --				
Emotion Vocab. & Skill ---------------------- Pro-social Skills & ---------------------------- Diversity Issues ----------------				
		Problem Solving		

Six to Eight Year Olds

Children six to eight years old are very verbal and able to discuss quite complex situations. They will be able to understand, learn, and internalize skills that the stories teach with fewer repetitions and fewer practice activities outside of the *Kids Like Us* doll stories. Although many of your children may not have much feelings vocabulary, they will easily pick it up and be ready to use the words in later stories. Once you have established caring and empathy as a norm, your students will eagerly work to solve the dolls' problems and strive to undo the incorrect assumptions and stereotypes they have come to believe.

These children will also have a much more complex social scene than younger children, and they will be influenced and aware of more of the world outside of their own class and homes. This can mean they will be able to bring in more information of their own to discussions about many different subjects, but it also will mean they may have formed more incorrect ideas and biases.

I recommend spending time observing and taking notes on the social scene in your class. It can be an eye-opening experience and can help pinpoint which issues would be most appropriate for doll stories.

All of the goals are important for these children to reach and all are appropriate for them to study. You can start with the goal of introducing words and skills to deal with emotions and progress from there at the rate your group is learning, continually returning to mirror stories, classroom skills, and undoing incorrect information and stereotypes whenever called for in your class. Thus you will develop your own timeline based on how your group progresses.

Finding time to teach these skills to children who are six to eight years old is difficult since there are so many other things they must accomplish. I know I have sometimes become so focused on getting in one more lesson on capital letters or the meaning of addition that I have forgotten to do any lessons on social skills. Although children of this age are the most ready and able to learn these important and often life-saving skills, we are less likely to put a priority on presenting the skills to them. It is unfortunate that the school system seems to think that by the age of five children have learned all the social and emotional skills they need and are ready to spend the rest of their educational time exclusively on academic work.

Social skills and academic skills go hand in hand. Time spent on *Kids Like Us* stories really is worth it. I encourage teachers to fit in a fifteen-minute *Kids Like Us* doll story twice a week right before recess, right after lunch, or anytime you can find a few spare minutes. One thing I have found to be true is that once my students have learned, through a few doll stories, to encourage each other to learn and to help each other celebrate their accomplishments, academic learning takes place at a much faster pace. And children who feel respected and safe in their classrooms can ask questions freely and try their best without fear of criticism or humiliation.

School districts can support this work in many ways. It costs so little for such an immense pay-off. They can make funds and training available for teachers to purchase dolls and learn to use them. School districts can also arrange storytelling partnerships where teachers can discuss the stories they have told and help each other plan the next ones. And they can encourage teachers to find a few minutes in their daily schedule to help children gain the skills they will need to relate effectively and without bias to everyone around them.

When you are beginning to tell *Kids Like Us* doll stories, it's helpful to evaluate how each story went. You can learn a lot by thinking about what you planned, what you actually said, how the kids responded, what happened that you didn't expect, and what didn't happen that you thought would.

Record keeping. Take a few notes about the story on the doll's Biography Page. Writing down the details of what happened in the story you just told will help you review it. This information will also be invaluable when you need to see which stories you have told. Also, if you found yourself adding little details about the dolls, such as loving pistachio ice cream, you can make a note of it on the Biography Page.

Some teachers like to keep a doll story journal, writing down their thoughts about how a story went, how their students reacted, and what they will try to do differently next time. This can also be a way to keep track of any issues that come up during one story that should be handled in another story at a later date. Or use an Evaluation Sheet (see page 213), which takes you through each stage of the story and makes it easy to jot quick notes.

Partnership. One of the best ways to help yourself review your storytelling experiences is to find a storytelling partner. Another teacher who is also a beginning *Kids Like Us* storyteller can be the most helpful and fun partner, although anyone interested in going over your stories with you will be a help. It can be fun

to describe your students' involvement with the dolls. Some of the student's insights and comments are amazing, and having a partner to relate them to makes it easier to remember them. It is also helpful to have someone to discuss where things went wrong.

Videotaping. The most helpful evaluation method is videotaping. Watching other storytellers with their dolls can tell you a lot about how to tell a *Kids Like Us* story. But watching yourself tell a story will give you more information than anything else. Seeing yourself tell the story and also being able to watch the children's responses and notice what you pick up on and what you miss will give you a clear view of the story.

It is very hard to tell the story, attend to all the children, ask questions, and also step back and evaluate what you are and are not doing. By placing a video camera where it can see you and at least some of your children and letting it record the storytelling session will provide the greatest evaluation tool. Then, with no one to distract you, you can sit back and watch the story from this new perspective.

I set up my students in a horseshoe-shaped formation on the carpet, with me in the center of the horseshoe and the camera at the opening. This allows the camera to see me and also catch most of the children's faces. Then I pretend the camera is not there and tell the story I have prepared.

Researching Identity
and Story Information

Many teachers feel at a loss when trying to give children authentic experiences with such features as a variety of cultures, languages, and physical conditions. Many teachers have not had these experiences themselves—children with physical challenges were not in our classrooms or our communities were segregated from communities that were different from our own. How, then, are we to do things better for this generation? How do we educate ourselves enough to be sure not to pass this deficit on to the children we are raising now?

It will take some work. *Kids Like Us* doll stories are an easy medium to help you present the world's diversity to your students, but you will have to do some research to learn the information you will present through this medium.

This research begins when you create the dolls' identities. You will need to know some things about the dolls you are planning to portray. If you find yourself thinking that this is a daunting task, don't panic. There are ways to learn what you need to know.

Take issues one at a time. When I began to tell *Kids Like Us* doll stories, I created a couple of dolls from cultures I knew about and researched one other that was present in my classroom. Then, over the next few months, I reached out to different sources of information and learned about cultures that were unfamiliar to me.

I did the same with other diversities. I represented a child who was Deaf in my collection from the start because I had worked with Deaf children and felt confident in creating this doll's identity and representing the issues that would be important to him. Eight months later I persuaded a parent to create a doll-sized wheelchair, interviewed someone at Easter Seals, borrowed a kid-sized wheelchair, and introduced Mickey who has cerebral palsy and mostly uses a wheelchair. He has been a part of my doll collection ever since. The time I spent on research about him is still paying off for every child who enters my program.

There are many other possible sources of information. Once you put your feelers out, you will find help in interesting places. Here are some sources I have found useful. More information on many of these sources can be found in the resources section of this book.

- parents of students
- observation of children and their families
- children's magazines that contain cultural information
- children's books
- children's videos

- university foreign student council
- university student unions for African American, Hispanic, Asian, Arabic, and Jewish students
- university departments: Hispanic Studies, Women's Studies, and so on
- churches, temples, mosques, and other religious centers
- Easter Seals Society
- special education teachers and specialists
- books for teachers
- Native American reservation information centers and presses
- Natives' programs; public school districts
- Women's History Project
- racism awareness workshops
- Gallaudet University
- Braille Institute
- community cultural centers
- peace and social change organizations
- doctors
- the public library
- Independent Living Centers (advocacy organizations for people with disabilities—one in every state)

These are just a few of the places you will be able to get information. If you become tuned in to the world of people around you, sources will appear everywhere you go. For example, I learned about Japanese taiko drumming from the school's architect. While waiting for my daughter at basketball practice, I had a conversation with a parent who grew up in Alaska. A baby-sitter told me about being Baha'i. A friend's visiting mother was willing to be recorded speaking and singing in the three languages of her childhood—Russian, Polish, and Yiddish. Because I am open to this information and trying to learn about everyone, I notice the opportunities when they come my way.

Two things to remember: First, when you have a chance to ask questions, make sure you ask about young children's issues (food, play, language, family customs), since these are what you will be representing with your *Kids Like Us* dolls. Second, although people are often happy to talk about themselves and appreciate someone who is open to learning about their experience, not everyone feels this way. Some people get tired of the burden of educating everyone about their lives. When asking people to give you information, you must be sensitive to their willingness to educate you by asking respectfully, "Would you be willing to tell me more about that? I would really like to learn about it." And always be able to take no for an answer.

When interviewing the parents of a child in your class, it helps to present your quest for information like this:

> "I would like to create a doll in my collection that represents a child from your culture (or a child that has your child's physical challenge). We will get to know this doll and at the same time get to know about this culture (or physical challenge). I want to represent this child's life as accurately as possible. Would you be willing to help me with this? I will not make the doll be exactly like your child or your family, of course, but information about your family will help me choose accurate characteristics for the doll and her family."

Remember that no one person represents an entire culture, and one family's experience with a medical condition will not mirror another's. If you have two or three families to use as information sources, by all means, talk to them! And remember not to get stuck in stereotypes. This is one reason it is a good idea to have two or more dolls representing a single culture—to show the diversity present within every supposedly homogeneous group. When a child asks a question about one of the dolls and you don't know the answer, stay calm. Try to think of it as a learning opportunity. Then you can answer with something like this:

> "That's a good question! I'm not sure why Jewish people wear a little cap sometimes. I'll have to ask somebody about that. When I find out, I'll let you know. Okay?"

> "Fiona would like to learn how to spell words to Henry in finger spelling. I think that's a great idea! But I don't know how to do finger spelling. How do you think we could find that out?"

> "Hmmm. I'm not sure about that. Let me think about what my opinion on that is and then we'll talk about it again. Is that all right?"

When you respond this way, you *must* be sure that you do get back to the topic. The children will understand and will see that learning is a lifelong process. This is good modeling.

It is best not to rely on this response too often, of course. Do your research before discussing a topic with your students. They will be learning a lot from your *Kids Like Us* dolls. It is only fitting that you learn from them as well!

Appendix 1: Sample Forms

Names	Race/Ethnicity	Physical Appearance/ Other Characteristics	Favorite Activities and Foods	Individual Behaviors

My Class

New

	Family Structure	Economic Class/Home/ Parent Occupation	Recent Family History	Family Culture/ Language	Religion
My Class					
New					

Kids Like Us Identity Planning Chart

Name	G / B	Age	Physical			Family			Behaviors/ Activities/Food
			Race/ Ethnicity	Physical Appearance	Other Characteristics	Family Structure	Class/Home Parent Occupation	History, Religion Culture, Language	

Kids Like Us First Introduction Planning Sheet

Doll(s) to be introduced:

Children who may need support:

1. Greeting the children

2. Basic facts

Name:
Age:
Gender:
Family structure:

3. Important characteristics to be introduced (one or two most important—plan the details)
languages, race, religion, special abilities, disabilities, parent's jobs, family history, home, some detail of the family's culture, issues central to the child's personality

4. Favorite activities and foods (choose one or two to tell a bit about)

5. Other dolls that are close friends (if any—plan what they do together)

Main goals:

Children who may need support:

Doll(s) to use:

1. Introduction:
basic facts about the doll (reminders)   **facts to prepare for this story**

2. Situation Setup (keep it short!)

3. Identify Feelings (ask, don't tell!)
Note a few feelings appropriate to the story; circle new vocabulary you will present.

4. Discussion/Problem Solving (ask questions to make them think)
List questions you can ask to help children think about each important issue.

5. Resolution (use children's ideas)
List important elements of story you will need to be sure to conclude.

_____'s Biography Page

Full Name: **Age:**   **Gender:**

Race/Ethnicity: **Physical Characteristics/Challenges:**

Family Structure: **Language(s):**

Class/Home/Parent Occupations: **Family History/Culture/Religion:**

Favorite Activities/Foods/Friends: **Special Behaviors:**

Date	Stories Told	New Details

_____'s Biography Page (continued)

Date	Stories Told	New Details

Main goals of story: **Date:**

Story line: **Doll(s) used:**

Five Steps: Write down some quick notes on how each step went. Use questions to help you.

1. **Introduction:** (Did the greeting get the kids' attention? Did a child have trouble passing the doll? Did the details interest the kids? Did it lead into the story well? Did any details distract?)

2. **Situation Setup:** (Was it planned well? Did I tell it easily? Was it simple enough? Was the story a good one for meeting the goal(s)? Did the children understand what happened?)

3. **Feelings:** (Did I remember to ask? Were the kids responsive? What words did they use? What words did I introduce? Did any express inappropriate emotions/strong reactions? Did I reflect the responses?)

4. **Discussion/Problem Solving:** (Make a short outline of the points the discussion centered on. The discussion did/did not help meet the goals(s). Why? Any surprises? What got the discussion off track? How did I handle it? Any child not understand? Any personal sharing? Was it too long/just right?)

5. **Resolution:** (Did I wrap up all the elements? Was it realistic? Did I use children's ideas?)

What the kids learned: (list skills practiced)

Vocabulary/skills to reinforce in class:

Other doll stories needed/follow-up activities:

Information I need to gather:

This step went well: _____ **because** _____
_____

This step didn't go well: _____ **because** _____
_____

This story was good for the children because: _____
_____

The children had a lot to say about this: _____
_____

The children didn't know about this: _____
_____

After the story I feel: _____ **because** _____
_____

How my doll stories are improving: _____
_____

I will make these changes next time: _____
_____

I will be sure to do these things again: _____
_____

Appendix 2: Sample Features for Kids Like Us Dolls

Sample Features

These sketches show a variety of features that can be used to paint dolls' faces. Eyes, noses, and mouths come in all shapes and sizes! The sketches can be reduced or enlarged, copied freehand, or transferred directly to a doll's face, using sewing carbon paper. Many thanks to Do Mi Stauber for drawing these sample doll features.

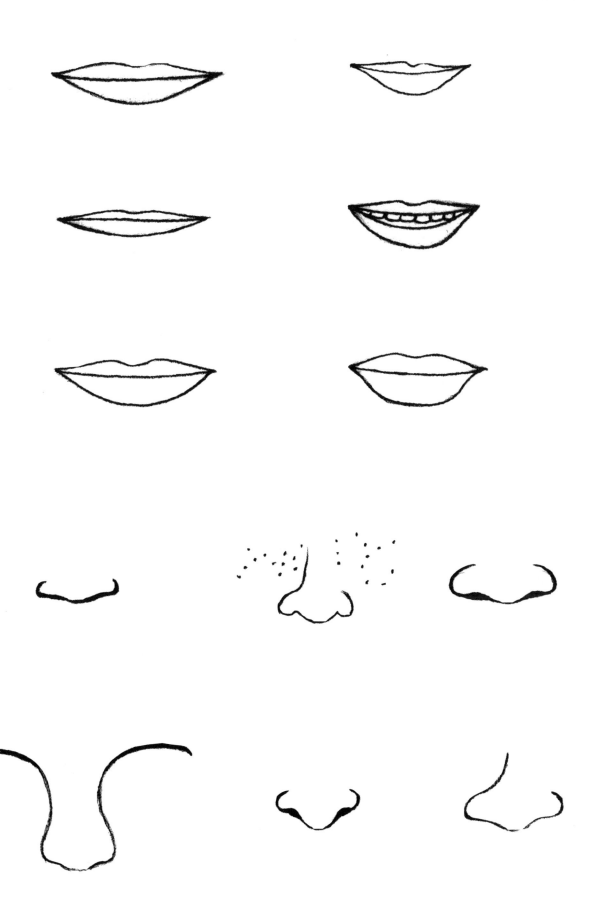

Resources

Dolls and Doll-Making Supplies

People of Every Stripe! P.O. Box 12505, Portland, OR 97212 (800-282-0612).

Makes high-quality cloth dolls with a huge range of accurate racial and ethnic features, hair, and skin colors. Includes dolls with physical disabilities.

Chapel Hill Training Outreach Project, 800 Eastowne Drive, Suite 105, Chapel Hill, NC 27514 (800-473-1727, www.chtop.com).

Activities to help young children understand and accept individual physical differences. Includes a training manual and pattern for cloth dolls. Their New Friends dolls each have a different physical disability.

Environments, Inc., P.O. Box 1348, Beaufort, SC 29901 (843-846-8155).

Early childhood catalog that includes the Earthchild family of dolls, which are 20-inch cotton dolls with painted faces and hair.

The Doll Book: Soft Dolls and Creative Free Play, Karin Neuschutz (Burdett, NY: Larson, 1982).

Good information on making doll hair as well as other construction techniques.

Magic Cabin Dolls, 1950 Waldorf NW, Grand Rapids, MI 49550-7000 (888-623-6557).

Excellent source of doll-making supplies, including material, hair yarn, and patterns.

Lakeshore Learning Materials, P.O. Box 6261, 2695 E. Dominguez Street, Carson, CA 90749 (800-421-5354).

This catalog has many high-quality multicultural and disability-aware materials, including posters, food, art materials, puzzles, puppets, and plastic dolls. They sell the best quality skin-colored paints.

General Curriculum

Anti-Bias Curriculum: Tools for Empowering Young Children, Louise Derman-Sparks and the ABC Task Force (Washington DC: National Association for the Education of Young Children, 1989).

An essential resource and an excellent introduction to anti-bias curriculum. Everyone should read this book.

Beyond Heroes and Holidays: A Practical Guide to K-12 Anti-Racist, Multicultural Education and Staff Development, Lee Menkart and Okazawa-Rey (Washington, DC: Teaching for Change).

This book is available from Teaching for Change, P.O. Box 73038, Washington, DC 20056 (202-238-2379).

Big As Life: The Everyday Inclusive Curriculum, Stacey York (St. Paul, MN: Redleaf, 1998).

An integrated curriculum that includes anti-bias attitudes and learning throughout the program.

Celebrate! An Anti-Bias Guide to Enjoying Holidays in Early Childhood Programs, Julie Bisson (St. Paul, MN: Redleaf, 1997).

An excellent book for teachers in the process of rethinking the role of holidays in their curriculum.

The Optimistic Classroom: Creative Ways to Give Children Hope, Deborah Hewitt and Sandra Heidemann (St. Paul, MN: Redleaf, 1998).

Information and activities to encourage self-esteem and to develop empathy and problem-solving skills.

Roots and Wings: Affirming Culture in Early Childhood Programs, Stacey York (St. Paul, MN: Redleaf, 1991).

Day-to-day guidance and lesson plans for multicultural education.

Teaching Tolerance, 400 Washington Avenue, Montgomery, AL 36104 (www.splcenter.org).

A free magazine full of first-hand accounts of teachers' experiences and a broad range of resources. Also distributes Starting Small, *a free book and video highlighting several programs across the country.*

Teaching Young Children in Violent Times: Building a Peaceable Classroom, Diane E. Levin (Cambridge, MA: Educators for Social Responsibility, 1994).

Excellent activities designed to create a supportive and caring classroom community.

We Are All Alike...We Are All Different, Cheltenham Elementary School Kindergarten (New York, NY: Scholastic, Inc. 1991)

This picture book uses photographs, children's drawings, and a simple patterned story to explain all that humans share as well as all the ways each person is unique.

Dealing with Feelings

Rhythm and Rhymes, Josh Greenberg (Albany, NY: Gentle Wind, 1985) (888-386-7664, http://www.gentlewind.com).

This tape features the "Mad Mad Polka," an excellent song for learning ways to release anger that are not harmful. Another song on the tape contains a fat joke, however.

Childswork/Childsplay, P.O. Box 61586, King of Prussia, PA 19406.

A catalog of posters, card games, and other good materials for anger management, conflict resolution, and learning about emotions.

Dealing with Feelings Series, Elizabeth Crary (Seattle, WA: Parenting Press, 1992).

> *These "choose your own solution" books show the effects of choices children can make when responding to strong feelings. Each time the book is read a different choice can be made.*

Everybody Has Feelings (Todos Tenemos Sentimientos), Charles Avery (Seattle, WA: Open Hand, 1992).

> *A photographic essay book of kids and their many feelings.*

Conflict Resolution

Peacemaking Skills for Little Kids, Peace Education Foundation, 1900 Biscayne Boulevard, Miami, FL 33132 (800-749-8838, http://www.peace-ed.org).

> *Songs, games, activities, posters with I-Care-Cat to teach respect and conflict resolution.*

CRU Institute (Conflict Resolution Unlimited), 845 106 Avenue NE, Suite 109, Bellevue, WA 98004 (800-922-1988).

> *Provides in-school training for teachers and students in conflict resolution and student mediation. Also teaches using "I messages," listening skills, and role plays. Provides training manuals and videos.*

Before Push Comes to Shove: Building Conflict Resolution Skills with Children, Nancy Carlsson/Paige and Diane E. Levin (St. Paul, MN: Redleaf, 1998).

> *This book is a good introduction to conflict resolution. Includes a full discussion of conflict resolution skills and how to reinforce them throughout the day.*

Children's Problem-Solving Book Series, Elizabeth Crary (Seattle, WA: Parenting Press, 1992).

> *This series of picture books deals with common conflicts. Readers make choices and see the result of their choices in the story line.*

Specific Issues

Adoption

Making Sense of Adoption: A Parent's Guide, Lois Ruskai Melina (New York: Harper, 1989).

> *Includes comprehensive information on talking about adoption with children.*

Being Adopted, Maxine B. Rosenberg (New York, NY: Lothrop, Lee and Shepard Books, 1984)

> *This picture book tells the adoption story of several children in their own words.*

Body Size

Radiance, P.O. Box 30246, Oakland, CA 94604 (510-482-0680).

A magazine for large women with positive information on living a large life. Some issues focus on large children and how to support them.

Council on Size and Weight Discrimination, Inc., P.O. Box 305, Mt. Marion, NY 12456, (206-923-9354, www.cswd.org).

A not-for-profit group that distributes information on how to recognize, avoid, and deal with size bias. Cathi Rodgveller is the contact for workshops and information about their Kids Come In All Sizes project.

Belinda's Bouquet, Leslea Newman (Boston, MA: Alyson Publications, 1991).

A picture book showing a young girl learning that people naturally come in all sizes.

I Like Me!, Nancy Carlson (New York, NY: Viking/Penguin 1988).

A happy story about a young pig who likes everything about herself, including her round belly.

Gender

Beyond Dolls and Guns: 101 Ways to Help Children Avoid Gender Bias, Susan Hoy Crawford (Portsmouth, NH: Heinemann, 1996).

The perfect introduction to gender bias issues. This small book describes the many ways we continue to encourage gender bias and explains simple ways to make changes.

Together and Equal: Fostering Cooperative Play and Promoting Gender Equity in Early Childhood Programs, Carol Hilgartner and Barbara Metzger Schlank (Old Tappan, NJ: Allyn and Bacon, 1997).

Curriculum planning and themed activities to allow teachers to weave cooperation and gender equity throughout their program.

Educational Equity Concepts, Inc., 114 East 32 Street, Suite 701, New York, NY 10016 (212-725-1803).

Curriculum materials for gender- and disability-aware education.

Boys Will Be Boys: Breaking the Link Between Masculinity and Violence, Myriam Miedzian (New York, NY: Anchor, 1992).

This book discusses how we are raising boys and what needs to be done to help them grow without violence.

What Is a girl? What Is a boy? Stephanie Waxman (New York: Crowell, 1989).

This picture book follows a simple pattern. It states a gender stereotype ("Some people think that boys don't...") and then shows through real-life examples that the stereotype is untrue ("but here's Tim, and he likes..."). It also explains about and shows the body parts that actually create each person's gender.

Exclusion

You Can't Say You Can't Play, Vivian Gussin Paley (Cambridge, MA: Harvard University Press, 1992).

One teacher's account of an innovative change in her classroom culture when she makes the rule that you can't say "you can't play."

No Red Monsters Allowed, Liza Alexander (Chicago, IL: Goldencraft).

This picture book shows how Elmo of Sesame Street feels when he is excluded from a group. It also shows others standing up against bias and how much better they feel when they do. This book is out of print, but may be available through libraries.

Families

The Way We Really Are: Coming to Terms with America's Changing Families, Stephanie Coontz (New York, NY: Basic, 1998).

A candid discussion about the changes family life has gone through in recent times, this book evaluates how today's families can best adjust to these changes.

Opening Doors: Lesbian and Gay Parents and Schools, (San Diego, CA: Family Pride Coalition, 1999).

A handbook for parents and educators that is available from the Family Pride Coalition, P.O. Box 34337, San Diego, CA 92163 (619-296-0199, www.familypride.org).

Family Diversity Projects, Inc. P.O. Box 1209, Amherst, MA 01004-1209 (413-256-0502, www.familydiv.org).

An organization that creates and distributes photo-text exhibits and books that represent the rich diversity of family life. Exhibits include In Our Family: Portraits of All Kinds of Families, Of Many Colors: Portraits of Multiracial Families *(also available in book form),* Nothing to Hide: Mental Illness in the Family, *and* Love Makes a Family: Portraits of Lesbian, Gay, Bisexual and Transgender Parents and Their Families *(also available in book form).*

Race/Culture

Through Indian Eyes, Beverly Slapin and Doris Seale, editors (Philadelphia: New Society, 1987).

Gives guidelines from Native American viewpoints for analyzing children's books.

Title 9 Natives Programs.

Find these programs through your local school district's Office of Indian Education. The programs will have information about the lives of Native American children in your area.

Skipping Stones, P.O. Box 3939, Eugene, OR 97403.

An international magazine for children 10–16. Includes information about children and cultures around the world as well as in the United States.

Constructive Playthings, 1227 E. 119 Street, Grandview, MO 64030-1117 (800-448-4115).

This company offers a collection of Judaic classroom materials, including books and puzzles.

West Music, P.O. Box 5521, Coralville, IA 52241.

A great resource for musical instruments and music from all over the world.

Children Just Like Me, Susan Elizabeth Copsey (New York, NY: DK Publishing, 1995).

A beautiful photographic display of children in countries all around the world. Shows and tells about things that really explain the children's lives, like their favorite foods and what they like to play.

Asian American Curriculum Project, 234 Main Street, San Mateo, CA 94401 (800-874-2242).

Asian American dolls and books for teachers and children.

African American Images, 1909 West 95 Street, Chicago, IL 60643 (800-552-1991).

Books and posters for adults and children. Also, products for celebrating Kwanzaa.

Arab World and Islamic Resources and School Services, 2095 Rose Street, Suite 4, Berkeley, CA 94709 (510-704-0517).

Teaching resources about Arabic cultures.

American-Arab Anti-Discrimination Committee (ADC), 4201 Connecticut Avenue NW, Suite 300, Washington DC, 20008 (202-244-2990).

Information source for helping to make classrooms supportive of Arabic children.

White Awareness: Handbook for Anti-Racism Training, Judith H. Katz (Norman, OK: University of Oklahoma Press, 1978).

Activities for people who are working on understanding racism.

All the Colors We Are: The Story of How We Get Our Skin Color, Katie Kissinger (St. Paul, MN: Redleaf, 1997).

A beautiful picture book that describes the reason for skin colors in a simple way.

Kids with Disabilities

Kids with Special Needs, The Learning Works, P.O. Box 6187, Santa Barbara, CA 93160 (800-235-5767).

Comprehensive resource that helps educators familiarize themselves with various disabilities and health conditions and explore ways to reduce children's fears about differences.

Gallaudet University Press (800-621-2736).

Publishes books on all topics relating to Deaf and hard-of-hearing people. Publishes picture books in sign language.

Signs for Me: Basic Sign Vocabulary for Children, Parents, and Teachers, Ben Bahan and Joe Dannis (San Diego, CA: Dawn Sign, 1990).

A beginning sign language book showing illustrations for common signs in a young child's vocabulary.

We Can Do It, Laura Dwight (New York, NY: Star Bright, 1998).

This picture book uses beautiful photographs of children with special challenges to show the things they can do.

Friends Together: More Alike Than Different, Rochelle Bunnett (New York: Checkerboard, 1992).

Posters show children of all abilities learning and playing together.

Friends in the Park, Rochelle Bunnett (New York, Checkerboard, 1992).

Photographic picture book showing children of all abilities together.

Braille Institute, 741 N. Vermont Avenue, Los Angeles, CA 90029 (800-BRAILLE).

Information on living with blindness.

National Easter Seals, 230 W. Monroe Street, Chicago, IL 60606 (800-221-6827).

A source of information about children with disabilities. Local offices may be able to connect you with adults who would be willing to visit your classroom or advise you on forming a doll's personality. Some groups will loan classes a child-sized wheelchair.

Gay and Lesbian Issues

GLSEN Bookstore 121 West 27th St. Suite 1003-B, New York, NY 10001 (212-627-7707, www.glsen.org).

A catalog of books and videos with information on dealing with gay issues.

It's Elementary, (Chasnoff and Cohen, 1995)

This video for teachers and administrators shows real examples of school activities, faculty meetings, and class discussions about homosexuality.

Index

T

tardiness, 11, 159
Taus, Kay, 4, 5
teasing, 146–147
    and cross-gender friendships, 56
    discussion/problem-solving step,
       141, 142
    and doll identities, 32–33
    full story example, 178–185
    glasses, ix–xii, xiii
    prevention of, 4–5
    situation setup, 86, 89, 92
    and standing up against bias,
       20–21, 93, 148–149
    See also anti-bias attitudes; bias;
       bias, standing up against
television, 9, 53, 69, 81, 127
theme studies, 6–7, 67–68, 106–107
trust, 150–151
turn-taking, 10, 118. *See also*
       classroom skills
two and three year olds
    and comfort with diversity, 16
    feelings step, 98–99
    full story example, 165–170
    story progression, 196–198

U

Umoja
    caring, 115–116
    introduction sequence, 52, 56–58
    and religion, 81, 129
unexpected comments, 8, 44–45,
       55–56, 69–70, 110
unit studies, 6–7, 67–68, 106–107

V

vegetarianism, 81
videotaping, 200
violence, 9, 10
vocabulary
    anti-bias, 8–9, 85–86, 134,
       138–139, 185, 199
    emotions, 8–9, 97–99, 109, 110,
       197, 198

W

waiting in line, 11
walking aids, 82
war, 14
wondering stories
    discussion/problem-solving step,
       130–131, 132–133
    situation setup, 82
worry, 71

Z

zoo animals, 106–107